Günther Plamenig

The 2%

You decide

Bottom up Publishing

Notes:

Günther Plamenig

The 2%

You decide

Copyright: Bottom up Publishing

Birkenstrasse 14

4142 Münchenstein - Switzerland

Email: bottomupverlag@gmail.com

Edition 1

Unabridged edition:

November 2025 Bottom up Publishing

Cover page: Yves & Günther Plamenig

Typesetting: Yves Plamenig

Consulting: Marketing Yves Plamenig

Marketing: Yves and Günther Plamenig

Thanks to everyone who contributed to the publication of this book.

A special thank you to Yves once again.

Printing: Libri Plureos GmbH, Friedensallee 273, 22763 Hamburg

ISBN 978-3-907720-74-5 EAN 9783907720745

Notes:

Table of contents:

Notes:

Notes:

Foreword:

There is a silent truth that hardly anyone speaks of, yet it determines the life of every single person: the vast majority remain average throughout their lives. They follow the same patterns, the same narratives, the same hopes and fears as millions of others—and wonder why their lives never achieve the depth, freedom, and fulfillment they secretly long for. Only a small minority—two percent—manage to break out of this invisible circle. Two percent who become not only financially independent, but also mentally, emotionally, and existentially free. Two percent who get there not by chance or luck, but because they have cultivated a completely different way of thinking and acting. This book is not a guide that promises quick fixes or superficial recipes. It is an invitation to a radical insight: the difference between the 98 percent and the two percent has nothing to do with education, background, or luck. It has to do with the way we see the world, the beliefs we hold, and the decisions we make every day. Average is not a fate, but a mental pattern. And likewise, exceptionality is not a privilege, but an opportunity open to everyone. The average person seeks security and finds dependence. They chase status and lose freedom.

They live in stories they did not write themselves and wonder why they are not the authors of their own lives. The two percent, on the other hand, have understood that money, success, and independence are not the goal, but the byproduct of a different way of thinking. They see money not as a number, but as energy. They do not fear failure, but recognize opportunities in it. They build their freedom not on external circumstances, but on inner clarity. This book shows why the average remains average—and what each person can change to break out of this invisible majority. It shows how deeply rooted beliefs work, why habits are more powerful than intentions, how our environment and culture keep us small, and why only a few find the courage to break their inner chains. It makes it clear that the boundary between mediocrity and freedom does not lie outside, but inside – in the way we think, feel, and act. But this is not a theoretical treatise. It is a journey that leads the reader step by step out of the confines of mediocrity. It is a mirror that shows how we are bound by unconscious patterns – and a map that describes how to break these chains. Each section of this book is written in such a way that it can not only be understood, but also experienced. Because true change does not come through information, but through transformation. If you are holding this book in your hands, it means that you sense that more is possible. That you suspect that the stories of "normal life" are not the whole truth.

That you know deep down that freedom is not reserved for the few, but is also within your reach. This book will not spare you; it will challenge you. It will show you the mechanisms by which the masses keep themselves small—and reveal the steps you can take to break free. In the end, you will understand: it's not about being better than others. It's about no longer being a slave to patterns that prevent you from living your own life. It's about not being one of the 98 percent who put security above freedom, but one of the two percent who have the courage to go their own way. Breaking out of the average starts here – with you, with your decision to no longer remain stuck in the stories of the masses. This book is your compass. You have to walk the path yourself.

Notes:

Notes:

Notes:

Chapter 1: The Myth of Average

Humans live in images. They are guided by ideas that have been instilled in them since childhood. One of the most powerful images is that of the so-called average. It creeps into our language, our standards, our expectations of ourselves and others. We hear about the average family, the average salary, the average student, the average life expectancy. Everything seems to fit into a large curve that distinguishes what is normal from what appears rare or deviant. The average seems harmless, almost reassuring, because it gives us security. It suggests that there is a middle ground where one can feel secure. But it is precisely this apparent security that captivates millions of people and prevents them from ever entering the sphere where the two percent who are truly financially independent live. The statistical measure of the average is an abstraction. It describes a number, a middle ground that is created by adding up many values. In mathematics, this is helpful because it allows us to simplify complex data sets. But in the life of the individual, the average becomes a prison when it is adopted as a yardstick for one's own existence. Because no human being is average.

Every human being is a unique case, an unrepeatable constellation of experiences, talents, influences, and decisions. Nevertheless, most people try to fit into this image, as if they had to prove that they belong exactly in this middle. It is a paradoxical dynamic: the majority of people cling to the idea of being average because they assume it means normality and security, while at the same time feeling the longing to be something special. Psychology is well aware of this mechanism. People constantly compare themselves, consciously or unconsciously. Experiments have shown that people judge their own income, abilities, or even life satisfaction less in absolute terms and almost exclusively in relation to others. Most people don't want to be at the bottom or the top, but somewhere in the middle. This "middle" is then elevated to an ideal, even though in reality it is nothing more than a statistical construct. This orientation toward the middle gives rise to the phenomenon we call the average. It stems from a deep need for belonging, for protection from deviation, for recognition by the group. But while the average is a form of self-reassurance from a psychological point of view, it acts like a trap from an economic perspective. Those who settle in the middle also orient themselves toward mediocrity in their thinking, actions, and aspirations. This is particularly evident in the financial world. The average person exchanges their time for money. They orient themselves according to the standards set for them: a regular job, a secure salary, a house or apartment, a car, a few vacations. All of this sounds like a good life. And in a way, it is.

But it is not independent. It depends on conditions, contracts, employers, banks, and political frameworks. The average person lives in a state of dependency that they often do not even notice because it is shared by so many. In contrast, there are the two percent who are completely financially independent. They exist beyond the average. They do not live on a monthly salary, but on structures they have built up. These structures continue to function even when they themselves are no longer working. They have taken the step of freeing themselves from the exchange of time for money and have organized their capital in such a way that it works for them. This difference is not a minor detail, but the fundamental dividing line between dependence and independence, between the average and the exceptional. It is often assumed that access to this exception is reserved for the privileged – those who have rich parents, who were allowed to attend an elite university, who had the right contacts at the right time. But history has disproved this narrative countless times. People from the humblest backgrounds, without academic education, without significant start-up capital, have managed to break away from the average. What united them was not their background, but their attitude. They thought differently about risk, about work, about money. They understood that the average is not a necessity, but a choice – one that millions make unconsciously. Scientific research in behavioral economics shows that people tend to stick to the status quo, even if it is disadvantageous in the long run. This is called the "status quo bias." It explains why many people prefer to remain in a mediocre but familiar situation rather than take the risk of gaining something through change. This clinging to the familiar is one of the main reasons why the average remains stable, why 98% remain so reliably in the middle. The two percent, on the other hand, have overcome this bias. They have learned to live with uncertainty, to see it as a field of possibilities rather than a threat. This reveals the core of the myth of the average: it is not just a statistical number, but a mental attitude that is deeply ingrained in our culture. We are trained to conform, to fall in line, not to want too much, not to step out of line too much. The school system rewards conformity, not creativity.

It rewards correct answers, not new questions. Society reinforces this logic by prioritizing stability over flexibility. Those who conform are perceived as reliable, those who break out are perceived as risky or even threatening. But it is precisely in this breakout that lies the path to the freedom that only the two percent know. So the question is not whether you were born average—most people are. The question is whether you remain average. And here lies the crucial truth: it does not depend on your education, your ancestry, or your background. It depends on your thinking, your actions, and your willingness to see through and leave behind the myth of average. Most people will not do this. They will continue to believe that average means security, while unconsciously remaining trapped in a subtle dependency. But those who have the courage to see the middle ground not as a benchmark but as an illusion open the door to another world. A world in which independence is not just a dream but a lived reality. The average is more than a number; it is a cultural construct, an invisible net that shapes our thoughts, feelings, and actions. When you live in a society that has been geared toward stability and conformity for generations, deviating from the middle is perceived not as an opportunity, but as a danger. It is like an invisible frame that directs all movements into certain paths. Those who think outside these paths are viewed with skepticism, sometimes ridiculed, sometimes even excluded. But it is precisely this exclusion that reveals something crucial: the average defends itself. It wants to preserve itself; it wants as many people as possible to remain within its boundaries so that order is maintained. This begins in early childhood. Children learn very quickly that reward and recognition are not necessarily linked to creativity or courage, but to the ability to meet expectations.

At school, the highest virtue is not the discovery of new things, but the repetition of the familiar. Those who follow the rules are praised as well-behaved. Those who ask too many questions or give unusual answers are perceived as disruptive. Even in these early experiences, the idea takes root that it is better to stay in the middle, better not to stand out, better not to stray too far. This conditioning solidifies over the years and becomes part of one's identity. Psychology calls this social conditioning. People do not develop their identity in a vacuum, but in constant interaction with their environment. Parents, teachers, friends, the media—they all send messages about what is acceptable and what is not. And almost all of these messages point to the middle ground. Society's statistics shape the individual by conveying that normality is synonymous with security and that deviation is synonymous with risk. But this apparent security harbors a subtle danger: those who focus too much on normality lose touch with their own uniqueness. They lose the ability to think outside the box and thus miss out on precisely those opportunities that could lead them out of the 98% circle. Scientifically, this mechanism can be summarized as "conformity pressure." Studies by Solomon Asch in the 1950s impressively showed that people are willing to accept obvious errors in perception tasks if the group they are in makes the same mistakes.

To this day, this phenomenon remains one of the most important tools for understanding human behavior. For most people, the urge to belong to a group exceeds the need for truth or individual integrity. In modern society, this manifests itself in consumption habits, career patterns, the way people spend their free time, and the goals they consider desirable. Everything is guided by the invisible hand of the average, which ensures that people do not stray too far from the others. Yet the middle ground is not objective. What is considered normal today may look completely different in a few years. A hundred years ago, it was normal for the majority of people to work in agriculture; today, it is considered normal for most people to work in offices. The average is therefore a moving target that shifts with the development of society. But it is precisely because it shifts that its deceptiveness becomes apparent: those who orient their lives toward belonging to the middle are orienting them toward a phantom. They are chasing a normality that is constantly in flux and yet can never provide security. The two percent who are financially independent have seen through this game. They have understood that it makes no sense to orient themselves toward a moving center. They have aligned their thinking with principles that are stable: value creation, independence, long-term perspectives. And they have freed themselves from the pressure to always belong. In a sense, they have developed the strength to live against the psychological gravity of society. They know that belonging is important to humans, but that it should not come at the price of self-sacrifice. The science of motivation provides interesting insights here. Research by Edward Deci and Richard Ryan on self-determination theory shows that people have three basic needs: autonomy, competence, and social connectedness. While most people overemphasize their social connectedness and are thus pulled toward the average, the two percent focus on autonomy. They want to create, decide, and be independent. This does not mean that they have no social relationships – on the contrary, they often maintain very strong networks. But they do not let their lives be determined by the pressure to conform, but by the desire for independence. It is precisely this difference that leads them to take paths that remain hidden to most people. It is interesting to note that many people who remain average rationalize their situation.

They tell themselves that they simply did not have the opportunities, that they are trapped in a certain system, that others were more privileged. These explanations provide short-term relief, but in the long term they prevent people from taking responsibility. They reinforce the belief that belonging to the 98% is inevitable. Psychologists refer to this as "learned helplessness." This concept, developed by Martin Seligman, describes the tendency to settle into passive patterns when one repeatedly experiences that efforts have no effect. Even if, objectively speaking, there is room for action, people then behave as if they have no choice. The two percent, on the other hand, operate from the opposite attitude. They believe in the effectiveness of their actions. They are convinced that decisions, even small ones, have a big impact in the long term. This conviction is not always rational in the sense of a guaranteed probability of success, but it is psychologically enormously effective. It leads these people to remain persistent, to persevere, to see setbacks not as a final failure, but as a stage on the way. This resilience is one of the most important factors that sets them apart from the average. Economic history is full of examples of this.

Entrepreneurs such as Ingvar Kamprad, the founder of IKEA, or Oprah Winfrey, who rose from poverty to become a media icon, show that background is not the decisive factor. What is decisive is the ability to break patterns and no longer remain average. What they have in common is not luck or a special educational qualification, but the willingness to go their own way, even if this way was not initially understood by others. They refused to accept the myth of the middle ground as the standard. Another aspect is the role of language. Language creates reality. Those who constantly talk about "normal," "usual," or "average" unconsciously construct a framework in which extraordinary possibilities hardly ever occur. The average then becomes not just a number, but a way of thinking. It determines how we see ourselves and what we believe to be possible. On the other hand, those who begin to change their language also open up new ways of thinking. It makes a difference whether you say, "That's how everyone does it," or ask yourself, "How could I do it differently?" This seemingly small shift in language has a big impact on what we perceive as our scope for action.

Research in cognitive psychology shows that such changes in language actually transform thinking. Using different words activates different neural networks, different images, different emotions. As banal as it sounds, the path out of the average often begins with the way you talk about yourself and your possibilities. Language is not only an expression of thoughts, it is also a tool for shaping new realities. And yet the power of the average is persistent. It is reinforced by the structures of our society: by school systems that reward conformity, by labor markets that demand conformity, by media that glorify average biographies, by consumption patterns that sell the same dreams to everyone. Those who want to escape this web need not only knowledge, but also courage. Courage to expose themselves to the judgment of others, courage to accept uncertainty, courage not to see immediate results. It is this courage that distinguishes the two percent, and it is precisely this courage that the average often avoids. The myth of the average does not persist because people are incapable of breaking out of it. It persists because it is comfortable. It offers apparent security, it spares responsibility, it justifies stagnation. But this comfort comes at a price: it costs freedom, it costs independence, and ultimately it costs the opportunity to truly take ownership of one's own life.

And that is precisely why it is worth questioning this myth – even if it is uncomfortable. Because beyond comfort lies the freedom that only the two percent who have broken away from the logic of the middle know. If we want to understand the average as a cultural pattern, it is not enough to look at it in terms of numbers and statistics. We need to take a deeper look at what it does to people, how it shapes their view of themselves and their possibilities. The average is an invisible yardstick that most people use to orient themselves, even if they are not consciously aware of it. It is embedded in proverbs, in advice, in well-meaning wisdom. "Do what everyone else does," "Don't be too extreme," "Don't overdo it" – these phrases seem harmless, but they are an expression of a way of thinking that sets mediocrity as the norm and as the limit. In this context, science refers to "social norms." These are unspoken rules that exist in every society and cause people to behave similarly, even if they don't have to. Such norms are not bad per se; they ensure coexistence and create reliability. But they also have a downside: they keep people stuck in patterns that are not questioned. In modern societies, this often means that life moves within a narrow corridor. You go to school, do an apprenticeship or study, look for a job, work for decades, and then eventually retire.

It is a life course that applies to millions, and that is precisely why it seems like a law of nature. Those who do not follow it are considered unusual, sometimes risky, sometimes even failures. But this is precisely where the mistake lies. The life course that the average person takes for granted is not a law of nature. It is the result of historical developments. The model of a secure job that carries you through to retirement emerged in the course of industrialization and became the norm in the 20th century. Before that, most people lived in completely different structures, often in self-employment, in family businesses, in changing forms of employment. Today's image of normality is therefore historically young and by no means a given. But because so many people live this way, it seems like the only right way. This shows why 98 percent of people remain average: they confuse habit with necessity. What many people do is perceived as the only thing possible. Psychologically, this is called the "bandwagon effect," the phenomenon that people believe something to be true or right because many others do it.

This effect is well known in economics. Trends that actually have little substance can stabilize through mere imitation. Entire markets emerge because people believe something is valuable simply because others are buying it too. The same is true of lifestyles. They gain their authority not through internal logic, but through the sheer number of people who follow them. The two percent have seen through this deception. They know that normality is a product of habit and that you can consciously decide to break out of these habits. This breakout does not happen overnight, but through a gradual change in perception and behavior. First, you have to see that the middle ground is not a law of nature, but a construct. Then you have to find the courage to seek your own path, even if it is unfamiliar. And finally, you have to persevere, even when you encounter resistance. Because the average defends itself; it will not be abandoned without a fight. It is interesting to note how closely language and thought are intertwined in this process. Those who remain average often describe their lives in passive terms. They talk about "having a job," "needing security," "being able to afford it." This language suggests that they experience themselves as dependent, that they adopt standards from outside. Those who break out of the average, on the other hand, use different terms.

They talk about "building something," "thinking in terms of possibilities," "shaping the future." Language reveals attitude, and attitude shapes action. Cognitive science shows that people are shaped not only by facts, but also by narratives. The stories we tell ourselves about ourselves influence what we believe is possible. If someone lives with the narrative that they are "just a simple employee," they will align their behavior with this image. They will avoid decisions that do not fit this narrative. On the other hand, if someone accepts the narrative that they are the architect of their own future, they will see and seize other opportunities. The difference lies not in objective circumstances, but in the inner story we tell ourselves about ourselves. This is a crucial point in explaining why it is so difficult to break away from the average: The inner story acts like an invisible script. It repeats itself unconsciously, day after day, leaving little room for anything new. These self-narratives are deeply rooted, often built up over years or decades. They cannot be changed simply by making a decision. They need to be slowly rewritten, a new learning process, a conscious replacement of old stories with new ones. The two percent have learned to actively shape their inner narratives. They allow themselves to think big, act differently, and take risks. Not because they are inherently more courageous, but because they have understood that the story they tell themselves determines the scope of their possibilities. Another mechanism that stabilizes the average is the fear of deviation. People fear not only failure, but also the judgment of others. Those who break out of their familiar framework risk ridicule, criticism, or envy. This fear is deeply rooted because belonging was essential for survival in evolutionary terms. In small tribal societies, exclusion could mean death. This is no longer the case today, but the old program continues to have an effect. It ensures that many people prefer to stay within familiar patterns, even if they make them unhappy, rather than risk being seen differently by the group. The two percent have not completely overcome this mechanism, but they have learned to deal with it differently.

They accept that criticism is part of the journey. They know that deviation provokes resistance, and they don't take this resistance as a sign of failure, but as confirmation that they are breaking new ground. This ability to deal with the judgment of others is one of the biggest hurdles for people who want to break away from the average. Because it means developing inner strength that does not depend on external recognition. Research on resilience has shown that people who have internal locus of control beliefs are better able to cope with adversity. They believe that they have influence over their lives, even when external circumstances are difficult.

This belief protects them from the passivity that many others fall into. In terms of financial independence, this means that the top two percent do not see money as something that comes to them by chance or is determined by external forces, but as something they can actively shape. They develop strategies, educate themselves, and implement ideas, even if these seem risky at first.

And this is precisely where it becomes clear that it is not school education or ancestry that determines membership of the two percent. It is inner convictions, attitude to life, and relationship to risk and responsibility. There are highly educated people who nevertheless remain average because they do not dare to leave the security of their jobs. And there are people without formal education who take extraordinary paths because they believe in their ability to shape their own destiny. Education can help, but it is no guarantee. Origin can create obstacles, but it is not destiny. What makes the difference is the decision to no longer remain in the middle, but to have the courage to forge your own path. Economics recognizes the principle of "cumulative advantages." Small differences at the beginning can create big differences over time. Those who start building capital early on will have an enormous advantage later on.

Those who have the courage to start their own projects early on gain experience that others do not have. This effect shows that it is not so much a one-time big opportunity that matters, but rather the sum of small decisions that accumulate over the years. Average people underestimate this dynamic. They see the success of the two percent and consider it luck or coincidence, while overlooking the fact that it is the result of hundreds, perhaps thousands, of decisions that have shaped a direction over the long term. The myth of the average persists not because it is natural, but because it stabilizes itself. It acts like a magnet that pulls everything toward the center. It makes use of psychological mechanisms such as pressure to conform, social norms, learned helplessness, and fear of deviation. It is reinforced by the language we use, the stories we tell ourselves, and the structures of our society. If you want to escape this magnet, you have to develop another force of attraction—the attraction of a vision that is stronger than the comfort of the middle.

This is precisely what distinguishes the two percent from the 98: they do not live for the average, they live for an idea of freedom that allows them to go beyond the norm. The average is not just a number, not just a social reflex, it is a psychological anchor that is deeply embedded in people. This anchor keeps them in a place they have not consciously chosen. It acts like an invisible hand that guides decisions without questioning them. And that is precisely where its power lies: most people do not realize that they are aligning themselves with a standard that they themselves have never defined. They unconsciously adopt what millions before them have done because it seems so self-evident that hardly anyone thinks to question it. If you take a closer look, the average is a web of beliefs that reinforce each other. One of these beliefs is that security is more important than freedom. It is so deeply woven into our culture that it is rarely questioned. Parents advise their children to choose a "secure" profession. Teachers praise those who do not stand out but are reliable. Social institutions rely on people fulfilling their role in the system without venturing into too many experiments. Security is thus declared a kind of supreme good, even though in reality it always remains relative. Because there is no such thing as absolute security. Jobs are lost, markets change, systems falter. But because so many believe in security, they orient their lives around it and thus remain in dependencies that they consider inevitable. The two percent who have been able to break away from this logic have understood that true security lies not in conformity, but in independence. Independence means not being dependent on an employer, not remaining dependent on the goodwill of an institution, not being trapped in a system that can change its rules at any time. Paradoxically, true security can only be achieved by letting go of supposed security. This requires courage because it means leaving your familiar comfort zone. But it is precisely this step that marks the line between the 98 percent and the two percent. Another part of the network that stabilizes the average is the belief that you have to accept your own limitations.

Many people tell themselves that they are simply not among the "chosen ones," that others had more talent, more intelligence, or more luck. This conviction is a relief because it relinquishes responsibility. It explains why people remain average without feeling guilty. But it is deceptive. Because it overlooks the fact that most limits are not objective, but self-constructed. Neuroscientific research shows that the brain is plastic, that it can change throughout life. Abilities are not fixed; they can be developed. And yet many people remain stuck in the belief that their possibilities are determined from birth. This shows how strongly beliefs shape our lives. Those who believe that they are not destined to become financially independent will not take any steps in that direction.

Those who believe that success is reserved for others will not seize the opportunities that come their way. Beliefs act like self-fulfilling prophecies. They generate behavior that confirms their own validity. The two percent have learned to question their beliefs. They have learned to replace old convictions with new ones. Not by indulging in illusions, but by empirically testing what is actually possible. They know that the limits of the average are not natural, but mental constructs. Psychology calls this the "mindset" effect.

Research by Carol Dweck has shown that people with a "growth mindset," i.e., the belief that abilities can be changed, achieve more than those with a "fixed mindset," who believe that everything is set in stone. This difference in thinking has enormous implications. It explains why some people see setbacks as learning opportunities, while others interpret them as definitive failures. The average is characterized by the fixed mindset, the two percent by the growth mindset. This difference may seem insignificant, but it determines whether someone settles permanently in the middle or finds the courage to leave their comfort zone. A third aspect that keeps the average alive is the illusion of normality. People believe that what the majority does is automatically the right thing to do.

But the majority is often wrong when it comes to long-term results. This is particularly evident in the financial world. Most people spend their money immediately or invest it in ways that yield little growth. They are guided by consumption patterns shaped by advertising and habits. Few think in terms of decades, and few let their capital work for them. The result is a stable majority that never really becomes independent and a small minority that finds its way to freedom. Economics describes this phenomenon as the "herd effect." It shows that people tend to do what the masses do, even if it is irrational. The two percent have learned to act against this herd effect. They know that independence does not come from conformity, but from thinking differently. They make decisions that may seem strange at the moment, but bear fruit in the long term.

They consume less when others consume, they invest when others are afraid, they build when others hesitate. This behavior requires not only knowledge, but also emotional strength. Because it is difficult to go against the movement of the majority if you are not internally stable. The ability to swim against the tide is one of the key differences that sets the two percent apart. The myth of the average also derives its power from the fact that it is comfortable. It allows people to stick to their routines without much effort and without confronting their own fears. This comfort is seductive because it is pleasant in the short term. But it prevents long-term freedom. Psychologically, this can be described as the "comfort zone trap." People prefer to remain in a state that is mediocre but familiar rather than venture into the unknown. But the unknown is where growth happens. Those who never leave their comfort zone remain trapped in mediocrity, even if they secretly want more.

The two percent have understood that independence can only be found outside the comfort zone. They consciously seek out experiences that challenge them. They know that uncertainty is not the end, but the beginning of development. And they have learned that courage is not the absence of fear, but the willingness to act despite fear. This attitude fundamentally distinguishes them from the 98 percent who remain in the middle. The question of why the average remains average is therefore complex. Psychological mechanisms such as conformity, learned helplessness, beliefs, and comfort zones keep it stable. Economic patterns such as consumerism and the exchange of time for money create dependency.

And it is cultural narratives such as the overemphasis on security that prevent people from breaking out. All of this together creates a web that seems so stable that most people do not question it. But it is not a law of nature. It is man-made, and therefore it can be changed. This is the crucial point that this book wants to make: everyone can break away from the average if they begin to recognize and break these patterns. It does not depend on school education, ancestry, or luck. It depends on the willingness to let go of old beliefs and break new ground. The two percent are not privileged from birth; they are privileged because they were willing to leave behind the thinking and behavior of the average. It is not an easy path, but it is a possible one. And everyone who takes it proves that the middle ground is not a straitjacket, but merely a myth that can be seen through. When we refer to the average as a myth, we do not mean just an abstract idea, but a whole network of narratives, self-images, social expectations, and economic structures that stabilize each other. The myth of the average is so powerful because it presents people not as exceptions, but as the rule. It says: this is how most people are, so you should be like that too. And this statement is not neutral, but normative. It makes mediocrity an obligation, elevating it to a standard from which to deviate seems not only unusual, but downright wrong. But the myth is not a law of nature. It is an agreement that has crept in over centuries and has become so self-evident that hardly anyone questions it.

This myth manifests itself in everyday life in inconspicuous details. It manifests itself in the way people talk about money. Many say they "earn" their money, implying that money is always the result of work performed. Time for money, performance for wages – this model is so deeply ingrained that it seems like an irrefutable law. But it is only a construct, an agreement within a certain era. In reality, money is nothing more than a store of value and a medium of exchange that can be separated from working time as soon as structures are created that generate value independently of the individual. The two percent have understood exactly that: they no longer earn their money in the literal sense through their own work, but rather let it flow to them through systems, investments, and ventures. The average person, however, remains stuck with the idea that money can only be earned through constant personal effort. This keeps them trapped in dependency. The myth is also evident in the way people talk about success. Success is often tied to external symbols: titles, status, and possessions that are visible. But these symbols are basically reflections of the average. They are what people consider success because the majority considers them to be so. A car, a house, a trip to certain places—these are all markers that reassure the average person because they signal belonging. They show that you can keep up, that you belong. The two percent have a different relationship to success. For them, it does not mean belonging, but freedom. It is not the symbol that counts, but the opportunity. Not what is seen, but what is made possible.

This difference is subtle, but crucial. Stories about education are also part of the myth. Many still believe that a high level of education automatically leads the way out of the average. Yet countless examples prove the opposite. There are academics who work in highly respected positions and yet remain completely financially dependent, while others without formal qualifications have created structures that give them independence. This does not mean that education is worthless – on the contrary, knowledge is always a resource. But it shows that education alone is not the key. Those who understand education within the myth of the average use it only to better adapt. Those who use education as a tool outside of this myth make it a basis for real change. The difference lies not in the diploma, but in the attitude. Another aspect is origin.

The average person believes that origin is destiny. Those born into wealthy circumstances have it easier, while those born into poverty are left behind. Statistically, a correlation between background and opportunities can certainly be demonstrated, but it is not an irrefutable law. Rather, history shows countless examples of people who had all the external disadvantages and yet found their way to independence. Background influences the starting conditions, but not the end result. The myth of the average, on the other hand, uses background as an excuse to justify stagnation. It says: I can't do it because I didn't have the right conditions. The two percent, on the other hand, say: I will find ways, regardless of where I come from. Scientifically, this attitude can be described in the concept of "internal locus of control." People with an internal locus of control believe that they themselves have influence over their lives. People with an external locus of control believe that external forces determine their lives. The average is shaped by external beliefs, the two percent by internal ones. This difference affects every decision.

Those who believe that they themselves are effective will act, will learn, will take risks. Those who believe that they are powerless will wait, will hesitate, will conform. Over years and decades, this creates a gap that ultimately seems insurmountable, even though it was the result of countless small decisions. It should also not be forgotten that the myth of the average is perpetuated by the systems themselves. Schools, companies, media—they all have an interest in keeping the average stable. Schools want predictable students who go through the program. Companies want reliable employees who fulfill their roles. The media want consumers who move with the flow of the masses. The average is the basis on which these systems function. That is why it is not only tolerated, but actively promoted. Those who stand out too much are viewed critically, sometimes even sanctioned. Those who underperform are excluded. In this way, the middle ground is constantly stabilized, while deviation in either direction is curbed. But amid all this, the fact remains that only two percent find their way to financial independence. This figure is not random. It reflects how rare it is to see through the myth and consistently take a different path. And yet it is also proof that it is possible. If it were completely impossible, these two percent would not exist. Their existence shows that the door is open—only very few walk through it. Why? Because it is uncomfortable, because it requires courage, because it means enduring the judgment of others and leaving the security of the middle ground behind. The key insight that everyone can take away is that belonging to the two percent does not depend on school education or ancestry. Nor does it depend on some mysterious talent or luck. It depends on whether you are willing to let go of average thinking. Whether you are willing to question old beliefs. Whether you are willing to accept uncertainty. Whether you are willing to put freedom above security. Anyone can develop this willingness, regardless of their starting point. It does not require any special external conditions, but rather internal decisions.

This turns the myth of the average into an invitation. It invites us to see through it and no longer allow ourselves to be bound by it. It invites us to accept mediocrity not as a law of nature, but as a cultural agreement that we can reject. It invites us to orient our lives not toward the middle, but toward our own possibilities. Most people reject this invitation because it is uncomfortable. But for those who accept it, a world opens up that is not limited by the average, but by one's own thoughts and actions. And that is precisely the message with which this first chapter ends: the average is a myth, and like any myth, it can be demystified. It is powerful as long as you believe in it. But those who see through it realize that it is only a construct that can be abandoned. The two percent are living proof of this. They have broken free from the logic of the average and thereby found a freedom that remains hidden to others. The path to this is open, but it begins with a decision: to no longer want to stand in the middle, but to have the courage to go your own way.

Notes:

Notes:

Chapter 2: The Psychology of Mediocrity

The phenomenon of the average is no coincidence; it is the result of psychological forces that are deeply ingrained in every human being. If we want to understand why the majority stays on familiar paths and only a small minority finds the path to independence, we must first look not at external structures, but at the internal mechanisms that control human behavior. The average is primarily a psychological pattern. It does not arise because people are too weak or too untalented, but because they are trapped in ways of thinking and feeling that they themselves do not understand. Psychology refers to cognitive biases, those systematic deviations in thinking that cause people to act irrationally and follow the same patterns over and over again. One of the strongest biases is the status quo bias. It describes the tendency to stick with what is familiar, even when there are objectively better alternatives. People fear change because change means uncertainty. This uncertainty triggers fear, and fear is one of the strongest human motivators.

People would rather remain in a mediocre but familiar situation than take the risk of stepping into the unknown. This explains why millions of people stay in jobs that do not fulfill them, in financial dependencies that burden them, and in patterns of life that keep them small. They do not fear the bad things they know, but rather the unknown, which they cannot assess. Another distortion is loss aversion. Studies by Daniel Kahneman and Amos Tversky have shown that people feel losses twice as strongly as gains. This means that the fear of losing something weighs more heavily than the joy of winning something. So when the average person has the choice between staying in a secure job or taking the plunge into self-employment, the fear of losing security outweighs the prospect of freedom. Loss aversion keeps the majority in mediocrity because it prevents them from taking risks, even if those risks would open the door to a better future. Added to this is the need for social belonging. Humans are social beings, and in evolutionary terms, the group was essential for survival. Those who were excluded had little chance of survival. This deep-rooted tendency is still evident today.

We want to belong, we want to be accepted, we don't want to be considered outsiders. But it is precisely this need that binds us to the average. Because, by definition, the average is what the majority does. If you want to belong, you have to conform. If you break out, you risk rejection, criticism, or ridicule. And because the fear of exclusion is so deeply ingrained, many people prefer to stay in the safe zone of mediocrity, even if they feel that they are not happy there. The average is therefore a psychological protection program. It offers security within the group, it offers the illusion of safety, it reduces the fear of loss. But these protective mechanisms have a downside: they prevent growth, they prevent freedom, they prevent people from developing their own potential. The two percent who have broken free from this protection program are not free from fear. But they have learned to interpret their fear differently. They see fear not as a sign to retreat, but as a sign that they are on the threshold of something new. They have learned to see the status quo not as a safe haven, but as a cage. They do not see loss as a catastrophe, but as part of the learning process. And they accept the possibility of exclusion because they know that belonging is not valuable if it comes at the price of self-sacrifice.

It is interesting to note that these psychological patterns operate not only individually, but also collectively. Societies develop their own average narratives that are deeply embedded in their culture. In Western societies, the narrative is often: "Go to school, get a degree, find a secure job, start a family, retire." This narrative is repeated so often that it seems like a law of nature. In other cultures, it may be different, but the core remains the same: the average becomes the norm that everyone should aspire to. Thus, mediocrity is stabilized not only by individual decisions, but also by collective narratives that are passed down from generation to generation. But these narratives are deceptive. They suggest security where in reality there is uncertainty. A "secure job" is not secure when entire industries disappear. A "reliable pension" is not reliable when political systems falter. A "normal life path" is not normal when it leaves millions unhappy. But because these narratives are collectively shared, most people believe they must be true.

The myth of the average is thus nourished by both individual psychology and the stories of society. The two percent have detached themselves from these stories. They tell their own stories. They do not believe in the dogma that you have to trade time for money your whole life. They do not believe that security can only be found through conformity. They do not believe that belonging is more important than self-determination. Their stories are about freedom, creativity, and independence. And it is precisely these stories that shape their behavior. Because, as psychology shows, people do not act according to objective truth, but according to the stories they believe to be true. This makes it clear that the average remains average because psychology keeps it stable. It is not external walls that keep us trapped in mediocrity, but internal programs.

And these programs can be changed. They are not fixed, they are learned. Everyone can learn to deal with fear differently, to evaluate losses differently, to define belonging differently. Everyone can tell new stories about themselves and thus open up new paths. But this requires awareness. As long as the mechanisms remain invisible, they act like invisible threads that guide us. Only when we recognize them can we cut them. The step away from the average is therefore not an external one, but first and foremost an internal one. It is the decision to no longer allow one's own psychological patterns to work unconsciously, but to consciously shape them. It is the decision to understand fear not as a warning against the wrong, but as an invitation to the new. It is the decision to seek belonging not through conformity, but through authenticity.

And it is the decision to write your own stories rather than simply adopting those of others. It is precisely at this threshold that the path of the 98 percent diverges from that of the two percent. When we look at mediocrity from a psychological perspective, we encounter a paradox: most people want a good life, they want to be content, successful and, in a sense, special, but at the same time they act in such a way that they remain average. They long for uniqueness, but their behavior is calibrated for conformity. This paradox cannot be explained by stupidity or a lack of ambition, but by deep-seated mechanisms of the human psyche. Mediocrity exerts a magnetic force because it conveys a sense of security. It is like an invisible herd in which one feels safe as long as one remains part of it. Social psychology has proven this phenomenon in numerous experiments. As early as the 1950s, Solomon Asch showed that people deny their own perceptions when the group claims otherwise. In his famous line experiments, participants clearly saw that one line was shorter than the other, but because all the other group members claimed the opposite, many went along with them.

They didn't want to deviate, stand out, or be alone. This experiment has lost none of its relevance. It shows how strong the pressure is to remain in line with the majority, even when the truth clearly contradicts it. Applied to life, this means that people feel unhappy in a system that keeps them down, but they conform because the majority does the same. Mediocrity is so stable because it constantly confirms itself. Those who live an average life see evidence everywhere that this is the right way to go. Friends, neighbors, colleagues—everyone does it similarly. And so a collective illusion arises: if everyone is going the same way, it must be right. This thinking is reinforced by what is known as "social proof," a principle described by Robert Cialdini in his research on influence. People orient themselves to what others are doing, especially in uncertain situations. The more others exhibit a certain behavior, the more it is perceived as normal, right, and valid. And because almost everyone stays within the average, the average seems to be the only option. But it is by no means the only option. It is a mental model that is so convincing that it is rarely questioned. And that is precisely where the tragedy lies: the majority do not live the life they actually want, but the life that is presented to them as safe and normal by the myth of the average. But this myth is deceptive.

The supposed security of mediocrity is a fiction. A job that you think is secure can be lost tomorrow. A pension that you think is guaranteed can be devalued by political decisions. A status that is considered stable can disappear in no time. The average does not protect against uncertainty, it only obscures it. The two percent have realized that uncertainty cannot be avoided, only the type of uncertainty can be chosen. The average chooses the uncertainty that it cannot control: dependence on employers, politics, markets, circumstances. The two percent choose the uncertainty they can shape themselves: the risk of entrepreneurship, the fluctuations of investments, the uncertainties of their own projects. The difference lies in whether one passively endures or actively shapes. Psychologically speaking, this is a question of control beliefs. People with external control beliefs feel helpless, while people with internal control beliefs see themselves as creators. The two percent belong to the second group, and that is precisely why they succeed in creating structures that enable independence. Mediocrity is also stabilized by the language we use. Those who say they "have to go to work" reveal a relationship of dependence. Work is then something that is imposed from outside, not something that one chooses for oneself. Language shapes reality. It shows how we see ourselves and what role we assign to ourselves. The average person talks about security, perseverance, and what they can afford. People outside the average talk about shaping, possibilities, and freedom. These differences in language reflect differences in thinking, and differences in thinking lead to differences in action.

Another psychological pattern that keeps the average stable is what is known as cognitive dissonance. People have a strong need for internal consistency. When their actions and beliefs do not match, they feel uncomfortable. To reduce this discomfort, they either adjust their actions or their beliefs. On average, the latter usually happens: Instead of radically changing their own lives, people adjust their beliefs. They tell themselves that they are satisfied, even if they are not. They convince themselves that independence is not possible anyway, even if they secretly dream of it. In this way, mediocrity is stabilized through self-deception. People cling to patterns that make them unhappy because the alternative seems too frightening to them. The two percent deal with cognitive dissonance differently. They use discomfort as a driver for change.

They allow themselves to feel the pain caused by the discrepancy between dream and reality and convert it into energy. They do not suppress their dissatisfaction, but confront it. This ability to deal productively with inner discomfort sets them apart from the 98 percent. While the majority tries to avoid contradictions, the two percent use contradictions as a driving force. The role of emotions should not be underestimated either. The average person is driven by emotions that provide short-term comfort but long-term paralysis. Fear, comfort, the need for harmony—all of these keep people on familiar paths. The two percent, on the other hand, have learned not to deny their emotions, but to master them. They feel fear, but they do not let it dominate them. They feel insecurity, but they use it as a sign of growth. They feel resistance, but they interpret it as proof that they are taking an unusual path. This emotional intelligence is not innate; it can be learned. It distinguishes those who remain passive from those who shape things. So when we ask about the psychology of mediocrity, we realize that it rests on three pillars: fear of uncertainty, longing for belonging, and the tendency toward self-deception. These three forces work together to keep people in the middle. They are powerful because they are deeply rooted in our evolution. But they are not immutable. People can learn to deal with uncertainty without freezing in fear.

They can redefine belonging without giving up on themselves. And they can resist the temptation to talk themselves into something that actually makes them unhappy. So mediocrity persists not because it is objectively the best option, but because it is psychologically the most comfortable. It saves decisions, it saves risks, it saves conflicts. But this saving is deceptive. It costs growth, it costs freedom, it costs the chance to lead a life that is truly independent. The two percent have realized that the price of conformity is higher than the price of risk. They have understood that you either endure the pain of uncertainty or the pain of lack of freedom. And they have chosen the former because it is the only one that leads to a future that is not limited by the myth of the average. Mediocrity has many faces, but at its core it is a psychological attitude. Those who live an average life unconsciously choose a certain way of seeing the world. This perspective does not develop overnight, but grows over years, fed by experiences, upbringing, culture, and social expectations. It takes shape through the repetition of small messages: Be careful. Don't take on too much. Keep your feet on the ground. Stick to what is tried and tested. These messages seem caring, even reasonable, but they carry a silent command: Don't go too far. Don't risk too much. Don't think too big. In this way, mediocrity is not only lived, but also passed on, handed down from generation to generation like an invisible chain. From a psychological perspective, there is a basic pattern behind this attitude: people strive for cognitive coherence. They want their inner world to match their outer world. If everyone around them lives by certain rules, they accept these rules as a matter of course. This desire for coherence explains why so many people don't even consider that there could be alternatives. The outside world becomes a mirror that reflects back what is supposedly normal and right. Individuals want to conform to this mirror so as not to fall out of the picture.

In this way, mediocrity stabilizes itself in a subtle way: it is not imposed, but voluntarily adopted because it seems to confirm one's own identity. It is interesting to note that it is precisely the adaptation to the average that creates a feeling of security, but one that is based on an illusion. People feel protected because they live like everyone else. But this security crumbles the moment external circumstances change. Those who base their existence on a single salary believe themselves to be secure as long as the salary comes in regularly. But when they lose their job, it becomes clear that this security never really existed. The average person lives in a system that promises stability but cannot guarantee it. The two percent, on the other hand, see through this illusion. They know that security only lasts if it does not depend on external factors, but on structures that they themselves have created. Psychology refers to this mechanism as learned security. People feel secure when they repeatedly experience that certain patterns work. If they go to work for years and are rewarded for it, then this pattern seems unshakeable. But in reality, it is only stable as long as the environment remains stable. The two percent have questioned this learned security. They have recognized that true stability can only be achieved by becoming independent of external conditions. That is why they build systems that can still function even if a single pillar collapses. Another aspect of the psychology of mediocrity is what is known as self-esteem economics. People protect their self-esteem by explaining away failures. Those who fail to break out of the average tell themselves that it would not have been possible anyway. This keeps their self-esteem intact, but the opportunity for change is lost. This psychological strategy is understandable because it avoids pain. But it keeps people trapped. They choose to protect their self-esteem at the expense of their freedom.

The two percent choose the opposite path: they are willing to risk their self-esteem in the short term by allowing mistakes, enduring criticism, and accepting setbacks. They know that true self-esteem does not come from avoiding failure, but from the ability to survive failure. A central area in which the psychology of mediocrity manifests itself is the fear of being judged by others. People want to be liked; they want to be accepted. This need for social validation leads them to make themselves small when they sense that their differences might cause offense. Those who break out of the average risk misunderstanding, envy, and ridicule. This fear paralyzes many and keeps them on familiar paths. But this is precisely where the key lies: The two percent have learned to live with this fear.

They know that not everyone will understand them, that not everyone will agree with them. But they do not allow this circumstance to influence their decisions. They accept that deviating from the average always creates social friction. And instead of bowing to this friction, they accept it as part of the journey. The psychology of mediocrity is also evident in the way people think about time.

The average person lives in the short term. They plan from paycheck to paycheck, from vacation to vacation, from year to year. Long-term thinking is difficult because it is abstract and the reward is far off. The two percent think differently. They are willing to sacrifice short-term comfort to gain long-term freedom. This thinking contradicts the human tendency toward immediate reward, which is described in psychology as "present bias." Studies have shown that people disproportionately prefer rewards that are immediately available over rewards that lie in the future. That's why many people don't save, don't invest, and don't think in terms of decades. The two percent, on the other hand, have learned to overcome this bias. They can imagine how their actions today will affect their freedom in ten or twenty years. They have the ability to think in long time frames, while the average person remains stuck in short cycles. The role of emotions is also central.

The average person avoids negative emotions and seeks short-term satisfaction. This pattern leads to the suppression of uncomfortable truths. Those who are dissatisfied with their job convince themselves that it would be the same everywhere else. Those who are in financial difficulties convince themselves that they are just unlucky. This suppression provides short-term protection, but it prevents growth. The two percent have a different relationship with emotions. They allow dissatisfaction to be felt and use it as a driving force. They see frustration not as an end point, but as an indication that change is necessary. This ability to not fear emotions, but to use them, is one of the psychological differences that separate them from the average. When you take all these factors together, you realize that the average is not the result of a lack of intelligence or talent, but of a network of psychological mechanisms. Status quo bias, loss aversion, the need to belong, self-esteem protection, present bias – they all work together to create a life that appears stable, but in reality is stagnant. The two percent have managed to see through this network. They are not free from these mechanisms, but they have learned to consciously control them. They know that fear of loss must not paralyze them, that belonging is not more important than freedom, that short-term comfort is not worth sacrificing long-term freedom. This shows that the way out of mediocrity is not a secret known only to a select few.

It is a decision that anyone could make. But because this decision means fighting against one's own psychological programs, most people do not take it. They remain in a comfort zone that pretends to offer security, when in reality it carries the greatest insecurity: the insecurity of not having truly lived one's own life. The psychology of mediocrity is not only a description of what people think, but also an explanation of how they feel and how they structure their own lives. Those who live an average life have certain emotional patterns that lead them back to the same paths again and again. These patterns are so powerful that they seem like invisible laws. But they are not natural, they are learned. And because they are learned, they can also be unlearned or broken. But to understand this, we need to delve deeper into the mechanisms that keep mediocrity so stable. One of these mechanisms is the fear of uncertainty. People like predictability. They feel more secure when they know what will happen tomorrow, even if tomorrow does not make them happy. This predictability gives life structure, and structure is confused with certainty. The average person believes that they are in control as long as they maintain the same daily routine.

But this control is deceptive because it depends on external factors. A job that seemed secure yesterday may be gone today. An income that seemed stable may be wiped out by a crisis. The belief that predictability means security is a fallacy. It prevents people from learning to deal with real uncertainty. The two percent are different in this respect. They have realized that uncertainty is unavoidable. Instead of fearing it, they learn to live with it. They accept that there are no guarantees and build their lives in such a way that they remain flexible. This attitude requires psychological strength because it means giving up illusions. It is easier to believe in the security of a system than to accept the truth that systems are unstable. But it is precisely this difference that determines who remains average and who overcomes it. Another mechanism that shapes mediocrity is the fear of rejection. People are afraid of being different from the group. They fear being excluded. This fear is deeply rooted in evolution because belonging used to be a matter of life and death. In the modern world, rejection no longer means death, but it is still perceived as a threat. That's why people prefer to conform rather than risk standing out. This conformity leads them to suppress their own ideas, dreams, and potential just to stay in the middle. The two percent haven't completely overcome this mechanism, but they've learned to interpret it differently.

They don't see rejection as a sign of failure, but as an indication that they are taking a different path. They understand that it is not possible to please everyone and that the price of conformity is often too high. Those who always want to please others ultimately lose themselves. Those who are willing to risk rejection gain authenticity. And authenticity is a force that attracts others, even if it irritates them at first. Mediocrity also thrives on the power of habit. Routines provide structure, they make decisions easier, they save energy. But they also hold us back. The average person lives in fixed habits that hardly ever change. They get up at the same time, take the same route to work, meet the same people, consume the same media, think the same thoughts. This repetition creates stability, but it excludes anything new. And new things are a prerequisite for growth. Those who remain in the same patterns cannot develop. Research on habits shows that they leave deep traces in the brain. Neural connections that are activated frequently become stronger. This means that the more often a behavior is repeated, the more likely it is to occur. That is why it is so difficult to change habits. It is not just a question of willpower, but a question of biological structure. But this is precisely where the challenge lies: if you want to break away from the average, you have to consciously break old habits and build new ones.

This process requires energy, patience, and repetition. The two percent are willing to do this work. They know that habits are the foundation of their future. The average, on the other hand, remains in patterns that stabilize them but also limit them. Another aspect of the psychology of mediocrity is rationalization. People seek explanations for why they are where they are. These explanations serve to protect their self-image. Those who remain average tell themselves stories such as: "I didn't have the right opportunities." Or: "I'm not the type to take risks." Or: "Others were luckier." These stories provide relief, but they make people passive. They take away responsibility and pass it on to external circumstances. Psychologists call this external attribution. The average attributes to the outside world. The two percent, on the other hand, attribute to the inside. They ask: “What can I do? How can I learn? What can I change?” These questions are uncomfortable, but they enable action. The role of emotions in dealing with money is also part of this psychology. The average person often associates money with fear, scarcity, or consumption. Money is either spent immediately to satisfy needs or viewed with concern because it is scarce. This emotional relationship keeps people in a cycle of dependency.

The two percent have a different attitude. They do not see money as a threat or a short-term pleasure, but as a tool. They view it more soberly, more rationally, more strategically. This emotional distance allows them to use money in a way that brings them long-term freedom. The average person also lives in a time structure that is characterized by external control. The calendar, working hours, social rhythms—everything dictates how time should be used. This external control is rarely questioned because it seems normal. But it leads people to view their lifetime not as their own property, but as a resource that belongs to others. The two percent, on the other hand, have reclaimed their time. They know that freedom means being able to control their own time. They are willing to work harder in the short term in order to be independent in the long term. This shift in how they deal with time is psychologically crucial. Because if you don't control your time, you don't control your life. When you look at these mechanisms together—the fear of uncertainty, the fear of rejection, the power of habits, rationalization, the emotional relationship to money, and the external control of time—you realize that mediocrity is a self-stabilizing system. It creates people who maintain it because they feel secure in it. And that is precisely what makes it so difficult to break through. But difficult does not mean impossible. It just means that awareness and determination are necessary. Psychology clearly shows us that the difference between the 98 percent and the two percent lies not in external circumstances, but in internal attitudes.

It is not education, background, or talent that makes the difference, but the way one deals with fear, habit, time, and responsibility. Mediocrity is a choice—an unconscious one, but still a choice. And anyone who begins to make this choice consciously has already taken the first step out of it. When we look at the psychology of mediocrity in all its depth, it becomes clear that it is not just a collection of individual errors in thinking, but a complete system that has become entrenched over generations. It is a system that affects not only individuals, but shapes entire societies. And because it has such a comprehensive effect, most people take it for granted. But the obviousness of mediocrity is precisely what makes it so dangerous. It makes us forget that it is only one possibility among many, that life does not necessarily have to be lived the way 98 percent of people live it. This system begins in childhood.

Children learn early on that conformity is rewarded and deviation is punished. The child who sits quietly is praised. The child who asks questions that don't fit the mold is reprimanded. Over the years, a psychological pattern emerges: you feel secure when you conform and insecure when you deviate. This pattern persists into adulthood, even if the sanctions become more subtle. Adults who take unusual paths no longer risk punishment from their teachers, but rather disapproval from society. And because this disapproval is painful, people prefer to stay in the middle. But the price for this is high. Those who constantly conform lose touch with their own individuality. They base their lives on the expectations of others and forget what they themselves actually want. This self-forgetfulness is a core characteristic of mediocrity. It makes people docile, but it also makes them unfree. And it is this lack of freedom that prevents them from belonging to the top two percent. Because freedom does not begin with money, but with the ability to take oneself seriously and go one's own way, even if it deviates from the norm. Psychology refers to this as internalized norms. Norms that originally came from outside are internalized so deeply that they are no longer experienced as foreign. People believe that they are their own convictions, when in fact they are only learned rules.

Those who live in mediocrity do not live according to their own standards, but according to those they have adopted. And as long as they do not recognize this, they remain trapped in it. The two percent differ in that they have learned to question these norms. They ask themselves whether what everyone else is doing also makes sense for them. They don't just accept things, they examine them. And it is precisely in this examination that the first step toward freedom lies. Another central element of the psychology of mediocrity is the way people deal with failure. The average person sees failure as proof that they shouldn't have tried in the first place. A failed project, a failed attempt, a lost investment – all of these are seen as warnings to be more cautious next time. The result is that people dare less and less. The two percent, on the other hand, see failure as a necessary stage. They know that without mistakes, you can't learn anything new. They do not fear failure because they understand it as part of the process. This difference in dealing with mistakes is crucial. It determines whether someone remains average or rises above it. Research on resilience confirms this.

People who see setbacks as challenges develop more strength, while those who see setbacks as defeats fall into passivity. Mediocrity is characterized by this passivity. It justifies it with phrases such as "You have to be realistic" or "It just wasn't meant to be." But in reality, it is not realism, but fear. It is the fear of failing again that prevents people from trying again. The two percent have come to terms with this fear. They do not make it disappear, but they do not let it control them. The relationship to time also distinguishes the average from the exceptional. The average person lives in short-term cycles. They think about the next paycheck, the next vacation, the next purchase. This way of thinking is understandable because immediate rewards have a stronger effect on the brain than distant ones. But it keeps you trapped in the present, which can never be more than mediocre. The two percent think in decades. They imagine how their actions today will shape their freedom in ten, twenty, or thirty years. This ability to think long-term contradicts the human tendency toward immediate reward, but it can be learned. And it is one of the most important psychological skills that makes the difference between dependence and independence. The psychology of mediocrity is also evident in our relationship with money. For most people, money is a means of satisfying immediate needs. They work in order to consume, and consumption serves to generate short-term feelings of happiness.

This relationship keeps them in a constant cycle: work, earn, spend. Money always remains scarce in this cycle because it does not grow, but is consumed. The two percent, on the other hand, see money as a tool. They do not spend it primarily on consumption, but use it to build structures. They do not see what each euro can buy today, but what it will make possible tomorrow. This shift in perspective is psychologically crucial because it radically changes behavior. The psychology of mediocrity is therefore a psychology of limitation. It limits thinking by placing security above freedom. It limits feeling by reinforcing fear of rejection and failure. It limits action by placing short-term rewards above long-term planning. All these limitations together keep the majority where they are. But they are not laws of nature. They are patterns that can be learned and therefore also unlearned. Every person has the ability to redefine their relationship to security, rejection, failure, time, and money. But few do so because it is uncomfortable. This is precisely the crucial point: the average person remains average not because they have to, but because they want to—unconsciously, but nevertheless willingly. They choose comfort over truth, the familiar over the possible, the collective over the individual. This choice seems harmless, but it determines their entire life. The two percent have made a different choice. They have had the courage to no longer be driven by psychological mechanisms, but to consciously control these mechanisms. They have accepted that fear, uncertainty, and failure are part of life, but they have decided that they are not obstacles, but tools. This chapter on the psychology of mediocrity ends with a clear insight: the difference between the 98 percent and the two percent lies not in external circumstances, but in internal attitudes. It is not origin, education, or luck that makes the difference, but the psychological ability not to blindly follow one's own patterns. Those who recognize this have taken the first step toward overcoming the myth of mediocrity. For the psychology that limits us can also be the psychology that liberates us—if we are willing to use it.

Notes:

Notes:

Chapter 3: The Power of the 2%

When you look at the two percent who are truly financially independent, there is a peculiar fascination in this small number. At first glance, it seems like an abstract statistic, but it is enormously meaningful. Two percent means that out of a hundred people, only two have taken the step out of dependence, while ninety-eight remain trapped in structures that hold them captive. This small minority lives beyond ordinary worries, beyond the daily question of whether their wages are enough to pay the bills, beyond the fear of losing their jobs. They embody a freedom that is almost unimaginable for the majority, and that is precisely why they have something mystical about them. But they are not supernatural beings, geniuses, or the chosen few. They are people who have learned to think, feel, and act differently. The power of these two percent lies not in their numbers, but in their influence. Those who are financially independent have the opportunity to shape their lives freely, make decisions according to their own standards, and build structures that change not only their own existence, but also that of others. This power is not manifested in ostentatious wealth, but in the ability to exist independently of external systems. Most people are bound by their economic situation to places, times, and dependencies. They have to work to live. The two percent, on the other hand, have reversed the relationship: they live, and their work, if it can even be called work, is an expression of their freedom.

It is interesting to note that these two percent are not necessarily the richest in the material sense. There are billionaires who, despite their enormous wealth, are trapped in dependencies – dependencies on markets, on political systems, on public opinion.

And there are people with comparatively modest wealth who are nevertheless completely independent because their structures are designed to enable freedom. This shows that the two percent is not about absolute numbers, but about quality of life. Independence does not necessarily mean unlimited wealth, but the ability to make decisions free from external constraints. The power of these two percent lies in the fact that they have broken away from the rhythm of the average. While the majority live from month to month, from paycheck to paycheck, from vacation to vacation, they have built structures that allow them to think and act for the long term. They are not under pressure to achieve immediate results, but can develop plans over years or decades. This long-term perspective gives them an enormous advantage, because it allows them to see and seize opportunities that remain hidden to the average person. Those who are caught up in everyday life only see the next step. Those who are free see the horizon. Psychology describes this difference as a shift in the time horizon. Average people operate in short cycles because their resources are limited.

They have to deal with the here and now because tomorrow is uncertain. However, this focus prevents them from developing long-term strategies. The two percent, on the other hand, have the luxury of expanding their thinking. They invest today because they know that the fruits will ripen tomorrow. They build, even if it takes years for results to show. This ability to think long-term is not a coincidence, but the result of conscious decisions. Another aspect of the power of the two percent is their inner independence. They have learned not to be swayed by the opinion of the majority. While the 98 percent are constantly seeking validation, the two percent act according to their own standards. This inner independence is a prerequisite for outer independence. Those who are constantly dependent on the judgment of others cannot make decisions that deviate from the norm. But the two percent consciously deviate because they know that freedom lies only where one does not follow the herd. Sociology refers to this as the phenomenon of minority power. Studies have shown that small, consistent minorities can exert an enormous influence on majorities.

When a small group persistently holds on to a conviction, the majority begins to question its own assumptions. The two percent embody precisely this minority power. Through their lives, they show that independence is possible. They are living proof that the average is not a given, but can be broken. Their existence is a silent but powerful message to the 98 percent: there is another way. This power is both inspiring and threatening. Inspiring because it gives hope that another life is possible. Threatening because it exposes the lie of the average. Anyone who sees the two percent realizes that there is no excuse for remaining mediocre. They realize that it is not a matter of origin or education, but of decisions. And it is precisely this thought that is difficult for many to bear. Because it takes away their excuse that their life is the way it is because it could not be any other way. The existence of the two percent forces people to confront their own responsibility. Psychology refers to this reaction as cognitive dissonance. When people are confronted with information that contradicts their self-image, they often react defensively. They criticize the two percent, they accuse them of being lucky, they declare their success unattainable.

All of this serves to keep their own image stable. Because accepting that they too could have acted differently would be too painful. The power of the two percent lies not only in their freedom, but also in the fact that they visibly challenge the structures of the average. But this power is not loud. It does not impose itself. It is more of a quiet force that works by example. People who live independently do not have to proselytize. Their lives themselves are the message. And this message has a profound effect because it shows that independence is not an unattainable ideal, but a lived possibility. Through their very existence, the two percent prove that freedom is not a dream, but can be a reality. This makes it clear that the power of the two percent does not lie in money alone. It lies in the combination of financial independence, inner strength, and long-term thinking. These three elements together create a freedom that goes far beyond what the average person knows.

They create the opportunity to lead a life that is not dictated by external circumstances, but by one's own choices. And that is precisely what makes the two percent so significant. They are not many, but they show what is possible when one has the courage to leave the average behind. The power of the two percent lies not only in their financial independence, but above all in the fact that they have developed a different perception of reality. While the 98 percent view the world through the lens of security, conformity, and short-term survival, the two percent have learned to shift their perception. They see opportunities where others see obstacles, they see long-term developments where others only see the next step, and they see freedom where the majority only sees uncertainty. This altered perception is not innate, but learned, and it is the foundation of the power that sets them apart from the masses.

Psychologically speaking, it is a change of perspective that is well documented in cognitive research. People tend not to perceive reality objectively, but through the lens of their beliefs, experiences, and emotions. This lens determines which possibilities become visible and which remain invisible. Those who are convinced that life is hard and unfair will find confirmation of this assumption everywhere. Those who are convinced that opportunities exist will discover them where others carelessly pass by. The two percent have consciously shaped their lenses so that they see opportunities, possibilities, and potential. This explains why they act where others remain stuck. A key difference lies in their attitude toward mistakes and setbacks. The average person sees a mistake as proof of their own incompetence. They interpret failure as confirmation that they should not have set out on the path in the first place. This attitude leads most people to give up after a few failed attempts. The two percent interpret mistakes completely differently. For them, mistakes are information, feedback, indications of necessary adjustments. They separate their self-esteem from their results.

They know that a failed project does not mean that they have failed as a person. This attitude allows them to move forward where others stand still. Research on "grit," or perseverance and passion for long-term goals, shows that this ability is one of the key predictors of success. Angela Duckworth's studies prove that it is not intelligence or talent that makes the difference, but perseverance. The two percent embody this principle. They persevere, they stick with it, they overcome setbacks. They know that the path to independence is not a straight one, but full of detours and obstacles. But they also know that every obstacle they overcome makes them stronger and brings them closer to their goal. Another aspect of their power lies in their relationship to risk. The average person fears risk and interprets it as danger. That is why they avoid it as much as possible. But risk is unavoidable. Even the average life is risky, even if it doesn't seem so. You can lose your job, fall ill, or become a victim of external circumstances. The supposedly risk-free life is full of invisible risks that are all the more dangerous because you don't consciously choose them. The two percent, on the other hand, consciously take risks. They choose the risks they take, and they do so with their eyes open. They see risk not as a threat, but as the price of admission to freedom. And because they choose it consciously, they can control it better. The power of the two percent also lies in the fact that they have learned to take responsibility radically. The average person tends to relinquish responsibility.

They explain failures with external circumstances, they look for the causes in the system, in politics, in other people. This attitude protects the ego, but it makes them passive. The two percent take responsibility even where they objectively cannot control everything. They don't ask first who is to blame, but what they can do. This attitude gives them power because it enables them to act. Even if they fail, they have the power to learn from their failure. The average person, on the other hand, remains powerless because they believe that others determine their fate. In research, this is referred to as the "locus of control" theory. People with an internal locus of control believe that they can control their lives. People with an external locus of control believe that external forces determine their lives. The difference between the two percent and the 98 percent can be pinpointed precisely here. The two percent have an internal locus of control. They feel responsible for their lives, and this feeling gives them the energy to shape them. The majority have an external locus of control. They believe that external circumstances dominate and therefore remain passive. The power of the two percent is also power over their own time. The average person lives at a pace set by others. Working hours, obligations, and social expectations determine the daily routine.

The two percent, on the other hand, have learned to organize their own time. They invest it in projects that give them freedom, not in routines that keep them trapped. Time is the scarcest resource in life, and those who do not control it are controlled by others. Control over one's own time is therefore perhaps the deepest form of power there is, and it is a characteristic that clearly separates the two percent from the majority. In addition, the two percent have the power to retell stories. Stories are the foundation on which cultures and identities are built. The average person lives in stories that deal with security, conformity, and normality. These stories are constantly repeated by the media, schools, and institutions.

They dictate what a normal life looks like and suggest that deviation is dangerous. The two percent reject these stories. They tell their own. Stories of freedom, of creativity, of courage. These new narratives shape their identity and thus also their actions. Those who tell themselves a different story begin to live differently. Their power also unfolds on a collective level. Although they make up only two percent, they have a disproportionately large influence. They create companies, innovations, and ideas that shape society. Through their actions, they show that there are other ways, and in doing so, they change the norms that the majority also follows. In sociology, this is referred to as the theory of "critical mass." Small groups can trigger big changes if they act consistently and remain visible. The two percent are an example of this dynamic. They are few in number, but their impact extends far beyond their numbers.

Ultimately, the power of the two percent is not just a question of wealth, but a question of attitude. It is the attitude of shaping one's own life instead of letting it be shaped. It is the attitude of understanding fear not as a limitation, but as a signal. It is the attitude of seeing time as a possession rather than an obligation. And it is the attitude of writing your own stories instead of repeating those of others. This attitude is open to everyone, but only a few embrace it. The message that emerges from this is clear: there is no natural reason to remain average. Everyone could learn to think differently, act differently, feel differently. But most people don't because the price is uncomfortable. The two percent have paid it, and in doing so, they have gained a power that goes far beyond material wealth. It is the power to be free, and freedom is the deepest form of influence a person can have. The two percent have a power that goes far beyond what can be measured in numbers.

This power is not only material, it is also psychological, cultural, and symbolic. It radiates because it embodies a possibility that seems unimaginable to the majority. The average person believes that one must come to terms with the circumstances, that one should be happy if one can make ends meet, and that it is presumptuous to want more. The two percent refute this assumption by their very existence. They are living counterexamples to the claim that there is no other way. Their power lies in their ability to shift norms. Societies are defined by what is considered normal. Normality is not a given; it is the result of collective habits. When the majority lives in a certain way, that way of life is declared the norm. But this norm is unstable because it can be shaken by individual, consistent exceptions. The two percent are such exceptions. By showing that one does not have to remain trapped in the cycle of work, consumption, and dependence, they shift what is considered possible.

They change the framework of what is conceivable, and that alone is a power greater than any fortune. From a psychological perspective, the two percent have a so-called model effect. In social psychology, we talk about social models who show other people how to do something through their behavior. Children learn not through instructions, but through role models. Adults are no different. We orient ourselves toward what others live. If most people remain average, then the average acts as a role model that forces conformity. But as soon as someone who lives differently becomes visible, a new space opens up. The existence of the two percent shows that you don't have to follow the rules of mediocrity. They show that freedom is possible, and this knowledge alone already changes the scope of action for the majority. The power of these role models is not always welcome. It also provokes resistance.

Because those who live an average life often see the two percent as a mirror that is painful to look at. It shows that they could have done more, that they chose to remain small. This mirror triggers defensiveness. That is why the two percent are criticized, ridiculed, sometimes even despised. But these reactions do not change the fact that their existence changes the way people think. They show that there are no excuses that justify a life of mediocrity. You can have excuses, but the fact that others have found freedom without better conditions exposes them for what they are: protective mechanisms for a self-image that masks one's own passivity.

The power of the two percent is also a power over the future. While the majority lives from day to day, the two percent create structures that can have an impact for generations. They create values that endure not only for themselves, but also for their children, their communities, and their society. This intergenerational dimension is what makes their power so sustainable. Those who are independent can use resources in such a way that they will still have an impact decades later. They are not only free for themselves, but also become the architects of a future that extends beyond their own lives. From an economic perspective, this is a fundamental difference. The average person consumes, while the two percent invest. Consumption ends in the moment, while investments have an impact on the future. This shift changes everything. It creates capital that has not only a financial but also a cultural impact. Because those who are free have the opportunity to promote other forms of work, education, and community. They are no longer part of the cycle that thrives on dependence, but instead create alternative structures. That is why the power of the two percent is not only private but also social. Another aspect lies in their ability to make independent decisions. Most people make their decisions under the pressure of external necessities. They have to work to pay their bills. They have to make compromises because they are dependent on their income. The two percent, on the other hand, have the opportunity to decide according to their own standards. They can choose what to do and what not to do, not out of compulsion, but out of freedom. This ability to make independent decisions is an expression of power that goes deeper than any amount of money.

Ultimately, power means being able to make your own decisions freely. Psychology calls this feeling self-efficacy. Albert Bandura described it as the belief that you are capable of shaping your own life. Self-efficacy is one of the strongest predictors of success. The two percent embody it in a radical way. They do not see themselves as victims of circumstance, but as creators of their own reality. And this attitude shapes their actions in a way that sets them apart from the majority. Because those who see themselves as effective act differently, look for solutions where others see problems, and persevere where others give up. The power of the two percent is also a power of distance. They can distance themselves from the mechanisms that determine the majority. They are not driven by the fear of not being able to pay their bills. They are not forced to trade time for money. This distance allows them to see life more clearly.

They don't have to react, they can act. They can choose which projects to pursue, which ideas to implement, which values to live by. The average person, on the other hand, is always driven, always in a hurry, always busy with the next thing. This drive prevents them from seeing the world clearly. The two percent, on the other hand, have the space to look at the big picture. This distance also has a spiritual dimension. Freedom means not only being financially independent, but also becoming inwardly free from the shackles that the majority invisibly wear. Those who are not constantly forced to follow the rhythm of the average have the opportunity to think more deeply about meaning, values, and their own lives. That is why the power of the two percent is not only economic, but also existential. It allows for a life that is not reduced to functioning, but to creating. And here lies the core: the two percent are not defined by their external circumstances, but by their attitude.

Anyone could develop this attitude. It requires courage, perseverance, and the will to leave one's comfort zone. But it is possible, regardless of origin, education, or luck. The power of the two percent is not a privilege, but a result. A result of decisions that anyone could have made, but that most do not make. This shows that the power of the two percent is not exclusive. It is open. It is accessible. But only a few seize it because it is uncomfortable. Those who seize it change not only their own lives, but also the world in which they live. For the existence of this minority changes the horizon of what is possible for everyone. It shows that mediocrity is not without alternative, but that beyond the average lies a freedom that is open to everyone. The power of the two percent does not unfold in noise or spectacle, but in a quiet consistency that is built up over years.

It is not the result of sudden strokes of luck or secret tricks, but the result of a different approach to the conditions of life. While the majority settles into existing structures, the two percent use these structures to break out of them. It is a paradoxical movement: they often start where everyone else starts, in the same schools, the same jobs, the same systems, and yet they gradually develop a different relationship to these systems. They do not see them as an end point, but as a starting point. If you want to understand why this small minority is so powerful, you have to look at how they think. The average person thinks in terms of limitations, the two percent in terms of possibilities. The average person is guided by what seems feasible, the two percent by what is desirable and can then be made feasible. This difference is not trivial. It changes the way you set goals, make decisions, and deal with obstacles. Those who think within limits immediately see why something cannot work. Those who think in terms of possibilities ask how it could work. This small difference in the question changes your entire life.

Scientifically, this difference can be explained by the concept of self-efficacy. People with high self-efficacy experience difficulties as challenges, not threats. They feel capable of exerting influence, even when circumstances are difficult. This belief is self-reinforcing: those who feel effective act more, those who act more experience more effectiveness, and this cycle intensifies over time. The two percent have cultivated this cycle. They have learned that they can produce results through their actions, even when there are setbacks. This belief makes them both resilient and creative. The power of the two percent is also evident in how they deal with resources. The average person views resources as something to be consumed. Time is used up, money is spent, energy is used up. The two percent see resources as something that can be invested and multiplied. Time can be invested in systems that free up time later.

Money can be invested in such a way that it grows. Energy can flow into projects that bear fruit in the long term. This different relationship with resources creates a leverage effect that has exponential effects over many years. Another aspect of their power lies in their relationship to risk. The average person avoids risk because they equate it with danger. But those who avoid risk also avoid opportunity. The two percent accept risk as inevitable, but they learn to calculate it. They look for ways to shape risks in such a way that they maximize opportunities and minimize losses. That doesn't mean they never fail. On the contrary, they fail often, but they do so in a controlled manner. They don't put all their eggs in one basket, but learn from every attempt. And it is precisely this learning that makes them more powerful, because it enables them to remain capable of acting in an uncertain world. Their power is therefore not merely economic, but also psychological. It is based on the ability to find stability in uncertainty, to see opportunities in risks, and to recognize lessons in mistakes. Average thinking is defensive; it protects what you have. The thinking of the two percent is expansive; it seeks what is possible. Over time, these two attitudes create worlds that can hardly be compared. The power of this minority also unfolds on a cultural level. They are the ones who bring in new ideas, create innovations, and change societies. The average preserves the existing, the two percent create the new. Without them, there would be no progress, no development, no change.

Their ability to think against the grain is what drives civilizations forward. And even though they often encounter resistance, history shows that it has always been a small minority that has initiated major upheavals. This cultural power is closely linked to their economic freedom. Those who are dependent can hardly afford to think outside the box. They risk too much. Those who are independent have the freedom to try new things, even if they are initially rejected. That is why financial independence is not only a private advantage, but a prerequisite for social innovation. The two percent have a freedom that the majority does not have: the freedom to experiment without their lives depending on immediate success. This freedom is the source of their creative power. The power of the two percent also has a symbolic dimension. They embody a possibility that seems unattainable for many. This embodiment is inspiring, but also disturbing. It inspires because it shows that more is possible. It disturbs because it exposes the excuses of the majority. This symbolic effect is perhaps the most profound aspect of their power. They don't need to preach or persuade—their lives themselves are the argument. They show that one is not forced to remain average. This reveals an uncomfortable truth: anyone could follow the path of the two percent, but most do not.

They do not do so because it is easier to have excuses. It is easier to believe that one has too little talent, that circumstances were unfavorable, that others were more privileged. These explanations are more convenient than taking responsibility. The existence of the two percent makes it clear that there are no definitive barriers, only barriers that we have accepted. And that is precisely where the power of this minority lies: it shows that freedom is a choice, not a gift. Ultimately, the power of the two percent is a quiet but profound revolution. It shows that life is not defined by the average, but by the opportunities one is willing to seize. It proves that it is possible to create structures that make people independent, even if the majority remains in the cycle of dependence. And it invites everyone to seize this opportunity, even if it is uncomfortable. Because the truth is: mediocrity is not a necessity, it is a choice.

And anyone can make this choice again at any time. The power of the two percent cannot be understood if it is measured solely by their material wealth. Money is undoubtedly an important tool, but it is not the essence of their freedom. The psychological, social, and cultural dimensions of their independence go much deeper. Most people only see the external results—houses, travel, time that is not dictated by external forces—but the decisive factor lies in the invisible: in attitude, in thinking, in inner freedom. For it is this inner independence that has made it possible to create outer independence. The average person remains average because they seek their power outside themselves. They believe that systems, governments, employers, or external circumstances determine what is possible. They live with an external focus of control that seems to give them security, but in reality creates dependence. The two percent have an internal focus of control. They are convinced that they themselves can set the decisive course, even when circumstances are adverse. This conviction is not naive, but guides their actions. It causes them to become active where others remain passive.

And it is precisely this action, repeated over many years, that creates the structures that make them independent. Psychologically speaking, the two percent have learned to see through the mechanisms of fear. The majority fear uncertainty and avoid it. They fear failure and interpret it as proof of incompetence. They fear rejection and organize their lives around pleasing others. These fears hold the average person in their grip, and they seem so normal that hardly anyone questions them. The two percent have developed a different way of dealing with fear. They know that fear is a companion to growth, not a signal to retreat. They know that failure means information, not identity. They know that rejection is inevitable when you go your own way. By not avoiding fear, but integrating it into their decisions, they take away its power to determine their lives. This ability gives them enormous inner freedom. And it is this inner freedom that is transmitted to the outside world. It allows them to consciously take risks, make investments, and create structures that do not depend on day-to-day circumstances. It allows them to pursue projects whose fruits will only become visible in years to come. It allows them to make decisions that are born not out of scarcity but out of abundance. While the majority live defensively, the two percent live offensively. They shape things instead of just reacting. This creative power also has a cultural dimension. Those who are independent can question values and norms. They do not have to conform to what the majority considers normal. They can tell their own stories, implement their own ideas, and go their own way. This cultural power is evident in the innovations that originate from minorities. It is almost never the large majorities that create something new. It is the small groups that are willing to deviate from the norm. The two percent belong to these groups. They are living proof that deviation is not only possible but necessary if a society is to develop further. At the same time, their power unfolds a symbolic force. They are projection screens. For some, they are role models, for others, the target of envy and criticism. In both cases, they have an impact. They change the thinking of the majority, whether they want it or not. Because their existence shows that freedom is not just a theoretical ideal, but a lived reality. It shows that origin, education, or luck are not the ultimate criteria, but that inner attitude, perseverance, and decisions are decisive. However, this does not mean that everyone will automatically follow the path of the two percent. Most will not do so because the psychological hurdles seem too high. It is more comfortable to remain average, to find excuses, to relinquish responsibility. But the power of the two percent lies in the fact that they prove that it is possible. They hold open a door that anyone could walk through if they wanted to. This open door is a silent challenge to the majority. It says: It's up to you. Not your background, not your degree, not your luck. You. Sociology describes this phenomenon as normative tension. The existence of a minority that lives differently creates tension in the consciousness of the majority. This tension can be resolved through conformity—by criticizing or devaluing the minority—or it can be used to question one's own life. Most choose the first path because it is easier.

But some allow themselves to be challenged by the tension. They begin to question their own patterns. They begin to see possibilities they didn't see before. And that's exactly how the power of the two percent works in the long term: not through coercion, but through inspiration; not through pressure, but through example. From an economic perspective, they create dynamics that extend far beyond their own lives. They create companies that provide jobs. They invest in projects that promote innovation. They change markets by setting new standards. Their freedom allows them to take risks that would be unacceptable to the majority. And that is precisely how progress is made. It can be said that without the two percent, there would be no movement. They are the troublemakers of the average, the engines of change. But perhaps their greatest power lies in the fact that they are not dependent on the approval of others. They don't need validation to follow their path.

That makes them untouchable. The average person lives by the judgment of the group, while the two percent live by the clarity of their own convictions. This independence of thought is the deepest core of their freedom. It allows them to do things that the majority would never dare to do because they are too fixated on the judgment of others. In the end, it becomes clear that the power of the two percent is not a magical quality, but the sum of many small differences in thinking, feeling, and acting. They have learned to take responsibility instead of giving it away. They have learned to use fear instead of succumbing to it. They have learned to think long-term instead of consuming short-term. They have learned to write their own stories instead of repeating those of others. This sum makes them free. And this freedom is the source of a power that is not based on domination, but on creation. This chapter on the power of the two percent ends with a simple but profound message: anyone can become part of this minority. There are no insurmountable external obstacles. There are only internal boundaries that one has accepted. The power of the two percent lies in the fact that they have not accepted these boundaries. And that is precisely why they are free.

Notes:

Notes:

Chapter 4: Why origin and education are not decisive

If you want to understand the difference between the two percent and the remaining ninety-eight, you inevitably come across a widespread belief: that success and independence depend primarily on background and education. It is an assumption that is deeply rooted in our culture, and it seems to be confirmed by countless examples. Those born into wealthy circumstances often have a better start in life, and those who have access to good education seem to be better prepared. But these observations, as superficially plausible as they may seem, do not explain why people with seemingly perfect conditions remain average, while others who start out with significant disadvantages find their way into the two percent. The idea that background or education is the deciding factor is psychologically comforting. It allows us to relinquish responsibility.

Those who were not born rich or do not have an outstanding educational qualification can reassure themselves with the explanation that independence is simply not meant for them. This belief stabilizes the average because it acts as a justification: you did not fail, you just did not have the right conditions. But reality repeatedly disproves this assumption. Stories of people who come from the humblest of backgrounds and yet have achieved enormous freedom show that background is not an insurmountable obstacle. And there are countless examples of academics with the best education who remain financially dependent throughout their lives. From a sociological perspective, background undoubtedly plays a role. It influences access to resources, networks, and knowledge. But this role is not deterministic. It creates starting conditions, not end points. People from favorable backgrounds can squander their opportunities, and people from unfavorable backgrounds can find ways to overcome these disadvantages. The difference lies in the attitude with which they view their circumstances. The majority accept their background as fate. The two percent see it as a starting point that can be shaped. The same applies to education. Here, too, the myth is strong: those who study, collect diplomas, and hold prestigious titles are supposedly better equipped to deal with the uncertainties of life. But reality shows that education alone is not the decisive factor. There are academics with doctorates who are stuck in mediocre jobs, and there are people without formal education who start businesses, build systems, and become independent. Education is a tool, but it is not the key. What matters is how you use this tool. Those who use education only to better adapt to existing structures remain average. Those who use it to break through or redesign structures can gain freedom. Psychologically, this difference can be explained by Carol Dweck's concept of "growth mindset" research. People with a static self-image believe that their intelligence, talents, and abilities are inherently limited.

They use education to prove what they can do, not to grow. People with a dynamic self-image, on the other hand, see education as a process that constantly expands their horizons. They seek out new challenges, see mistakes as learning opportunities, and use knowledge to create opportunities. The two percent belong to the second group. For them, education is not a degree, but a toolbox that can be expanded and used again and again. The fixation on origin and education is also evident in social narratives. The stories of successful people are often told in a way that emphasizes their background or education. The fact that they studied at elite universities or come from privileged families is highlighted. This suggests that these factors are the key to success. But these narratives overlook the many counterexamples. They overlook the entrepreneurs who dropped out of school and still built empires. They overlook the artists who came from poverty and still gained influence. They overlook the thinkers who broke new ground against all conventions. The majority ignore these examples because they are uncomfortable. They accept the excuse that background and education are the deciding factors because this explanation is less painful than admitting that it is their own attitude that is to blame. The truth is more complex. Origin and education create starting conditions, but they are not a guarantee and not a criterion for exclusion.

They offer advantages or disadvantages, but what matters is how you deal with them. Those who come from wealthy backgrounds may have more security, but this security can make them complacent. Those who come from difficult backgrounds may have fewer resources, but this scarcity can foster creativity and perseverance. Education can open doors, but it can also trap people in conformity. Lack of education can create obstacles, but it can also strengthen the urge to seek knowledge on one's own terms. The two percent are proof that neither background nor education are ultimately decisive. What unites them is not a common starting point, but a common attitude: the conviction that they can shape their own destiny. This attitude leads them to do more with favorable conditions and overcome unfavorable ones. The average person, on the other hand, allows themselves to be defined by their circumstances. They say, "This is who I am, this is my life, this is how it must remain." And it is precisely this statement that keeps them stuck. This reveals a central truth: if you want to become independent, you have to stop using your background or education as an excuse. These factors are real; they cannot be denied.

But they are not the end of the story. They are chapters that can be continued. And only those who are willing to view them not as fate but as a starting point can walk the path to the top two percent. The idea that background and education determine success and independence seems so obvious that it is rarely questioned. Almost everyone grows up with this narrative: those who grow up in a wealthy family have better opportunities, and those who enjoy a good education will automatically be more successful.

This way of thinking is so deeply rooted that it seems like a law of nature. But on closer inspection, it becomes clear that this is less an objective truth than a cultural narrative that stabilizes the average. Psychology describes such cultural narratives as "implicit theories." They are assumptions about the world that are so deeply ingrained in us that they no longer appear as beliefs, but as reality itself. Those who believe that origin determines life act accordingly.

Those who believe that education is the key behave accordingly. But like any implicit theory, these narratives are changeable. They can be broken if we recognize that they are not natural, but culturally constructed. A look at history makes this clear. Time and again, there are examples of people who have achieved extraordinary freedom despite all external conditions. They grew up in poverty, had little access to education, and yet they created structures that made them independent. Likewise, there are countless examples of people with the best education who remained trapped in the structures of mediocrity. This observation shows that although background and education influence starting conditions, they are not definitive determinants. They explain differences, but they do not explain why someone belongs to the top two percent.

From a sociological perspective, this is referred to as "structural opportunities" versus "individual action." Structural opportunities arise from background and education. They create possibilities, facilitate access, and offer resources. Individual action, however, determines whether these opportunities are used, wasted, or newly created. The average is carried by structures, while the top two percent actively shape them. They take advantage of favorable structures, but they are not dependent on them. And when no structures exist, they create their own. Research on social mobility shows that upward mobility is possible, even if it becomes statistically less likely the more unfavorable the starting conditions are.

But statistics describe probabilities, not necessities. They say nothing about individuals. Every person can be the exception, and the two percent are precisely these exceptions. They show that statistics are not destiny. For while the majority accept their origins as an explanation for their situation, the two percent question whether this explanation is compelling. A similar pattern can be found in the approach to education. Education is undoubtedly valuable; it broadens horizons, imparts knowledge, and connects people. But education is only as effective as the attitude with which it is used. The average person views education as a duty, as a means to an end, to achieve better positions within existing structures.

The two percent view education as a tool that empowers them to create their own structures. They do not learn in order to conform, but to become independent. This difference is crucial. It explains why education alone is no guarantee of freedom. The psychology of learning makes this difference clear. Learning is not just the absorption of information, but the transformation of perception. Those who learn to pass exams anchor knowledge superficially. Those who learn to solve problems integrate knowledge deeply. The two percent have cultivated this second form of learning. They see every piece of knowledge as a resource that can be applied. The average person, on the other hand, sees education as a certificate, as confirmation that they meet the requirements. This keeps them within the framework of the system, while the two percent expand the framework itself. Origin and education therefore only act as amplifiers, not as determinants. They can make the path easier or more difficult, but they do not define it. The decisive factor is how one deals with them. A wealthy family home can provide security, but it can also lead to complacency. A lack of resources can create obstacles, but it can also promote creativity and perseverance. A good education can open doors, but it can also create pressure to conform. A lack of formal education can be limiting, but it can also lead to self-taught individuals taking unusual paths. It is not the condition, but the interpretation of the condition that makes the difference. The two percent stand out precisely because they do not see conditions as end points, but as starting points.

They do not allow themselves to be defined by what was, but by what could be. They know that they can continue writing their story, regardless of how it began. The average person, on the other hand, accepts history as complete. They say, "This is who I am because this is who my family was" or "This is my life because my education determines it." This attitude is where the real difference lies. Psychologically, this difference can be found in the concept of attribution. The average person attributes externally: my background and education determine who I am. The two percent attribute internally: I determine what I make of my background and my education. It is this internal attribution that creates the ability to act. It turns the same conditions into completely different life stories. This makes it clear that background and education do have an influence, but they are not the final authority. They are contexts, not judgments. They can open or close doors, but they can never replace the key to freedom. This key lies in attitude, in the willingness to take responsibility, in the ability to interpret and shape conditions. The two percent have understood this, and that is precisely why they belong to this small minority. The idea that background and education are decisive factors in determining a person's place in life is so deeply ingrained in our minds that it seems like a law of nature. This notion is fed by observations that seem obvious at first glance. We see that children of wealthy parents often have a better start in life, that they have access to networks, resources, and high-quality education. Similarly, we see that people with academic degrees often attain more prestigious positions.

All of this reinforces the belief that the course is set early on and that individual effort is ultimately secondary. But on closer inspection, this narrative crumbles. For every example that confirms this assumption, there are countless counterexamples that refute it. Psychology explains this phenomenon with the concept of confirmation bias. People tend to select and interpret information in a way that supports their existing beliefs. Those who believe that background is decisive will primarily notice stories that confirm this belief: the entrepreneur who took over the family business, or the lawyer whose parents were lawyers themselves. The fact that there are countless people who had completely different starting points and still became independent is overlooked or dismissed as an exception. This stabilizes the belief in the power of background, even though it does not provide a complete explanation.

A similar pattern can be seen in education. Societies that place a strong emphasis on formal qualifications unconsciously convey the message that knowledge is only valid in certified form. Diplomas, titles, and certificates become symbols of competence. But knowledge alone does not guarantee independence. Education can open doors, but it says nothing about whether someone will actually walk through those doors. The majority use education to establish themselves within the system, not to question it. The two percent, on the other hand, use education—of whatever kind—as a tool for shaping their lives. They understand that knowledge is most valuable when it is applied, not when it hangs on the wall as a certificate. Sociological studies on social mobility show that there are indeed correlations between origin, education, and life course.

But correlation is not causation. The fact that many children of wealthy parents are also wealthy later in life does not mean that origin automatically guarantees prosperity. It simply means that certain starting advantages increase the probability. But probabilities are not laws. Every person is more than a number in a statistic. And this is precisely where the difference between the average and the exception begins. The average accepts probabilities as fate. The two percent recognize that statistics are not a judgment on their own lives. Attitudes toward background and education reveal whether someone remains average or not. The average person says, “I didn't have the right conditions, so I couldn't do it.” The two percent say, “My conditions were what they were – and I decided to make something of them.” This difference in interpretation changes everything. It determines whether background is seen as a shackle or a starting point, whether education is used as a tool for conformity or as a creative force. The psychology of the so-called “growth mindset” provides a clear explanation here.

People with a static self-image believe that their abilities and opportunities are fixed. They see background and education as determinants that can hardly be changed. People with a dynamic self-image, on the other hand, understand abilities as changeable and developable. For them, background is a starting point, not a limitation, and education is a process, not a final destination. The two percent embody this dynamic self-image. They grow from challenges instead of being intimidated by them. Another aspect that illustrates the difference is the role of personal responsibility. The average person often uses background and education as justification for relinquishing responsibility. They say, "It wasn't in my hands." This attitude protects self-esteem, but it takes away the power to change. The two percent take responsibility even when external factors play a role. They ask, "What can I do?

How can I make the best of these circumstances?" This responsibility is uncomfortable because it leaves no room for excuses. But it is the foundation of freedom. When you look at the stories of many people who have become independent, it is striking that their backgrounds were often not favorable. Many of them had neither financial security nor access to excellent education. What they had in common, however, was the will not to accept their circumstances as final. They used what they had and developed strategies to compensate for missing resources. This creativity, this persistence, this constant search for ways forward – none of this comes from background or education, but from attitude. Conversely, there are people who start out with the best conditions and yet never cross the threshold to average. They have everything that, from an outside perspective, is needed for a successful start: financial resources, networks, excellent education. But they remain trapped in dependencies because they never learned to take responsibility for themselves. Their favorable background makes them complacent, their good education makes them conformist.

They do not use their advantages to become independent, but to settle into the system as comfortably as possible. This shows that background and education not only open up opportunities, but can also harbour pitfalls. They can become a support, but also a shackle. The difference lies in how you deal with them. Those who regard background and education as a definitive definition remain average. Those who see them as a starting point have the opportunity to go beyond that. The power of the two percent lies in the fact that they have recognized this distinction. They do not allow themselves to be limited by external attributions. They know that background and education have an influence, but they also know that the decisive factor always remains their attitude. It is this realization that gives them the freedom to create structures that make them independent. And that is precisely why they are living proof that background and education are not decisive – only how one deals with them. If you think more deeply about why the myth of background and education is so persistent, you realize that it is not only based on individual beliefs, but also fulfills a social function. It is a narrative that stabilizes existing structures. Those who believe that only those "born into the right circumstances" or "highly educated" can achieve freedom accept the order as it is.

This belief protects the system from too much change because it makes most people feel that their situation is inevitable. Psychologically speaking, this is a form of learned helplessness. People who are convinced that they are determined by their origins or educational background see no point in making their own efforts. They come to terms with their place in the middle because they believe that they cannot act differently anyway. But this learned helplessness is not natural. It arises from repeated experiences in which external factors appear to dominate. When children grow up in an environment of poverty and lack of opportunity, they easily internalize the belief that their lives must remain that way. When young adults see that degrees act as a ticket to certain professions, they believe that without these degrees, everything is blocked. These experiences are real, but the interpretation that follows is crucial. The two percent have learned to see this interpretation not as fate, but as a challenge. They accept the harshness of their circumstances, but they refuse to believe that they are final.

A key difference between the average and the exceptional lies in how they talk about their past. The average person recounts their origins as an explanation for their present. They say, "I am this way because my parents were this way" or "I couldn't do it because I didn't have a good education." This narrative stabilizes their self-image and protects them from the painful realization that they could have done more. The two percent, on the other hand, talk about their origins as a starting point. They say, "I come from there, and that's exactly why I decided to go my own way." This narrative transforms background from a shackle into a driving force. It turns disadvantages into sources of energy and obstacles into motivation. Research on resilience confirms that it is not objective conditions that determine the course of one's life, but the subjective meaning one attaches to them. Two people can grow up in almost identical circumstances and yet follow completely different paths.

One remains trapped in dependency, the other finds ways to independence. The difference lies not in the circumstances, but in the interpretation. This interpretation is not simply a rational process, but an emotional act deeply rooted in the psyche. Those who have learned to see difficulties as challenges develop resilience. Those who see difficulties as confirmation of limitations remain bound. A similar pattern can be seen in relation to education. The average person sees education as an end goal. A degree is seen as a guarantee of security, an education as a ticket to society. But in reality, education is never complete. It is a process that lasts a lifetime. Those who limit themselves to following the path of conformity with a diploma in hand remain within the framework of the system.

The two percent see education as a tool that must be constantly sharpened and expanded. They do not learn to meet expectations, but to open up new opportunities. They are often self-taught because they have realized that knowledge is not only imparted in institutions, but is accessible everywhere if you remain open. Modern research on "self-directed learning" shows that this ability is crucial. People who actively shape their own education develop greater flexibility and a stronger sense of control. They are not dependent on curricula or certificates, but create their own knowledge. This attitude is characteristic of the two percent. They seek information, apply it, reflect on it, and adapt it. In this way, education becomes not a stamp, but a living tool. The claim that background and education are decisive is so persistent because it shifts responsibility to external factors. If success depends on background, then the parents or society are to blame. If it depends on education, then the school system is responsible. This shift relieves the individual of responsibility, but it also renders them powerless.

It takes away their power to shape their own lives. The two percent do the opposite. They take responsibility even when it is inconvenient. They accept that external factors have an influence, but they refuse to give these factors sole power over their lives. It is interesting to note that this very difference also explains why people with very favorable starting conditions often remain average. Those who believe that their background or education already defines them sufficiently lose the urge to take responsibility themselves. They rest on their advantages instead of using them as a basis for further action. In this way, background becomes a cushion that is comfortable but paralyzing. Education becomes a trophy that is proudly displayed but no longer used. In this way, apparent advantages can turn into invisible limitations. The two percent have a different attitude. They do not see their background as a cushion, but as a resource. They do not see education as a trophy, but as a tool. And that is precisely why they succeed in finding their way to freedom, regardless of their starting conditions. It is this attitude that makes the decisive difference, not the objective circumstances. This shows that believing in the power of background and education is one of the greatest illusions of the average person.

It acts like an invisible net that holds people in their position. But this net only exists as long as you believe in it. The two percent have torn this net apart by ceasing to regard background and education as limitations. They have realized that the key to independence always lies in their own hands – regardless of where they were born or what certificates they hold. One of the greatest deceptions of our time is that people believe their background or school education determines the course of their lives like an inevitable script. This assumption has a relieving function: it takes responsibility away from the individual and shifts it to what is long past or to what could only be passively received. But precisely because it is so relieving, it is also so dangerous. It lulls you into a false sense of security, it reassures you, it explains why you stay where you are. The average person lives in this explanation as if in a warm but cramped room. They know that they are limited, but they accept this limitation because they believe it is natural. The truth is different. Origin and education are not insignificant; they undoubtedly shape experiences and open or close doors. But they are never the last word. They are starting points, not end points.

And this is precisely where the decisive difference between the two percent and the remaining ninety-eight percent lies. While the majority sees origin and education as a definition, the two percent sees them as raw material. Raw material can be used to build something, but it does not determine what will ultimately be created. Psychology shows that people tend to define themselves through stable identity narratives. Those who say, "I am the child of poor parents, and therefore my life is limited," have inscribed themselves into a narrative that binds them. Those who say, "I don't have a high level of education, so I can't be successful," have limited their opportunities through a story they tell themselves. These stories are more powerful than reality because they determine how people act. Those who believe they are limited will not act, and this is precisely how the limitation becomes a self-fulfilling prophecy. The two percent have learned to tell different stories.

They define their origins not as a burden, but as a starting point. They see a lack of education not as a flaw, but as a motivation to learn for themselves. They understand that no external condition is as powerful as the internal decision to make something different out of it. And by telling these stories over and over again, they change their identity, and with it, their actions. It is this shift in storytelling that makes the difference: the majority justifies why they remain average, while the minority tells how they rise above the average. Research on social mobility clearly shows that although there are correlations between background, education, and success, there are always people who break these correlations. Statistically improbable does not mean impossible. Everyone who belongs to the two percent is a living counterargument to the claim that background and education determine everything.

They show that statistics are not destiny. They are proof that attitude and decisions weigh more heavily than starting conditions. The real problem with the average lies not in external circumstances, but in internal attitude. Those who accept their background as fate will not strive to break out of it. Those who see education as a definitive ticket will stop learning once they have that ticket in their hands. It is this internal limitation that keeps the average average. The two percent have broken through it by recognizing that nothing is final as long as you are alive. Every background can be reinterpreted, every education expanded.

Nothing is complete as long as one is willing to move forward. Another aspect that becomes clear here is the connection between responsibility and freedom. The average person shifts responsibility outward, to parents, teachers, society, systems. But in doing so, they also shift the possibility of freedom. Because those who are not responsible are also not free. The two percent take responsibility radically. They accept that they reap the fruits of what they sow, regardless of the quality of the soil. This responsibility is difficult, but it sets them free. It turns background into a starting point and education into a tool. The emotional dimension should not be underestimated either. The average person clings to their background and education because it gives them a sense of identity and security. They can say, "I am this way because my circumstances were this way." This explanation may be painfully limiting, but it is also reassuring because it makes life seem predictable.

The two percent forego this reassurance. They face the uncertainty that arises when one no longer accepts background and education as an explanation. They know that uncertainty is the price of freedom. And they are willing to pay that price. This makes it clear why background and education must not have the final say. They are stages, not goals. They are framework conditions, not judgments. They are chapters, not the whole book. The average makes them end points, the two percent make them starting points. And that is precisely where the decisive difference lies. At the end of this chapter, we are left with a simple but radical realization: Origin and education do not determine whether you belong to the two percent. They can make the path easier or more difficult, but they do not determine it. What matters is the attitude with which you walk it. Those who take responsibility, who see their origins not as a shackle but as a driving force, who use education not as a qualification but as a tool, have the opportunity to become independent. The two percent are living proof of this. They show that freedom is not tied to conditions, but to decisions. They show that no one is condemned by their background and no one is defined by their education. They show that everyone has the opportunity to become more than they believe they can be. And that is precisely why the average is average: because it does not recognize that it has this opportunity. The two percent have recognized it, and they have acted on it.

Notes:

Notes:

Chapter 5: The invisible chains of everyday life

One of the most subtle and at the same time most effective forms of power is that everyday life binds people without them noticing. The routines, habits, and apparent givens in which the average person lives act like invisible chains. They are neither loud nor brutal, but quiet and steady. They hold people captive, not because they have to, but because they are used to living that way. This is precisely the secret of inertia, which keeps the average person average. People believe they are free to make their own decisions, but in fact they are moving along paths that have long been mapped out. These invisible chains consist of the repetitions of everyday life. You get up, go to work, earn money, spend it, go to sleep—and the next day the cycle begins again. This rhythm provides security, but it also binds. It conveys a sense of order, but at the same time it prevents anything truly new from emerging. The average person confuses this order with freedom because it gives them stability.

But in truth, it is a form of imprisonment. Those who always follow the same paths rarely experience the possibility of taking other routes. From a psychological perspective, this phenomenon can be explained by the concept of "habitualization." Humans are creatures of habit. They adjust their behavior to be as energy-efficient as possible. What has been learned once becomes automated in order to save energy. This automation is useful because it makes everyday life easier. But it has a downside: it blinds us to alternatives. Those who live in automatism for too long forget that they even have a choice. This is precisely why the routines of the average person are so powerful. They do not appear as chains, but as normality. The two percent have learned to question this normality. They recognize that habits are tools, not laws of nature. They consciously use routines to create stability, but they are always ready to change them when they no longer serve a purpose. The average person, on the other hand, defends their routines, even if they are restrictive. They say, “That's how it's done” or “It's always been that way.” These phrases encapsulate the power of everyday life, which perpetuates itself. A particularly effective invisible bond is the link between work and consumption. The average person lives in a cycle in which they exchange time for money and immediately spend that money again. This cycle seems inevitable because it is the foundation of modern societies. But it is a trap.

Those who sell all their time have no time left to create structures that could make them independent. Those who consume all their money have no means to use it productively. Thus, they remain trapped in the rhythm of working and spending without ever getting ahead. The two percent have broken this cycle. They understand that work is not only a means of consumption, but also an opportunity to build systems. They do not see money as a reward for effort, but as a resource that can grow. They forego short-term consumption in order to create long-term independence. This renunciation often seems incomprehensible to the average person because they are used to satisfying their needs immediately. But this is precisely where the invisible chain lies: in the habit of focusing on short-term gratification, even if it makes you unfree in the long term. Another aspect of these chains is the social dimension.

People orient themselves to their environment. Those who are surrounded by people who live average lives adopt their patterns. They follow the same habits, adapt to the same expectations, and repeat the same explanations. In this way, the social environment stabilizes the invisible chains of everyday life. The average person controls themselves because they are constantly reminded that their life is “normal.” And normality has enormous power. It turns chains into something that is taken for granted. But the two percent have learned to escape this pull. They actively seek out other role models, they create new environments for themselves, they cultivate habits that are not determined by the average. They know that normality is nothing more than the sum of collective habits. By questioning this sum, they break free from the invisible chains.

In the end, it becomes clear that everyday life is not a neutral structure, but an invisible power. It holds the majority captive because they do not recognize that their routines are prisons. The two percent have seen through this prison. They know that freedom means consciously choosing routines and changing them at any time. That is precisely why they are independent. The most subtle form of bondage is that which is not recognized as bondage. People who live in political systems that openly oppress them feel the pressure they have to resist. But the invisible chains of everyday life are more deceptive because they do not appear as chains, but as normality, even security. The average person does not realize that they are bound because they move in patterns that have been familiar to them since childhood. It is precisely this familiarity that makes them so strong. From early childhood, people are socialized into routines. They learn to get up in the morning, go to school, then to work, to be diligent, to do their tasks, to earn their money, and then to spend it. This sequence is rarely questioned because it forms the basic framework of social life. It conveys a sense of order and predictability. But there is also a trap in this order: it leaves little room for questions about alternatives. Those who ask these questions are often considered dreamers or troublemakers. Thus, the invisible chains are stabilized by the fact that they are defended by the majority. Psychologically, this phenomenon can be described using the concept of "social normalization." People orient themselves toward how others live and take these lifestyles as a yardstick for what is right and normal. Those who deviate risk rejection, and it is precisely this fear that keeps most people within the average. They repeat what they have learned, not because it gives them freedom, but because it gives them social validation. In this way, everyday life is stabilized not only by habits, but also by the expectations of others. The link between work and identity is particularly effective in this context. The average person defines themselves by what they do for a living. Work becomes the central source of meaning and value. Those who work are considered hard-working and useful, while those who do not feel inferior.

This pattern is so strong that it is hardly ever questioned. But it is binding because it forces people to exchange their time for money in order to feel valuable. The invisible chain consists of the belief that without this kind of work, one has no meaning. The two percent have broken this pattern. They understand that work is not the goal, but the tool. They realize that their value does not depend on whether they are busy from morning to night, but on whether they create structures that make them independent. They often work harder than the average person, but they work with a different goal in mind. They don't just want to earn money, they want to create freedom. This perspective changes the entire approach to work and robs the invisible chain of its power. Another component of these chains is consumption. The average person lives in a rhythm where consumption serves as a reward for work.

You work to buy, and you buy to feel free for a short time. But this freedom is an illusion. It only lasts as long as the consumption continues, and then the cycle begins again. So you remain trapped in a system that makes you believe that happiness can be bought. The invisible chain is that consumption is not recognized as an addiction, but as normality. The two percent also see through this illusion. They know that consumption does not liberate, but binds, when it becomes an end in itself. They do not forego enjoyment, but they are not dependent on it. They do not use their money primarily for short-term satisfaction, but for long-term freedom.

They invest, while the average person consumes. This difference seems small, but it changes everything. For while the average person becomes more deeply entangled in the cycle with every purchase, the two percent build a little more independence with every investment. The invisible chains of everyday life are therefore not made up of visible obstacles, but of invisible patterns. They are all the more powerful because hardly anyone questions them. The average person lives in them as if in a house they never leave because they believe it is the whole world. The two percent, on the other hand, step outside. They recognize that everyday life is only one of many possible forms of life. This realization is the first step toward freedom. The invisible chains of everyday life are so powerful because they appear to be normal. What everyone does seems like a matter of course that does not need to be questioned.

Humans are social beings, and their perception of what is right or wrong, possible or impossible, is strongly determined by what they see repeatedly in their environment. When the majority lives according to the same routines, these routines seem like a law of nature. They are no longer questioned, but simply accepted. This is precisely where the insidious power of the average lies: it does not need to actively control or punish, it works through mere repetition and confirmation. A classic example of this is the idea that you have to get up in the morning, have a permanent job, work your hours, and be paid regularly for it. This structure seems so self-evident that it is hardly ever perceived as a restriction. It is considered normal, even desirable. Those who have a secure job are considered successful. But this rhythm, as secure as it may seem, is a form of dependency. It forces people to constantly exchange their time for money, without the possibility of ever leaving this cycle behind.

The invisible chain lies in the fact that people no longer question this exchange. In this context, psychology refers to cognitive dissonance reduction. People tend to explain their behavior in a way that is consistent with their self-image. So those who live their entire lives in this rhythm begin to believe that there are no alternatives or that other paths are risky and irresponsible. In this way, they unconsciously stabilize their own chains. You justify what you do, even if it makes you unfree. The average person says, "That's just how it's done." This statement is not only a description, but also a justification that protects your own behavior from any questioning. Another element of these invisible chains is the structure of consumption. Societies are set up in such a way that consumption is rewarded not only economically, but also socially. Those who consume show that they "belong." New clothes, new gadgets, new vacations become symbols of success. The average person lives in a cycle in which consumption serves as validation: you work to consume, and you consume to feel alive and valuable. But this cycle is a trap. It devours resources without ever creating freedom.

The feeling of reward is only short-lived, and as soon as it fades, the cycle begins again. The two percent have broken this cycle by not seeing consumption as an end in itself. They consume consciously, but they invest more than they spend. They know that true value lies not in short-term satisfaction, but in long-term freedom. While the average person spends money to buy recognition, the two percent use money to create independence. This difference is invisible as long as you are caught in the cycle, but it makes a decisive difference over the years. Time itself is also bound by invisible chains. The average person lives according to a calendar that is determined by external factors. Working hours, vacation time, weekends—life is divided into predefined blocks.

Freedom is reduced to small islands: a few weeks of vacation, a few free hours in the evening. But even here, there is an illusion. People believe that they are free when they are not working, but in reality, this freedom is limited from the outset. It is not self-determined, but assigned from outside. People remain within a framework that they have not created themselves. The two percent understand time differently. They know that time is the most important resource that cannot be renewed. That is why they do not sell it permanently, but invest it to create structures that will give them more time later. They work intensively, but with one goal in mind: to free themselves from the exchange of time for money. The average person, on the other hand, thinks in terms of hours that are sold, while the two percent think in terms of systems that can grow. This different view of time is one of the strongest chain breakers there is. Another invisible strand of these chains lies in social expectations. The average person bases their life largely on how they are perceived by others. They don't want to stand out, cause offense, or be criticized. That's why they quietly follow the paths taken by the majority. This conformity is comfortable because it avoids conflict, but it comes at the cost of freedom.

Those who always do what others expect do not live their own lives, but lives determined by others. The invisible chain here is the fear of rejection. The two percent have learned to overcome this fear. They know that it is impossible to please everyone. They understand that rejection is the price of independence. Instead of seeking the approval of the masses, they seek clarity about their own goals. They no longer allow themselves to be bound by the expectations of others, but create their own standards. This inner freedom manifests itself outwardly as independence, and it is precisely this that has enabled them to break free from the chains of mediocrity. This shows that the invisible chains of everyday life do not consist of coercion, but of habit, consumption, time structures, and social expectations. They are effective not because they are imposed, but because they are accepted and repeated. The average remains trapped because it believes there is no alternative. The two percent have broken these chains because they have stopped taking the familiar for granted. The invisible chains that bind the average in everyday life do not act like iron shackles, but like familiar patterns. They are not painful, but comfortable. This is precisely where their power lies: you don't feel them as long as you follow them. Only when you try to break out of them does their strength become apparent. Anyone who has ever tried to change a habit knows how tough the resistance from within can be. This resistance is no coincidence, but the result of deeply ingrained psychological mechanisms that orient people toward security and repetition.

Behavioral research shows that habits are laid down in the brain like tracks. The more often a behavior is repeated, the stronger the neural connections that support it become. Over time, the behavior becomes automatic, without having to think about it consciously. This automation is an enormous relief because it frees up the mind. But it also makes you unfree if the behavior no longer serves what you actually want. The average person lives predominantly in such automated tracks. They repeat what they have always done, not because it is the best thing to do, but because it is the easiest thing to do. One example of this is how we deal with money. Most people get used to spending their income immediately at an early age. Bills, consumption, small rewards – at the end of the month, the money is gone and the cycle begins anew. This habit is so strong that it seems like a law of nature. It is rarely questioned because it is deeply rooted in everyday life. The two percent have broken this habit. They have learned to see money not only as a means of spending, but as a resource that can grow. But to get there, they had to break an invisible chain: the habit of always consuming everything immediately. Another invisible chain is the structure of time. The average person bases their life on fixed routines that are dictated by external factors: working hours, weekends, vacation times. This structure provides security, but it also limits. It prevents people from organizing their time freely. Those who always live within these boundaries forget that time could also be used differently. The two percent have learned to see their time as capital, not as a predetermined sequence.

They consciously decide how to use their hours and build systems that give them more time later on. This approach to time is a form of liberation that overwhelms the average person because it requires personal responsibility. Social expectations act like a particularly strong chain. The average person lives in constant fear of being judged by others. They adapt in order to belong, to find recognition, to not be excluded. This adaptation is so deeply internalized that it is hardly even consciously perceived. People choose professions, homes, and lifestyles that are accepted by those around them. People do not live according to their own standards, but according to the expectations of the group. The two percent have broken these chains by overcoming their fear of rejection. They know that it is impossible to please everyone and that true freedom is only possible if one is prepared to endure criticism. The power of these invisible chains is particularly evident in the fact that they are defended by the majority. Anyone who tries to break free from them encounters resistance, not only within themselves, but also from outside. Friends, family, colleagues—they all reflect back that the familiar is right. Anyone who lives differently is quickly considered unusual, risky, perhaps even irresponsible.

In this way, the average protects itself. It guards its own chains by sanctioning deviations. This is what makes breaking free so difficult, but also so meaningful. The two percent have endured this resistance. They have learned that freedom only comes when you are willing to stand up against the inertia of everyday life and the expectations of the masses. They have consciously broken routines, questioned consumption habits, changed the structure of their time, and overcome the fear of rejection. These steps are uncomfortable, but they lead to a freedom that goes far beyond everyday life. In the end, it becomes clear that the invisible chains of everyday life exist not through force, but through habit. The average person does not hold on to the average because they cannot, but because they do not want to. They remain in the familiar because it is easier to repeat familiar patterns than to break new ground. The two percent have found the courage to leave this comfort zone. And that is precisely what sets them apart: they have realized that freedom does not begin where everything is comfortable, but where one consciously breaks the invisible chains.

The invisible chains that bind the average person are so difficult to break because they do not act like external walls, but like an internal agreement. People who live average lives defend their own chains as if they were part of their identity. They believe that they could not survive without them, that their life would fall apart if they left their familiar paths. This identification with the chains is perhaps the deepest form of imprisonment. It prevents people from even recognizing the shackles as such. Social psychology describes this phenomenon as "internalized norms." These are rules that originate from outside, but are internalized to such an extent that they are no longer perceived as foreign. They do not appear as pressure, but as a matter of course. Those who have learned throughout their lives that you have to work to be recognized no longer experience this as an external demand, but as their own conviction. Those who have learned that consumption brings happiness believe in it, even if experience shows the opposite. These internalized rules are the strongest chains because they cannot be broken from the outside. They must be recognized and broken from within. The two percent have gone through this process of inner liberation. They have realized that many of the beliefs they grew up with are not objective truths, but cultural stories.

They have begun to question these stories. Does work really always have to mean exchanging time for money? Does happiness really have to lie in consumption? Does normality really have to mean living like the majority? By asking these questions, they began to see the invisible chains. And only those who see the chains can break them. But this process is painful. It requires questioning the familiar, giving up the security of normality. It is easier to remain in familiar structures, even if they make you feel unfree, than to step into the unknown. That is why the majority remains average. They know they are trapped, but they prefer to endure the familiar rather than risk the unknown. The two percent have found the courage to endure this pain. They have accepted that freedom means uncertainty, that new paths offer no guarantees. They have understood that you can only grow if you leave the old behind. The invisible chains of everyday life consist not only of routines, consumption, and social expectations, but also of language. Language is a powerful tool that creates realities. The average person says things like “That's how you do it” or “There's no other way.” These statements are not descriptions, but self-hypnosis. They program the consciousness to believe that alternatives do not exist.

The two percent have changed this language. They don't say “That's not possible,” but “How could it be possible?” They don't say “That's how you do it,” but “That's how I do it.” This small shift in language alone changes thinking and thus action. Emotions also play a central role. The average person clings to invisible chains because they provide security. Even if they make you feel unfree, they feel familiar. Familiarity conveys calm, and this calm outweighs the freedom that uncertainty brings. The two percent have learned to live with this uncertainty. They have left their comfort zone and gone through the fear. They have understood that fear is not a signal to retreat, but an indication that one is entering new territory. In the end, it turns out that the invisible chains of everyday life only have power as long as one believes in them. They do not exist as objective walls, but as collective agreements. The average person remains bound because they believe them to be immutable.

The two percent have realized that you can start breaking them at any time. It is not an easy path, but it is possible. Anyone could take it, regardless of their background or education. This makes it clear that the invisible chains of everyday life are the real prison of the average person. They hold them captive, not through external force, but through internal consent. Those who do not question them remain trapped in the cycle of work, consumption, and conformity. Those who see them and are willing to break them enter the path to freedom. The two percent have taken this step, and that is precisely why they belong to the small minority that is independent. They are proof that the chains are not real, but only work as long as you believe in them.

Notes:

Notes:

Chapter 6: The Science of Decision

There is an invisible point in every person's life where they decide whether to remain average or to set out on the path to independence. This point is rarely a dramatic moment, a clear cut that can be easily identified in retrospect. Rather, it consists of countless small decisions that add up over the years. Every choice a person makes has the potential to bring them closer to freedom or deeper into mediocrity. This is precisely where the invisible power of decisions lies: they do not shape life all at once, but like drops of water that change the landscape of existence stone by stone. The psychology of decision-making is a field that has been intensively researched for decades. Time and again, it has been shown that humans are not purely rational beings, as was long assumed.

Rather, they make decisions based on habits, emotions, and unconscious patterns. The average person lives precisely according to these patterns. They repeat what is familiar, they make decisions out of fear of loss, they choose the shortest path to reward. These patterns seem reasonable to them, but in reality they are automatisms that keep them average. The two percent have learned to break through these automatisms. They have understood that decisions are not just reactions, but tools. While the average person limits their choices through fears and habits, the two percent expand their spectrum by consciously reflecting. They don't ask, "What is safe?" but rather, "What brings me closer to my goal?" This difference is subtle, but it has a massive impact over the years.

A person who makes decisions every day that maximize security remains in a cycle of dependency. A person who makes decisions every day that enable freedom moves step by step toward independence. A key to understanding this difference lies in the concept of loss aversion, as described by Daniel Kahneman and Amos Tversky. People tend to weigh losses more heavily than gains. The average person therefore makes decisions that avoid losses, even if this means missing out on greater gains. This attitude keeps them safe, but also mediocre. The two percent, on the other hand, have learned to consciously deal with this tendency.

They accept that losses are part of the process and base their decisions not on avoiding pain, but on gaining freedom. The ability to take a long-term perspective also plays a decisive role here. The average person makes short-term decisions. They ask themselves: "What will give me security, comfort, and recognition today?" The two percent, on the other hand, think in terms of decades. They ask: "Which decision today will secure my freedom in ten years?" This long-term perspective changes the yardstick by which one acts. It requires patience, discipline, and a willingness to give up short-term gratification in order to achieve long-term independence. The average person usually fails at this point because they cannot bear the pain of sacrifice. The two percent, on the other hand, accept it as the price of freedom. From a neurobiological perspective, this difference can be explained by the activity of different areas of the brain. Short-term decisions are strongly influenced by the limbic system, which is responsible for emotions and rewards. Long-term decisions, on the other hand, require the activity of the prefrontal cortex, which is responsible for planning, self-control, and abstraction. The average person lives predominantly in the limbic system: they react to immediate stimuli, to fear, to pleasure, to social confirmation. The two percent have learned to activate their prefrontal cortex by consciously reflecting and planning. This is not an innate ability, but a trained one. Anyone could develop it, but most people don't because it takes effort. The science of decision-making shows that freedom does not depend on big, heroic moments, but on the sum of small, conscious choices. The average person makes these choices unconsciously, while the two percent make them consciously. This is precisely where the difference lies. Decisions are like invisible switches. They steer life onto paths that only become clearly different after years. But once you are on a path, it becomes more difficult to leave it with each subsequent decision. That is why the average is so stable: it consists of a thousand small decisions that all lead in the same direction. The two percent are not independent because they had better starting conditions, but because they have learned to make different decisions. They have learned to trade the short-term pain of sacrifice for the long-term joy of freedom. They have learned to overcome their fear of loss and consciously take risks.

They have learned to think not in terms of days and weeks, but in terms of years and decades. This attitude has shaped them, and it is what sets them apart. Decisions seem like insignificant moments, yet they are the invisible architects of life. Most people are not consciously aware of them because they believe that their lives are shaped by major events: choosing an education, starting a job, entering into a relationship, perhaps moving house or inheriting money. But in reality, it is the many small decisions made every day that form the foundation on which our entire lives rest. The question of whether to get up an hour earlier in the morning, whether to save or spend money, whether to read or be entertained, whether to give in to a fear or overcome it – all of this seems insignificant at the moment, but it adds up to a structure that seems almost unchangeable over the years. This is precisely why the science of decision-making is so central to understanding why only two percent become independent and the average person remains in their role. Cognitive psychology has shown that humans are not the rationally calculating machines that classical theories have long portrayed them to be. Rather, they are beings who act under the constant influence of emotions, social norms, and cognitive shortcuts. Decisions are not made based on sober logic, but mostly according to patterns that originate in the past. We gravitate toward what is familiar and avoid what seems new or uncertain.

This is the mechanism that keeps the majority in the average. Freedom requires new decisions, risky paths, and crossing boundaries. But those who have learned to put security above all else will never achieve freedom. Behavioral economics has impressively described this pattern. People prefer short-term rewards, even if long-term gains would be much greater. This behavior is called present bias. The average person lives by it: they choose immediate consumption over long-term investment; short-term convenience over long-term development; the quick feeling of belonging over the slow development of independence. These decisions seem small, but they add up to a life marked by dependence. The two percent have learned to consciously overcome present bias. They cultivate the ability to delay gratification, which psychologists have identified as one of the strongest predictors of success. Studies such as the famous "marshmallow experiment" show that children who are able to postpone immediate gratification are more successful, healthier, and more stable later in life. But whether or not you have this ability is not a matter of fate. It can be learned and trained.

The two percent have done just that: they have learned to resist short-term temptations in order to gain long-term freedom. Another mechanism that shapes the decisions of the average person is the so-called "status quo bias." People tend to prefer the existing state of affairs, even if alternatives would objectively be better. The average person clings to the familiar because it is comfortable. Change triggers fear, and fear paralyzes. That is why most people remain in the same jobs, the same routines, the same social circles, even if they feel that these things make them unfree. The two percent have learned to break through the status quo bias. They don't see change as a threat, but as an opportunity. They know that progress is only possible if you leave the status quo behind. Decisions are therefore not merely acts of choice, but acts of self-creation. Every person constantly recreates themselves through their decisions. The average person creates a life that is riddled with dependencies because they make decisions in such a way as to maintain short-term security. The two percent create a life of independence because they make decisions in a way that builds long-term freedom. This difference is not the result of a single moment, but the sum of thousands of small divergences. Neuroscience shows that decisions are plastic. The brain changes as a result of the decisions we make repeatedly. Those who repeatedly choose to follow the easy path create pathways that automate this path. Those who repeatedly choose to take the difficult but more rewarding path create pathways that strengthen resilience and foresight.

In this way, the brain becomes a mirror of one's own decisions. It adapts to the life one chooses, making it more likely that one will stay on the same path. This explains why it is so difficult to break away from the average: the brain itself is programmed by decades of decisions. But it also explains why it is possible: the same plasticity allows new pathways to be created when you start making different decisions. The two percent do not differ in terms of superior intelligence or exceptional talent, but in terms of the discipline to make conscious decisions. They reflect on what they do and check whether it brings them closer to their goal. They accept that every decision has a price, and they are willing to pay that price. The average person, on the other hand, tries to make decisions without a price – they want security without risk, reward without sacrifice, recognition without independence. But it is precisely this attitude that keeps them trapped, because it distances them from reality. This shows that the science of decision-making is not an abstract theory, but an everyday practice. Every person decides whether to remain average or to develop beyond that – not in one big moment, but in the countless small choices they make every day. Those who recognize this have already taken the first step toward freedom. For the invisible chain of mediocrity lies not in circumstances, but in the way we make decisions. If we want to understand why only a small proportion of people find their way to freedom, while the vast majority remain average, we need to take a closer look at the mechanics of decision-making. Decisions are not merely conscious acts; they are embedded in a web of emotions, memories, expectations, and social influences.

The average person believes they are making free decisions, but in reality they are following unconscious patterns that guide them without their knowledge. It is precisely these unconscious patterns that are the invisible threads from which the web of mediocrity is woven. Research in cognitive psychology has shown that people do not weigh up most of their decisions rationally, but make them using so-called heuristics – mental shortcuts that enable quick judgments but often contain systematic biases. One of these heuristics is the "availability heuristic." People judge probabilities based on how easily they can think of examples. If the average person repeatedly hears stories that self-employment is risky, that investments are dangerous, that most people fail, then this shapes their decisions. They avoid risk, not because they have calculated it rationally, but because the horror stories are more present in their minds than the success stories. The two percent have learned to recognize and correct these distortions. They know that perception is not reality, and they consciously check whether their decisions are based on facts or distorted impressions. Another example is the "confirmation bias." People seek information that supports their existing beliefs and ignore contradictory information.

Those who believe that it is impossible to become financially independent without a privileged background will find evidence of this everywhere: in statistics, in their environment, in the media. But those who are open to counterexamples will discover countless stories of people who have overcome precisely this hurdle. The two percent are willing to examine and change their beliefs. The average person, on the other hand, clings to their beliefs because they provide security, even if they limit them. The science of decision-making also shows that emotions have a stronger effect than rational arguments. Decisions are prepared in the limbic system long before the mind justifies them. This explains why the average person often makes decisions that reassure them in the short term but make them unfree in the long term. They buy something to relieve stress. They stay in a job they hate because the uncertainty of a change triggers fear. They say yes when they mean no because they fear rejection. These are all emotional decisions disguised as rational ones. The two percent have learned to understand their emotions without blindly following them. They use fear as a signal, but not as a limit. They recognize the impulse for short-term gratification, but they consciously choose long-term freedom. From a neuroscientific point of view, this difference is a training of the prefrontal cortex. This area of the brain is responsible for controlling impulses, planning scenarios, and pursuing long-term goals. The average person makes little use of it because they live predominantly in reaction mode. The two percent, on the other hand, have learned through repeated practice to increase the distance between impulse and action. They do not decide immediately, but reflect, examine, and weigh things up. This ability to delay is the key to freedom. It allows decisions to be made not only out of fear or desire, but out of clarity and foresight. But social influences should not be underestimated either. Decisions are rarely made in isolation. They arise in the context of groups. The average person bases their choices heavily on what those around them think. They make decisions that ensure they don't rock the boat, that they belong, that they don't stand out. This social conformity is deeply ingrained in humans because it was once essential for survival. But in modern societies, it is often a trap. It forces people to take paths that do not set them free, simply because everyone else is taking them.

The two percent have learned to be aware of this dynamic. They know that every big decision inevitably means being different. They accept the price of social irritation because they know that conformity would keep them trapped in the average. The science of decision-making thus reveals that freedom is not a question of intelligence or luck, but a question of how we deal with internal and external influences. Those who are guided by emotions, distortions, and social expectations remain mediocre. Those who learn to recognize and consciously control these influences have the opportunity to become independent. This process is exhausting because it requires constant self-reflection. But it is possible, and that is precisely where hope lies. The two percent are not distinguished by better circumstances, but by more conscious decisions. They know that every choice is a switch that steers life in a certain direction. They know that it is not the big events that determine fate, but the sum of small decisions made day after day. The average person underestimates these small decisions, the two percent overestimate them – and that is precisely why they are free.

It is one of the great illusions of the average person that decisions only carry weight when it comes to the big questions in life – choosing a career, starting a family, buying a house or planning for retirement. This fixation on the big picture obscures what is really important: that it is the many small, seemingly unspectacular decisions that make the difference between freedom and mediocrity over the years. The science of decision-making impressively shows that the path to the top two percent is not marked by a few heroic deeds, but by the sum of everyday choices. Behavioral psychology refers to these as "microdecisions." These are the inconspicuous moments when you choose whether to invest an hour or waste it, whether to save or spend your money, whether to distract yourself with superficialities or educate yourself, whether to give in to convenience or take the uncomfortable but more rewarding path. Each individual micro-decision seems trivial, but it is like a drop falling on a stone. Over time, it hollows out the shape of life.

The average person underestimates these drops, but the top two percent know their power. Neuroeconomics has proven that decisions are recorded in a kind of mental account. Every time you make a decision that serves short-term pleasure, you strengthen the account of impulsivity. Every time you make a decision that serves a long-term goal, you strengthen your self-control account. Over time, this results in a tendency: people who always make short-term decisions program their brains for dependence. Those who make long-term decisions program them for freedom. This plasticity explains why the path out of mediocrity is difficult, but not impossible. Those who begin to make different decisions change their neural account and thus the basis for their future actions. One particularly impressive mechanism is the "commitment strategy." It describes the ability to commit oneself to a decision in order to overcome future temptations. The two percent consciously use such strategies. They commit themselves to actions that secure their long-term goals, even if the temptation to deviate from them is great in the short term. The average person, on the other hand, drifts along. They hope that they will be strong enough in the moment of temptation – and fail again and again because they have not structured their decisions in advance. This difference explains why the same people repeatedly end up in consumption, routines, and dependencies, while others, who are not stronger but more conscious, free themselves. The social dimension of decision-making reinforces this mechanism. The average person is guided by the behavior of those around them. They see that everyone around them is working, consuming, conforming—and they unconsciously decide that they must act the same way.

The two percent have broken free from this mirror. They know that social imitation is a powerful mechanism, and they consciously choose who they observe and learn from. Instead of imitating the average, they look for role models who are already independent. They choose a different environment, and this environment changes the quality of their decisions. Scientifically, this is supported by the theory of social comparison processes. People constantly orient themselves by how they relate to others. The average person compares themselves downwards or sideways – with people who live similarly or are slightly worse off. This stabilizes them because they feel validated. The two percent compare themselves upwards – not in the sense of envy, but in the sense of inspiration. They look for people who are further ahead and let their example shape their own decisions. This difference in orientation changes a person's entire decision-making structure. But perhaps most importantly, decisions are not just actions, they are self-definitions. Every decision a person makes sends a signal to their own consciousness: “This is who I am.” Those who repeatedly choose to give in to comfort tell themselves the story: “I am someone who gives up.” Those who repeatedly choose to act for freedom are telling themselves the story: “I am someone who shapes things.”

These stories are powerful because they shape our self-image. And our self-image, in turn, determines how we make decisions in the future. The average person underestimates this feedback loop, but the two percent consciously use it. This makes it clear why decisions are the real foundation of freedom. They are not a reaction to external circumstances, but the ongoing creation of one's own life. The average person remains passive and drifts along, while the two percent recognize the power of choice and take responsibility. It is this act of responsibility that sets them apart from the average. The science of decision-making reveals that freedom is not a sudden state that befalls you, but the result of a long chain of conscious choices. Every single person has the potential to change the direction of their life. But whether or not they use this potential depends on the decisions they make every day. The average person underestimates this power because they believe that it is major events that determine fate. They look at luck, background, and external circumstances. The two percent, on the other hand, have realized that it is the inconspicuous, everyday decisions that set the decisive course. One of the deepest insights in decision-making research is that decisions are never neutral. Even refraining from making a decision is a decision—the decision to leave everything as it is. The average person confuses passivity with security. They believe that by doing nothing, they are avoiding risks. But in reality, they are choosing mediocrity without realizing it. The two percent know that not making a decision has just as many consequences as making one. They take responsibility for this, even if it is uncomfortable. In economics, this is referred to as opportunity cost.

Every decision means giving up another possibility. The average person hardly considers these costs. They only see what they gain, not what they lose when they choose the comfortable option. They stay in their secure job and lose the chance to build their own structures. They consume immediately and lose the chance to grow their capital. They stay in their familiar environment and lose the opportunity to discover new horizons. The two percent consciously factor these costs into their calculations. They see not only the obvious, but also what they are missing out on. As a result, they make decisions that are more rewarding in the long term. Philosophy describes decisions as acts of self-determination. Every person is defined by the choices they make. Freedom is therefore not only the absence of coercion, but also the conscious choice of one's own direction. The average person avoids this responsibility because it means burden. They say, "I couldn't help it." In doing so, they relieve themselves of the weight of choice, but at the same time they lose the possibility of freedom. The two percent accept the burden.

They take responsibility for their decisions, even when they make mistakes. This attitude sets them free because it gives them the power to choose again and again. In psychology, this is referred to as self-efficacy—the belief that you can shape your own life. This belief is nourished by decisions. Those who repeatedly experience the impact of their decisions strengthen their confidence in their own effectiveness. However, those who remain passive weaken it. The average person undermines their self-efficacy through repeated non-decisions. The two percent strengthen it by acting, even if they fail. They know that failure is not the end, but information they can use for their next decision. This closes the circle: Decisions are not just pragmatic acts, they are existential statements. They say, "I take responsibility for my life." The average person rarely says that. They shift responsibility outward, they wait, they hope. The two percent say it constantly, through every choice they make. They don't act because it's easy, but because they know that action is the only way to create freedom. So, at the end of this chapter, it becomes clear: the science of decision-making is the science of freedom. It makes it clear that no person is defined by their background or education, but by the way they make decisions. It shows that every day offers new opportunities, that every small choice counts, that freedom does not arise suddenly, but is built piece by piece. The average person remains trapped because they do not use this power. The two percent are free because they have recognized it.

Notes:

Notes:

Chapter 7: Money as energy – How the 2% understand money in a completely different way

For most people, money is a necessary means of shaping their lives, paying bills, affording things, and feeling a certain sense of security. But hardly anyone recognizes that money is more than just a medium of exchange. For the average person, it is a resource that comes and goes, like water in a river, which you have to scoop up with your hands and immediately pour back out again. For the two percent, however, money is not just a means, but an energy. An invisible force that can be multiplied, transformed, and converted into completely new forms. They see money not as a goal, but as a tool; not as a reward, but as a source of energy that generates movement. It is precisely this difference that makes them independent, while the average person remains trapped in the cycle of work and consumption. Science helps us understand this difference. Economists describe money as a universal medium of exchange, a unit of account, and a store of value. But these definitions are only superficial. Psychologists and sociologists point out that money also has a symbolic character. It embodies power, recognition, status, even love and belonging. People project countless meanings onto money that go far beyond its practical use. The average person is particularly susceptible to these projections.

They believe that money defines their self-esteem. They feel rich when they can consume and poor when they have to go without. In doing so, they turn money into an emotional mirror. The two percent, however, detach themselves from this projection. They do not see money as a substitute for self-esteem, but as energy that acts independently of emotions and social attributions. The energy of money is evident in the fact that it generates movement. Those who put money into circulation create momentum: companies are founded, ideas are realized, structures grow. The average person, however, converts money almost exclusively into consumption. They transform energy into short-term satisfaction that immediately evaporates. The two percent, on the other hand, invest. They put their money to work, transforming energy into new energy. It is as if they plant a seed, while the average person eats their seeds immediately. The difference between consumption and investment is invisible at the moment, but it unfolds over the years with dramatic consequences. An important psychological mechanism that explains this difference is the concept of delayed gratification.

Studies show that people who are able to postpone short-term rewards are more successful in the long term—not only financially, but in all areas of life. The average person fails precisely at this point. They cannot hold on to the energy of money. It burns in their hands because they want to convert it into consumption immediately. The two percent, on the other hand, cultivate patience. They understand that money unleashes its greatest power when it has time to work. They don't spend it immediately, but use it in such a way that it grows. They trust in the process of accumulation, while the average person is fixated on immediate gratification.

Neuroscience also supports this observation. Money activates the same reward centers in the brain as food or drugs. It creates pleasure as soon as you receive or spend it. The average person remains trapped in this primitive cycle. They use money to feel rewarded and repeat this cycle until they consider it normal. The two percent, on the other hand, distance themselves from this neurological seduction. They do not use money to generate short-term pleasure, but to build structures that will later give them lasting independence. This ability to control their own reward system is perhaps the greatest strength of the two percent. Historically, the same difference can be seen. Entire cultures have failed because they only consumed money and did not invest it. Societies that hoarded surpluses to build walls or luxuries disappeared. Societies that invested surpluses—in infrastructure, education, trade—grew and shaped history. This pattern is repeated on a smaller scale in individuals. The average is like a society that immediately burns its surpluses in consumption. The two percent are like cultures that invest surpluses and thereby strengthen their foundations. The key point is that money should not be understood as a static quantity.

It is like electricity: without a conduit, it fizzles out; with a conduit, it can light up entire cities. For the average person, money is an object. For the two percent, it is a flow. This flow can be directed, multiplied, transformed. Those who have money have the opportunity to create movement – not only in their own lives, but in the lives of others. The average person misses this opportunity because they reduce money to the moment. The two percent, on the other hand, think in terms of processes. They know that money does not stand still, but that once set in motion, it can multiply.

This makes it clear that the difference between the average and the two percent is not in the amount of money someone has, but in the way they understand it. The average person understands money as a reward. The two percent understand it as energy. The average person wants to spend it. The two percent want to move it. This difference is subtle, but it changes your entire life. Because those who understand money as energy do not use it to validate themselves in the short term, but to build structures of freedom in the long term. If you want to understand the meaning of money in depth, you have to go beyond the superficial idea that it is printed paper or numbers on a screen. Money is not a substance in its essence, but a symbol that represents energy. It is solidified work, concentrated time, stored possibilities. For the average person, this idea remains abstract because they experience money only as a means of consumption. They work, they receive an amount, and they exchange this amount for goods, services, or status symbols. Money flows through their hands like water they cannot hold. They see it coming, they see it going, and they believe that is its nature. But the two percent understand money on a different level. They see not only the symbol, but the energy bound within it. For them, money is not the end point, but the starting point; not the reward, but the resource that enables new realities. Economics describes money functionally: as a unit of account, a medium of exchange, a store of value. But this definition falls short when it comes to explaining why the average person remains poor and why the two percent become free. Because in truth, it is not the function of money that determines its potential, but the meaning we attribute to it. For the average person, money means security and consumption. For the two percent, it means energy and creative power.

This difference in meaning is crucial because it shapes behavior. Those who view money only as security cling to it and fear losing it. Those who view it only as consumption spend it immediately. Both attitudes prevent money from growing. However, those who view money as energy understand that its value lies not in holding on to it or spending it, but in putting it into motion. Psychology shows that people learn their relationship with money in childhood. Children who experience money as scarce often develop the attitude that they must use it immediately when it is available because they fear it will disappear again. Children who experience money being used as a means of power often develop an ambivalent relationship with it – they long to possess it, but at the same time feel guilty when they have it. The average person carries these impressions with them throughout their life without questioning them. They repeat patterns that do not stem from their own decisions, but from the stories of their parents, their environment, and their culture. The two percent realized at some point that these stories are not the truth, but merely programs. They began to consciously change their relationship with money. One crucial idea plays a role here: money is not something you have, but something you move. If you think of money as electricity, it becomes clear that it is only useful when it flows through wires, when it powers devices, when it is in motion. A power storage device that is never discharged is worthless. Similarly, a sum of money that is only hoarded or consumed is energetically dead. Only when money is invested does it unfold its power. The two percent understand this intuitively.

They understand that money can work for them when it is tied up in structures that generate new value. The average person, on the other hand, sees money only as a static possession. They believe that they must either hold on to it or spend it. In this way, they consume energy instead of using it. From a neurobiological perspective, money acts as a stimulus that activates the reward system. Simply seeing or receiving money triggers the release of dopamine. The average person remains at the mercy of this mechanism. They spend money because they want to feel the rush that buying something creates. They work not to create freedom, but to repeat this cycle of reward and satisfaction. But like any rush, this one is short-lived, and so they must endlessly renew the cycle. The two percent, on the other hand, recognize the mechanism and do not allow themselves to be controlled by it. They cultivate a different form of reward: not buying, but building. Not spending, but growing. They derive joy not from consumption, but from multiplication. This shifts their entire reward system.

Sociology provides another perspective. Money is also a means of communication. It says something about what a society values.

The average person uses money to signal belonging. They buy what others buy, they live how others live, they define their value by mirroring their environment. The two percent, on the other hand, do not use money primarily as a signal to the outside world, but as a tool for the inside. They do not ask, "How am I seen?" but rather, "How can I shape things?" Money does not serve to buy recognition, but to create freedom. This different form of communication fundamentally distinguishes them from the average person. History also confirms this pattern. Great entrepreneurs, investors, and philanthropists have never seen money as a goal, but as a source of energy. They have understood that money can be used to initiate processes that extend far beyond the individual. They have recognized that money can be multiplied when it is put into motion. The average person, on the other hand, sees money only as something to be possessed or lost. They view it as static, not dynamic. And that is precisely what keeps them in mediocrity.

At the end of this section, it becomes clear that money is not a thing, but an energy. The average person consumes it, the two percent use it. The average person sees money as a reward, the two percent see it as a tool. This difference is the key to independence. Because those who only spend money remain dependent, while those who move money as energy gradually break free from the chains of mediocrity. If you want to understand why the majority of people remain financially dependent and only a small minority achieve true freedom, you have to realize that it's less about knowledge and more about attitude. Money is not a rigid object, but a process, a flow that can be set in motion again and again. The average person experiences money as a reward for performance, as a means of immediately fulfilling desires or covering needs. In doing so, they reduce it to a linear logic: work – wages – consumption. This logic seems reasonable, but in reality it is a trap. Because it ties the energy of money to the finiteness of one's own labor. Those who live this way remain trapped in a cycle of effort and reward, without ever crossing the threshold to independence. The two percent have broken through this logic. They understand that money must remain in motion, that – like any energy – it only unleashes its power when it is transformed rather than consumed.

Instead of endlessly exchanging their own labor for money, they build systems in which money itself becomes the worker. They let money flow, grow, and multiply. And because they do so, they free themselves from the direct dependence that paralyzes the average person. This difference can be explained scientifically with the principle of the multiplier. Economists describe how capital multiplies when it is invested productively. An invested amount creates jobs, generates demand, yields interest or returns, and thus generates further streams of income. The average person hardly experiences this process because they consume money immediately. They interrupt the flow before it can arise. The two percent, on the other hand, prolong the flow by seeing money not as an end point, but as a starting point. This difference is also deeply rooted psychologically. The average person experiences money emotionally.

For them, it is associated with fear or desire. Fear of losing it, or desire to enjoy it immediately. These emotions drive them to either hoard money or spend it. Both block their energy. Money that is only hoarded stagnates. Money that is spent immediately disappears. The two percent have learned to detach their emotions from money. They view it soberly, almost objectively, as a form of energy that needs to be set in motion. This distance allows them to make rational decisions where the average person reacts impulsively. It is interesting to note that even people with a high level of education and a large income often remain stuck in average thinking. They earn a lot, spend a lot, and yet remain dependent. Because the decisive difference lies not in the amount of income, but in the way it is understood and moved. A person with a modest income who understands money as energy can build independence step by step. A person with a high income who understands money as a reward remains trapped in the same cycle despite all the sums involved. From a neuroscientific perspective, this means that the two percent have learned to consciously change their dopamine control. They experience joy not from consumption, but from growth. They derive satisfaction not from owning something immediately, but from seeing how money generates energy that multiplies. This shift in the reward system is no small matter. It changes the entire way of thinking, feeling, and acting when dealing with money. The average person chases the short-term thrill.

The two percent cultivate the long-term joy of independence. From a sociological perspective, this way of thinking is disruptive. It breaks with the norm that money is primarily used for self-expression. The average person buys to be seen. They consume to signal belonging. The two percent, on the other hand, use money in a way that supports structures that endure regardless of outside opinions. For them, money is not a stage, but a foundation. They know that status is deceptive, but freedom is lasting. That's why they don't spend money on recognition, but on freedom. The idea of money as energy can also be found in spiritual traditions. Even in ancient writings, wealth is understood not only as possession, but as a flow that passes through people. Those who dam it up lose it. Those who channel it wisely increase it. This view is remarkably consistent with modern systems theory and economics. For systems in which energy remains in flux grow. Systems in which energy stagnates decay. The two percent act in accordance with this principle, even if they do not express it in spiritual terms. They keep the flow alive. In the end, it becomes clear that the difference between the average and the two percent is not a secret, but a different way of understanding money. The average sees money as wages, as a reward, as consumption. The two percent see money as energy that can be shaped, moved, and multiplied. This difference changes everything—not just the bank account, but the whole life. Because those who understand money as energy stop chasing it and start making it work for them. There is a quiet, barely noticed truth about the difference between the two percent and the average: it is not the amount of income that determines whether someone becomes free or not. It is the way they understand and direct the invisible energy of money. The average person believes that freedom is only possible if you earn a lot. That's why countless people chase higher salaries, bonuses, and supposedly secure career paths. But experience shows that even people with very high incomes can live in constant dependency, often even more so because their consumption adapts to their income.

They earn more, they spend more, they remain trapped in the same cycle. The two percent prove the opposite. Many of them started with little. What set them apart was not the amount, but their attitude: they saw money not as a reward, but as energy to be shaped. The energy of money unfolds in motion, not in stagnation. Those who merely hoard money block its flow. Those who spend it immediately burn it. The two percent have understood that money is like water: it must circulate, but in the right channels. It must not seep away, and it must not overflow. This balance requires awareness, discipline, and an understanding that money is a tool that changes its form when you use it. The average person experiences money passively—they receive it, they lose it, they long for more. The top two percent experience it actively—they direct it, they multiply it, they transform it into structures that serve them. Psychology describes a phenomenon that highlights this difference: so-called "mental accounting." People tend to put money into boxes – salary for fixed costs, bonuses for luxuries, credit cards for spontaneous desires. This way of thinking tempts us to treat money differently depending on which mental account it is in.

The average person is guided by this illusion and spends impulsively depending on the box. The two percent, however, view money independently of its source. They always see it as energy that is either increased or consumed. They are not blinded by mental drawers, but ask themselves how each amount can best be put to work to create freedom. Neuroscience explains this difference through the connection between emotion and money. The average person is caught in a reward system that thinks in the short term. Every purchase triggers dopamine, while every investment initially feels like a loss because the reward is deferred. The two percent have learned to reprogram this mechanism. They do not derive pleasure from quick consumption, but from long-term growth. They have trained their brains to value the growth of opportunities more than the moment of purchase. This training is not innate, but the result of repetition, reflection, and conscious decision-making.

Anyone could go through it, but most people remain in the comfort zone of the quick fix. From a sociological perspective, money is also a form of language. It communicates belonging, status, and power. The average person uses money to speak the language of conformity: they consume in order to belong, they use brands and symbols to show that they meet expectations. The two percent speak a different language: they don't use money to prove something to others, but to gain independence. Their money communicates freedom, not belonging. They don't buy symbols, they create substance. Economic history provides impressive examples. Rich cultures and dynasties did not survive because they had enormous resources at their disposal, but because they understood how to use these resources as a source of energy. Where surpluses were invested—in trade, education, infrastructure—periods of prosperity ensued. Where they were spent only on luxury and consumption, decline followed. This same pattern is repeated on an individual level. The average person lives like a culture that burns its surpluses in pomp and circumstance. The two percent live like cultures that transform surpluses into foundations. The crucial point is that money does not merge with identity for the two percent.

The average person defines themselves by their possessions: who they are depends on what they have or do not have. This identification ties their self-esteem to their bank balance. If this fluctuates, so does their inner sense of security. The two percent separate their identity from money. They see it as a resource, not as a self-definition. Their value does not depend on how much they own, but on how consciously they use their energy. It is precisely this inner distance that gives them the freedom to make courageous decisions that the average person avoids out of fear. This difference can also be described philosophically. The average person views money materialistically – as something you can have or lose. The two percent view money processually – as a flow that needs to be shaped. This change in perspective is radical because it completely changes the relationship between people and money. Those who see money as a thing fight for possession. Those who see it as a flow direct movement. And those who direct movement gain power that goes beyond possession. This shows that the decisive difference lies not in numbers, but in meanings. The average person remains a prisoner of their emotions, their social reflections, and their unconscious patterns. The two percent free themselves by understanding money as energy that can be directed. This insight is not a theory, but a practice that begins in everyday life—with every decision about whether to consume or increase energy.

There is probably no topic that is as riddled with misunderstandings and projections as money. For the average person, it is a source of worry, longing, and conflict, while for the two percent, it is a tool for creation. This difference stems not only from different knowledge or educational backgrounds, but from a fundamentally different perspective. The average person sees money as a reward, while the top two percent see money as energy. This shift in thinking is so profound that it steers entire lives in different directions over the years. This is particularly evident in how differently the two groups deal with uncertainty. The average person fears uncertainty because they see money as a protective shield. They save to feel secure, they spend to compensate for stress, and they lose both the moment external circumstances change. This spiral of fear keeps them trapped because they believe that money can provide security in the sense of invulnerability. But that is an illusion.

No amount of money can protect them from illness, loss, or social upheaval. The two percent know this, and that is precisely why they use money differently. For them, money is not security, but movement. For them, security does not come from holding on, but from building structures that make them independent. Psychologically, this difference can be explained by the concept of control beliefs. The average person usually has an external control belief:

they believe that their fate depends on external factors – their employer, the market, the state, luck. The two percent have an internal locus of control: they are convinced that their actions, their decisions, and their handling of money make the decisive difference. This conviction changes everything. Because those who believe that they cannot make a difference behave passively. Those who believe that they can shape things behave actively. For the two percent, money becomes an expression of self-efficacy, while for the average person it remains an expression of dependence. Research on emotions in dealing with money also confirms this difference.

Studies show that fear and greed are the strongest driving forces for the average person. They fear losing money and are eager to spend or multiply it quickly without having a system behind it. This emotional fluctuation makes them susceptible to manipulation—advertising, trends, promises of quick profits. The two percent, on the other hand, cultivate serenity. They do not allow themselves to be driven by short-term emotions, but stick to long-term processes. They understand that money needs time to unfold its energy and that panic or euphoria are only disturbances in the flow. From a sociological perspective, money is often a means of self-expression for the average person. They buy to be seen, they consume to belong, they define themselves through symbols that are meant to signal to others that they are successful. But these symbols are fragile. They lose their luster as soon as someone else surpasses them or as soon as fashion changes. The two percent, on the other hand, do not see money as a language of conformity, but as a language of freedom. They invest in values that exist independently of the opinions of others. Their freedom grows, while the average person only cultivates their image. The historical dimension also illustrates the difference. Entire nations have understood how to use surpluses to create independence – they invested in education, infrastructure, and innovation. Other nations burned their surpluses on luxury, wars, or waste.

One path led to freedom, the other to ruin. The same mechanism applies in the lives of individuals. Those who only consume money build nothing. Those who understand money as energy lay foundations that last. Philosophically speaking, this reveals a profound paradox: the average person chases money in order to be free and remain trapped. The two percent use money to free themselves from money. The more systems they build that generate income independently of their direct labor, the less money plays a role in their self-esteem. They no longer need it to prove themselves because they have understood that freedom lies not in having, but in being able. They can decide how they live, and that is where true power lies. From a spiritual perspective, money is a form of energy that intensifies when it is moved in harmony with inner clarity.

Those who act out of fear lose. Those who act out of clarity win. The average person acts out of scarcity, the two percent out of abundance. This difference is subtle, but it determines the direction of life. Scarcity creates narrowness, abundance creates expansiveness. Scarcity seeks security, abundance creates opportunities. So, at the end of this chapter, it becomes clear: money is not a neutral thing, but an energy that is guided by the attitudes of the people who use it. The average person remains bound because they either hold on to money or burn it immediately. The two percent free themselves because they let money flow without being controlled by it. They understand that money is not the goal, but the means, and that freedom begins when money is understood as a tool for movement and creation.

Notes:

Notes:

Chapter 8: The illusion of security – Why permanent employment and status symbols are deceptive

Security is one of the strongest human needs. Since time immemorial, humans have sought protection from uncertainty, danger, hunger, and cold. In modern societies, this need has taken on other forms. Fireplaces and sturdy huts have been replaced by employment contracts, insurance policies, and material status symbols. People feel secure when they believe their income is stable, when they own a house, when they drive a car that signals respect. But the truth is that these forms of security are illusions. They calm the nervous system and allay fears of chaos, but they are no guarantee of stability. It is precisely when we believe we are secure that we are most vulnerable. The average person clings to these illusions.

They believe that a permanent job protects them from the uncertainties of life. They believe that status symbols prove their worth and secure them recognition. But both are deceptive. A permanent job gives a feeling of continuity, but it ties people to dependence on an employer whose decisions they cannot control. Status symbols may earn them recognition in their social environment, but they make them dependent on opinions that are constantly changing. Security based on external structures is always uncertain. Psychology explains this behavior through the principle of cognitive bias. People overestimate the stability of what they know.

Those who are employed today believe that this will still be the case in ten years. Those who own a house believe that this guarantees security. But in reality, both depend on factors that cannot be controlled: economic fluctuations, corporate decisions, social changes, personal misfortunes. The average person represses this uncertainty because it is too frightening. They look for symbols that calm their fears, even if they have no substance. The two percent have seen through this illusion. They know that a permanent job is not a guarantee, but a relationship of dependency. They know that status symbols have no real value, but only generate short-term recognition. They do not seek security in external structures, but in inner freedom and self-created systems. They understand that true security does not lie in contracts or things, but in the ability to react flexibly, build structures, and act independently. From an economic perspective, this pattern is particularly evident in times of crisis.

When companies cut jobs, millions of people lose their supposed security in one fell swoop. Houses can lose value, status symbols can become a burden. It is precisely in such moments that it becomes clear how fragile the things to which the average person ties their security are. The two percent are less affected by this because they have not tied their security to a single system. They diversify, they create income streams that do not depend on a single source, and they measure their value not by external symbols but by their independence. From a philosophical point of view, too, the search for security is a paradox. Because life itself is change. Security in the absolute sense does not exist. Those who seek it are fighting against the nature of life. That is why the attempt to secure oneself often ends in even greater uncertainty. People cling to contracts, to things, to symbols – and lose the ability to act flexibly.

The two percent have understood that freedom is worth more than security. They know that you cannot escape the flow of life, that you can only learn to navigate it. This makes it clear that the average person remains trapped in the cycle of illusion because they believe that external structures protect them. The two percent are free because they know that true security does not lie in permanent jobs or status symbols, but in the ability to think and act independently. In the modern world, security has become a guiding principle that shapes entire life plans. People choose careers not because they fulfill them, but because they are "secure." They buy houses not because they live freely in them, but because they have been told that property means security. They invest in status symbols not because they have intrinsic value, but because they hope that the judgment of others will give them a sense of stability. But the more you examine this concept, the clearer it becomes that it is a deceptive construct. Security, as the average person understands it, does not exist in the form in which it is desired. Industrial psychology impressively describes how the idea of secure permanent employment has developed over the last hundred years. In the post-war period, it was indeed a promise: large companies offered lifelong employment, stable pensions, and social security.

But this reality has changed radically. Today, the job market is volatile, companies are constantly changing, and technologies are displacing entire industries. The "secure job" has long since become a myth, but the average person continues to cling to it because they know no alternative. They cling to the image of permanent employment as if it were a rock in a storm, when in reality it is just a sandbank that will disappear with the next tide. Economic data confirms this uncertainty. Even large corporations regularly cut thousands of jobs, merge, or relocate jobs to other countries. Globalization has created a dynamic in which stability hardly exists anymore. But instead of acknowledging this as reality, the average person represses the danger. They reassure themselves with the thought that their employment contract protects them, even if it only applies as long as it serves the company. The two percent see through this illusion. They know that dependence on a single source of income never means security, no matter how solid it may seem. True security lies in diversity, in flexibility, in the ability to build multiple streams of energy. Psychology also confirms that clinging to this illusion creates more fear than it takes away. People who believe that their security depends solely on their employer are constantly in a state of subliminal worry about losing this source. They live in latent insecurity, even if they do not want to openly admit it.

Their fear manifests itself in stress, insomnia, and dependence on routines that give them a false sense of stability. The two percent, on the other hand, do not share this fear because they know they have multiple options. They feel free because they do not make their income dependent on a single factor. Status symbols are a second major illusion. The average person believes that a certain car, a certain watch, a certain place of residence gives them security – not in an objective sense, but in a social sense. Those who possess these symbols believe that they are recognized, respected, perhaps even untouchable. But this security is even more deceptive than a permanent job. It depends entirely on the opinions of others, which can change at any time. Status symbols lose their value the moment a new model appears or society sets different standards. They are like sandcastles that crumble with the next wave. Sociologists refer to this as "symbolic capital." It is capital that exists not in real values, but in meanings. A car is not just a vehicle, but a sign. Clothing is not just fabric, but a symbol.

But symbols are fragile. They do not guarantee freedom, but bind people even more strongly to the opinions of others. The average person clings to them because they believe it makes them more stable. In reality, it makes them more vulnerable. Because those who derive their sense of security from symbols lose it as soon as the symbols fade. The two percent know this. They invest their money and energy not in symbols, but in systems. They do not buy signs of recognition; they build structures that exist independently of opinions. From a philosophical point of view, this reveals the paradox of security. People seek something that does not exist in absolute form. Life is change, it is movement, it is risk. Security in the sense of guaranteed stability is an illusion. But instead of acknowledging this truth, the average person builds a world of permanent jobs and status symbols to simulate a feeling of security. This feeling is real—but it is not stable. It is similar to the feeling of a child who closes their eyes and believes they are invisible. Reality remains as it is, even if you ignore it. The two percent have accepted this truth. They seek security not in immutability, but in adaptability. They know that a system that can change is more stable than one that remains rigid. That is why they create structures that can respond flexibly, they constantly educate themselves, and they diversify their income streams. Their security lies not in the illusion of control, but in the real ability to move. From a spiritual perspective, too, the search for external security is a dead end. True security does not come from things or contracts, but from inner clarity.

Those who know that they are rooted in themselves do not need symbols to feel stable. The two percent live this truth: they derive their security from trust in their own ability to shape their lives. The average person seeks it externally, and as long as they do so, they remain dependent. This shows that permanent jobs and status symbols are the two great illusions that bind the average person. They are reassuring, but they do not liberate. They provide a feeling, but no substance. They are projections that are supposed to satisfy the need for security, but in reality only create dependence. The two percent have recognized that security begins when you let go of illusions and choose freedom. If you examine the concept of security in depth, you come across a fascinating insight: it is less an objective reality than a psychological construct. People talk about security when they feel stability, predictability, and protection. But this feeling is always subjective; it is a perception, not a fact. What is considered secure today may be gone tomorrow. What is perceived as protection today may turn into a shackle tomorrow.

It is precisely in this mechanism that lies the trap into which the average person repeatedly falls. The modern world of work is the best example of this illusion. Permanent jobs convey a feeling of stability: a regular income, fixed working hours, social security. But behind this façade lies a deep dependence. For the supposed security only exists as long as the company exists, as long as the market remains stable, as long as the employer decides that the workforce is needed. The moment these conditions change, security crumbles. Millions of people have experienced exactly this in economic crises. Jobs that were considered unshakeable disappeared overnight. But surprisingly, this did not stop people from believing in permanent employment. The average person continued to cling to it as if it were their last resort. Psychologically, this can be explained by the need for cognitive consistency. People want to experience a world that is orderly and predictable. They repress facts that contradict this image and hold on to beliefs even when reality has long since disproved them. Permanent employment is precisely such a belief. It is the symbol of order, of predictability, of a world that remains stable. Those who believe in it feel reassured. But this reassurance comes at a high price, because it ties people to structures that can let them down at any time. Even more deceptive is the security that comes from status symbols. A house, a car, certain clothes, a prestigious job title—all of these give the average person the feeling of having arrived. But what does "arriving" mean in a world that is constantly changing? Status symbols are like masks that give the wearer meaning for a moment, but can slip off at any time. Their value is not real, but depends on the recognition of others. They can generate admiration, but also envy. They can create a sense of belonging, but also pressure. Above all, however, they are transient. The car loses its value, fashion changes, the title becomes relative. Security based on such symbols is a mirage. Sociologically speaking, this is a phenomenon of social comparison. People orient themselves towards the possessions and status of their fellow human beings. Those who have more seem to be more secure. Those who have less seem to be more vulnerable.

But this comparison is endless. There is always someone who has more, and so one's own security is constantly shifting upwards. The average person does not recognize this. They believe that the next symbol will finally bring the stability they long for. The two percent have long understood that this race is endless and pointless. They do not chase status, but build substance. Economics provides another argument against the illusion of security. Assets that are tied up in a single asset are risky. A job is a source of income, but only one. A house is a possession, but tied to a market that can fluctuate. Those who put all their eggs in one basket are playing with uncertainty, even if they believe the opposite. The average person makes precisely this mistake: they tie their entire existence to a few symbols and believe that this makes them secure. The two percent, on the other hand, spread their investments, diversify, and build systems that rest on several pillars. Their security does not come from a single symbol, but from a network of possibilities.

From a spiritual point of view, too, the search for security in the outside world is misguided. Because nothing in the outside world remains the same. Everything changes, everything passes. Those who cling to things cling to transience. The two percent seek security within: in self-confidence, in knowledge, in the ability to deal with uncertainty. They have accepted that life offers no guarantees. It is precisely this acceptance that sets them free. The average person, on the other hand, refuses to accept this truth.

They want a security that does not exist and pay for it with their freedom. Philosophically speaking, one could say that security is the religion of the average person. It gives them stability, structures their life, and promises salvation from fear. But like any religion, it can also be illusory if it is based on false foundations. The two percent have abandoned this religion. They have no need for illusions because they have learned to live with reality as it is: uncertain, changeable, open. In the end, it becomes clear that the illusion of security is a trap that the average person is afraid to leave. But the more tightly they cling to it, the more dependent they become. The two percent are free because they have understood that security does not lie in permanent jobs and status symbols, but in the ability to dance with uncertainty. The longing for security is a universal human need. But hardly any other need is so susceptible to deception. People seek stability, consistency, something that lifts them out of the chaos of unpredictability. But life itself is movement, change, risk. Those who seek absolute security are looking for something that does not exist. This is precisely where the illusion that binds the average person so tightly arises.

They construct a network of permanent jobs and status symbols that makes them believe they are protected. But in reality, they only become more entangled in dependencies that can be torn apart at any time. The world of work provides a striking example. For decades, young people were taught that the best decision for their lives was to find a secure job. Parents advised their children to pursue a "sensible career," to find a "good job," preferably in the civil service or in an established company. This narrative has shaped generations. But reality has long since changed. Companies are merging, jobs are disappearing due to automation, and entire industries are being transformed by technological innovation. The supposedly secure job has become a plaything of global forces that no individual can control. The average person, however, clings to the old narrative because they cannot bear the truth: that security in this form does not exist. Psychologically speaking, this is a form of repression. The fear of uncertainty is so great that people prefer to cling to an illusion rather than face reality. Deep down, they may know that their job is not secure forever, that their house could lose value, that their status is only temporary. But they push this realization into their subconscious and continue to live as if everything were stable. This psychological game comes at a high price.

It ties up enormous energy in maintaining the illusion and prevents new opportunities from being seen. The two percent differ precisely on this point. They are willing to accept the fear of uncertainty. They do not repress it, they face it. They know that fear does not disappear by ignoring it, but by transforming it through awareness. Instead of clinging to symbols, they use uncertainty as a driving force to create structures that are flexible and independent. Their security does not lie in nothing happening, but in being able to respond to anything. Status symbols act as the shiny masks of this illusion. The average person believes that they are secure if they wear the right symbols. A certain car, a certain place of residence, a certain lifestyle are supposed to prove that they belong, that they have made it. But status symbols are not securities, they are only reflections. Their value depends on the judgment of others, and that judgment is fleeting. Admired today, ridiculed tomorrow, forgotten the day after tomorrow—symbols lose their power that quickly. Those who rely on them are building their sense of security on sand. Sociologically speaking, this can be explained by the mechanism of social comparison. People feel secure when they believe they are better off than others. But this comparison is endless. There is always someone with more, and so one's own security remains fragile. The average person lives in this endless race.

They believe that the next symbol will finally reassure them. But as soon as they have it, a new goal emerges. The two percent have seen through this game. They know that comparisons never end and that true security cannot come from outside. That is why they invest not in symbols, but in substance. Economically, the fragility of permanent jobs and status symbols becomes apparent in times of crisis. When markets collapse, status symbols immediately lose their value. When companies cut back, permanent jobs are the first to go. At times like these, it becomes clear how little substance there is behind the illusions. But instead of learning from this, the average person keeps returning to the same patterns. They long for a feeling of security and accept dependence in return.

Philosophically speaking, this is why so many people remain restless inside despite all their material achievements. They build their lives on foundations that do not hold. They believe that they gain control by attaching themselves to symbols, but in reality they lose the only control that matters: that over their own attitude. The two percent have learned this lesson. They have realized that the search for external security is an escape from inner truth. Those who see through them free themselves not only financially, but also existentially. This reveals why permanent employment and status symbols are deceptive. They provide short-term reassurance, but in the long term they take away freedom. They give a feeling, but no stability. They are illusions that the average person defends because they are not ready to accept reality. The two percent, on the other hand, have stopped seeking illusions. They do not base their security on external symbols, but on inner clarity and structures that they can shape themselves. When you look at the illusion of security in all its depth, you realize that it is more than just an individual misunderstanding. It is a cultural narrative that shapes entire societies and guides generations. People grow up believing that a secure job, a home of their own, and visible status symbols are the most reliable foundations for a good life. This belief is repeated so often that it is hardly ever questioned. But it is precisely because it seems so self-evident that it is so dangerous.

It causes people to organize their lives according to patterns that do not set them free, but rather shackle them. The world of work has systematically reinforced this illusion. Companies benefit from employees who believe that their security lies in loyalty to their employer. Those who believe this narrative question less, are more willing to compromise, and remain even when conditions are no longer favorable. But this loyalty is asymmetrical. Companies do not act out of loyalty, but out of economic interests. A "secure job" only exists as long as it is profitable. This truth is suppressed because it raises the fear that one is never really secure. The average person prefers to live in the illusion, even if it makes them dependent. From a psychological perspective, the illusion of security acts as a mental shield. It takes the edge off the existential fear that every human being carries within them. Those who believe they are secure can relax and settle into routines. But this relaxation is deceptive. It prevents people from recognizing their real possibilities. They live in a cocoon that protects them from reality, but also from growth. Only those who have the courage to let go of this protective shield experience what real stability means: the inner strength to deal with uncertainty. Status symbols play the role of visible anchors. They convey the feeling that you have made it, that you are stable, that you can rely on something. But these symbols are empty. Their value is not absolute, but relational. They only have meaning as long as others recognize them. Thus, the supposed security they provide is in reality complete insecurity.

Because it does not depend on substance, but on the opinion of the masses, and that can change at any time. Those who base their identity and sense of security on symbols live in constant dependence on the eyes of others. Sociologically, this is reflected in the dynamics of consumption. Societies are constantly producing new symbols that promise security. Today it is the house in the suburbs, tomorrow the electric car, the day after tomorrow perhaps something completely different. The spiral continues to turn, and the average person follows it because they believe that the next possession will finally make them stable. But the two percent have realized that this spiral is endless. They opt out by no longer seeking security in external factors, but in their ability to shape, learn, and react. From an economic perspective, the illusion of security is particularly fatal because it forces people into inflexible structures.

Those who put all their eggs in one basket of permanent employment have no reserves when that source dries up. Those who invest their entire fortune in a single house are vulnerable when the market crashes. Those who invest everything in status symbols lose immediately when their value declines. The two percent know that security does not come from fixation, but from flexibility. Not from a single source of income, but from the ability to use multiple avenues. Philosophically speaking, the illusion of security is an expression of the human refusal to accept the nature of life. Everything changes, everything passes. There is no such thing as absolute security. Those who seek it seek stagnation, and stagnation in a dynamic world is synonymous with regression. The two percent have stopped seeking stagnation. They have learned that true security does not lie in the absence of danger, but in the presence of inner strength. From a spiritual perspective, the illusion of security is the great deception of the ego. It wants control, it wants guarantees, it wants predictability. But life eludes this control. The more the ego reaches for security, the greater the fear of losing it. The two percent let go. They accept uncertainty as part of existence and, paradoxically, experience a deeper peace as a result. For those who no longer fight to hold on to security become free to take life as it is.

In the end, it becomes clear that permanent employment and status symbols are not sources of security, but masks of insecurity. They provide short-term reassurance, but create long-term dependency. The average person remains trapped because they don't dare to let go of the illusion. The two percent have the courage to see through it. They know that true security does not lie in contracts or things, but in the ability to act independently, think flexibly, and develop inner strength.

Notes:

Notes:

Chapter 9: Trading time for money – The main pattern of the 98%

There is a pattern so deeply ingrained in the lives of the average person that it is hardly ever questioned: the idea that you have to trade time for money. This principle is taken for granted, as a law of nature in the world of work, as an inevitable order. It is instilled in us as early as school: children learn that they are rewarded for performance, that their hours are translated into grades, and that later on, the workplace is the logical continuation of this mechanism. Those who work receive money. Those who don't work don't get any. This linear thinking shapes generations and is rarely questioned. But this is precisely where the core difference lies between the 98% who remain in the cycle of dependency and the 2% who achieve financial freedom. At first glance, the mechanism of exchanging time for money seems logical and fair. Work means effort, hard work, commitment – and you should be rewarded for it.

But this logic has a crucial flaw: it inextricably links income to one's own labor, to the hours one makes available, to the presence one provides. Since time is the only resource that is irretrievably limited, this model inevitably leads to a dead end. Those who earn money solely through the direct investment of their time can never go beyond the limits of their lifetime. They may increase their hourly wage, they may advance their career, they may take on more responsibility – but the mechanism remains the same: they sell part of their lifetime in order to earn an income. From a scientific point of view, this is referred to as linear value creation. In a linear model, income is directly proportional to effort. Those who work twice as much earn twice as much. Those who work less earn less. This model creates an apparent fairness, because it seems to reward performance. But in reality, it is a trap, because it does not allow you to leave the cycle. After all, every person has only twenty-four hours in a day, only limited energy, only a finite body. Those who rely exclusively on this mechanism will never achieve freedom, but will remain stuck in the hamster wheel of linear exchange. The two percent see through this trap. They recognize that exchanging time for money is the primary cause of dependence.

That is why they build systems in which their income no longer depends directly on their presence. They invest in structures, in capital, in processes that generate money even when they are not present. They create mechanisms that run independently of their daily time. This transition from linear to exponential thinking is the crucial difference that separates them from the masses. Psychology shows why it is so difficult for the average person to break out of this pattern. People are conditioned to link reward directly to effort. Even children receive pocket money for doing chores, and students receive praise for completing assignments. The logic of "first perform, then be rewarded" is so deeply ingrained that it is perceived as natural. Those who try to think differently often encounter resistance—not only from outside, but also from within.

This is because it feels unfamiliar to receive money without having directly sacrificed time for it. Many experience feelings of guilt or doubt when they receive income from sources that are not directly related to their efforts. The average person confuses this conditioning with morality. They believe that only hard work is valuable and overlook the fact that value is also created through systems, ideas, and investments. Neuroscience explains this phenomenon through the functioning of the reward system. The brain reacts strongly to immediate correlations: action – reward. This correlation provides security because it is predictable. That is why the average person prefers activities where they immediately feel that their efforts are being rewarded – whether through salary, recognition or consumption. Income that is generated indirectly seems strange, uncertain, perhaps even unfair to them. The two percent, on the other hand, have learned to reprogram their reward system. They derive pleasure not only from immediate rewards, but also from long-term effects. They experience satisfaction in seeing systems grow, even if they are not constantly involved. From a sociological perspective, exchanging time for money is a means of keeping the majority dependent.

Societies are built on the labor of their members, and the link between time and wages ensures that this labor remains reliably available. The average person internalizes this structure as normality. They believe that there is no alternative and even defend it morally. Those who do not work within this system are considered outsiders, lazy, or rule breakers. The two percent consciously place themselves outside this norm. They accept the stigma because they know that freedom is only possible if you have the courage to break through the collective illusion. Economically, it is clear how unproductive the linear model is. Even highly paid professions—doctors, lawyers, managers—are still essentially tied to the exchange of time for money. They earn a lot, but they have to be present to do so. As soon as they stop investing their time, their income dries up. The two percent, on the other hand, build structures that continue to run independently of their time.

They know that real wealth does not lie in hourly wages, but in the ability to decouple income from one's own lifetime. From a philosophical point of view, this reveals a deep contradiction. Humans have only one life, only a finite number of hours. When they sell these hours, they sell the most precious thing they possess. They give away their lifetime to acquire symbols that give them a false sense of security or status. But time does not come back. The two percent have understood that if you want to be free, you must not sell your time. You can only invest it – in structures, in relationships, in ideas that will outlast your own lifetime. At the end of this section, it becomes clear that exchanging time for money is the main pattern that keeps the 98% trapped on average. It is not the amount of income that makes the difference, but the logic behind how it is earned. As long as people believe that they can only earn money by selling their time, they remain dependent. Only when they understand that money can be tied to systems rather than hours does the path to freedom open up. The idea of exchanging time for money seems so natural to most people that they never question it. It is an unwritten law that is instilled in childhood and cemented by society. From an early age, people learn that their efforts are measured in hours, that they can expect a certain wage for every hour of work, and that this exchange is the basis of their lives. This pattern becomes so ingrained that it almost seems like a natural truth. But it is neither a law of nature nor an inescapable reality, but rather a cultural construct that binds 98% of people and has been abandoned by 2%. When you realize how much this mechanism shapes your life, you recognize its full significance.

The average person plans their life according to hours and wages. They consider how many hours they have to work in order to afford certain things. They calculate how much vacation they can take, how much free time they can afford without their income suffering. Their entire thinking is permeated by the idea that time is a currency that is used to obtain money. This thinking is so deeply ingrained that it distorts the perception of freedom itself. For as long as you exchange time for money, you remain a prisoner of a finite resource. Work psychology clearly shows how this exchange shapes our attitude towards life. People who work on an hourly wage or in fixed salary structures strongly associate their identity with their job. Their self-worth depends on how much they work and how much they get paid for it. Those who work overtime feel more valuable because they believe they are contributing more.

Those who work less feel guilty or inferior. In this way, the center of life shifts: it is not being, but doing that determines value. One's own existence is justified by performance, and performance in turn is quantified by money. The two percent have recognized this mechanism and consciously broken with it. They understand that time is the most precious resource a person has because it is irretrievable. Money, on the other hand, is reproducible, renewable, replaceable. So those who sell their time to obtain money are exchanging the precious for the replaceable. This insight is not only philosophical but also of great economic significance. It opens up the possibility of other models in which money does not depend directly on one's own lifetime. From an economic perspective, exchanging time for money is a linear model that does not allow for scaling. A person can only work a limited number of hours per day.

Even if they increase their hourly wage, they remain limited by linearity. The two percent leave this model behind by creating structures that have an exponential effect. They invest in systems that generate income without their own time being the limiting factor. Whether through capital investments, businesses, or intellectual property, in all cases they decouple income from direct presence. However, the psychology of the masses clings to the security of the linear model. It seems fair, it seems just, it seems controllable. If you work for an hour, you know what you will get in return. This predictability conveys a sense of stability, even if it is actually a shackle. Because predictability prevents growth. Those who only do the predictable do not dare to take leaps. The two percent accept uncertainty because they know that this is the only way to achieve growth. They accept that income is not linearly predictable in order to build structures that go far beyond what an hourly wage could ever achieve. From a sociological perspective, the exchange of time for money fulfills an important function for the system. It keeps people predictable and available. It ensures that labor remains plannable, that the majority feeds their energy into the cycle that sustains society. From this perspective, the exchange of time for money is less an economic necessity than a social structure that stabilizes power relations. The average person does not recognize this. They believe that this is the only option and even defend it.

Those who live differently, who build systems that no longer exchange time for money, are often viewed with suspicion, as if they were breaking the rules of the game. But the rules of the game are not natural laws, but man-made constructs. Historically, the exchange of time for money only took its current form with industrialization. Before that, people often lived in different structures: farmers, for example, produced crops that functioned independently of hours, craftsmen built works that lasted independently of daily wages. It was only wage labor in the industrial age that made the exchange of time for money the dominant form.

The two percent have this historical awareness. They know that what was once created can also be abandoned. From a philosophical point of view, the exchange of time for money is a form of self-objectification. People turn themselves into commodities, selling parts of their lifetime like objects. They no longer treat their lives as a unique flow, but as a stock of hours that can be used up like coins. This view alienates them from themselves. They no longer see themselves as beings that live, but as resources that are consumed. The two percent have broken through this alienation. They do not view their lives as a quota of hours, but as an opportunity to create structures that exist independently of their own efforts. At the end of this section, it becomes clear that exchanging time for money is the pattern that keeps the average person in a cycle of dependency. It seems stable, it feels predictable, but it is the invisible barrier that prevents growth. The two percent have broken through this barrier by learning to invest their time rather than sell it. This is the key to freedom. The belief that time must be exchanged for money is not just an individual pattern, but a collective myth. It shapes the thinking of entire societies, influences education systems, labor markets, and even the way people perceive their self-worth. It is so deeply ingrained that it is hardly ever questioned. People take it for granted, even consider it a moral imperative. Those who work earn money. Those who do not work do not deserve any. This narrative seems to create order, but it has a destructive flip side: it binds the majority to a system that can never set them free. The psychology of this pattern is fascinating.

Even children learn that their time is valued. They sit in classrooms for hours, their attendance is recorded, their performance is translated into grades. Later, these patterns are transferred to the world of work: timetables become working hours, grades become salaries. People grow up with the conviction that their value is measured in units of time. This leads to a deep connection between identity and work. Those who work a lot feel more valuable. Those who work little feel guilty. Life thus becomes an endless barter transaction: time in, money out. But this exchange is deceptive. Because time cannot be multiplied. Every person has only a finite number of days. Money, on the other hand, can be multiplied, renewed, reproduced indefinitely. So those who sell their time to earn money are selling the most precious thing they have in exchange for something that could theoretically be multiplied infinitely. This imbalance remains hidden from the average person because they are trapped in linear logic. They believe that income must necessarily follow from hours worked and do not realize that in doing so, they are committing the greatest theft against themselves: the theft of their own lifetime. The two percent have recognized this connection. They know that if you want to be free, you can't trade time for money. Instead, they trade knowledge, systems, capital, and ideas for money. They don't use their time to sell it piece by piece, but to create structures that generate income independently of their presence. This difference seems insignificant, but it changes everything. It shifts the center of life from working within the system to designing systems. From an economic perspective, exchanging time for money is the weakest model of value creation. It is linear, limited, and dependent on the performance of the individual. Even those who earn above-average incomes eventually reach their limits. Doctors, lawyers, managers—they all ultimately exchange their time. When they stop working, their income dries up. Only those who build structures that run without their own presence can escape this logic. That is exactly what the two percent do. They use money as energy that keeps structures running, even when they themselves are not present.

Neuroscience explains why it is so difficult for the average person to break out of this pattern. The brain loves predictability. Exchanging time for money is simple, understandable, and predictable. An hour of work brings a certain reward. This simple pattern reassures the reward system, even if it is actually a shackle. Income from passive structures, on the other hand, is more unpredictable, fluctuates, and requires patience. The brain initially perceives this as uncertain and reacts with fear. The two percent have learned to tolerate this fear. They accept that growth takes time and is not immediately visible. This allows them to reprogram their reward system: they derive pleasure not from immediate payouts, but from long-term freedom. From a sociological perspective, exchanging time for money is also a form of control. Societies benefit when the majority channels their energy into predictable paths. Hourly wages discipline people, make them available, and keep them in structures that support the system. Those who deviate from this pattern are often stigmatized. The self-employed, the investor, the entrepreneur—they are all viewed critically because they do not play by the rules. The average person reacts with mistrust, sometimes with envy, sometimes with moral outrage. But this mistrust only protects the illusion. It keeps the cycle stable, trapping the majority. From a philosophical point of view, this pattern reveals a deep tragedy. Because the person who sells time sells their freedom. They give their days, their hours, their life for symbols that give them a false sense of security or status. But the time they give away never comes back. The two percent have understood that time must not be a commodity. It can only be an investment.

It must not be sold, but used to build structures that will last. From a spiritual point of view, this means that the average person lives in an illusion. They believe they are buying security, when in reality they are selling their freedom. They believe they are gaining recognition, when in fact they are placing themselves in a position of dependency. The two percent live in a different reality: they accept uncertainty today in order to gain freedom tomorrow. They do not exchange time for money, but time for opportunities. At the end of this section, it becomes clear that the main pattern of the 98% is the exchange of time for money. It is the invisible chain that binds them to mediocrity. The two percent have broken this chain by learning to decouple income from their lifetime. This is the key to independence – and the reason why the average remains average.

If you look at the structures of modern life with open eyes, you will see that the pattern of exchanging time for money is not just an economic practice, but a cultural paradigm that shapes all areas of thought and feeling. It is so deeply rooted that most people no longer see it as one option among many, but as the only way to earn money. This dogma has become so internalized that it is hardly noticeable how unnatural it actually is. For nothing in nature works according to the principle of selling time as a resource. Plants grow, rivers flow, stars shine – none of them give up their time, but work through cycles and energies that sustain themselves. Humans, however, have forced themselves into a structure in which they treat their own lifetime as a commodity to be traded on an invisible market. Psychology explains why people so willingly accept this absurdity. They fear uncertainty more than the loss of freedom. They would rather exchange the most precious thing they possess – their hours, their lifetime – for a feeling of predictability than face the uncertainty that would come with true freedom.

This behavior can be described by the concept of loss aversion: people feel potential loss much more strongly than potential gain. The loss of security seems more threatening than the possibility of gaining freedom. That is why most people remain in a model that makes them inwardly dissatisfied, but at least gives them the feeling that they know what will happen at the end of the month. But this supposed stability is deceptive. Those who sell their time always live on the edge of uncertainty, even if they don't want to admit it. Illness, dismissal, old age – all of these can immediately interrupt the flow of income. Precisely because time is so closely linked to money, the average person's life is accompanied by a silent fear that they rarely express openly. This fear manifests itself in stress, chronic tension, and the feeling of always having to do more in order not to fall behind. The cycle of work and reward, which appears stable on the outside, is often a cycle of fear and exhaustion on the inside. The two percent differ fundamentally in this respect. They know that life offers no guarantees and accept this uncertainty. But instead of fearing it, they use it as a driving force. They understand that freedom can only arise where one is prepared to relinquish control and create systems that function independently of one's own time. Their security lies not in contracts, but in structures that generate income even when they are not personally present. They have a different relationship to risk: for the average person, risk is a threat; for the two percent, risk is an opportunity. Sociologically speaking, the pattern of time exchange is a form of collective discipline. It keeps millions of people in a structure that guarantees the functioning of society and the economy.

Those who work eight hours a day remain bound, predictable, and calculable. The hourly wage is not only an economic instrument, but also a psychological one. It conveys the feeling that work is directly rewarded, thus preventing people from asking whether there might be other ways. Anyone who thinks outside this system is quickly considered deviant, a dreamer, or even a threat to order. From an economic perspective, the exchange of time for money creates an invisible ceiling that hardly anyone breaks through. Even if the hourly wage increases, the limit of one's own time remains. People can increase their income, but never indefinitely, because their lifetime is limited. This model prevents exponential growth. The two percent have recognized that wealth is not created by working more hours, but by leverage. They use capital, ideas, and networks to generate income that is not tied to the clock. From a philosophical point of view, trading time is a form of self-objectification. People reduce themselves to a number of hours that they can sell. They become a resource that is used up, like oil or wood.

This way of thinking alienates them from their own dignity. They are no longer beings with infinite inner depth, but workers, employees, functionaries. The two percent have overcome this alienation by no longer measuring their lives in hours sold, but in opportunities created. From a spiritual perspective, exchanging time for money is one of humanity's greatest illusions. It makes people believe they can buy security, when in reality they are selling their freedom. Every hour exchanged for money is an hour that will never return. The average person lives in this illusion because they lack the courage to seek other paths. The two percent live outside this illusion because they have learned that time should not be sold, but only invested. In the end, it becomes clear that exchanging time for money is not only an economic model, but also a trap of thinking that binds the average person. It conveys a feeling of security, when in reality it creates the greatest uncertainty: dependence on a resource that is irretrievably lost. The two percent are free because they have recognized this trap. They know that money can be multiplied, but time cannot. And that is why they do not use their time for sale, but to build structures that give them freedom. When you look at the core of the average life, you always come across the same structure: time is exchanged for money as if it were a currency that could be reproduced indefinitely.

But the truth is the opposite. Time is irretrievable, it slips away with every moment, and that is precisely why exchanging time for money is the greatest loss a person can inflict on themselves. The average person does not recognize this because they live in routines that reassure them. They get up in the morning, go to work, sell their hours, and at the end of the month receive a sum that makes them feel that their life is okay. But this feeling is a fiction, a fragile construct that is in reality based on dependence and limitation. Psychology shows that people live in patterns that give them a sense of security. They get used to the idea that work and wages are inextricably linked. This pattern reassures them because it creates predictability. But this predictability comes at a high price.

It costs them the freedom to determine their own time, it costs them the chance to build structures that exist independently of their presence. The average person prefers to live in predictable dependence rather than uncertain freedom. The two percent have the courage to choose the opposite. From an economic perspective, exchanging time for money is the model of scarcity. It assumes that income is only generated when a person is physically present, expends energy, and gives of their time. As a result, income always remains limited. Even those who earn a lot can only achieve as much as their time allows. The two percent have abandoned this model by learning to decouple income from their time. They know that real wealth does not lie in hourly wages, but in building systems that function even without them. From a neuroscientific perspective, trading time is closely linked to the reward system.

The average person feels satisfaction when they are immediately rewarded for work done. This pattern is deeply ingrained because it signals security to the brain. But it is also a prison because it limits thinking to short-term correlations. The top two percent have learned to reprogram their reward system. They derive pleasure not only from immediate rewards, but also from the freedom that arises in the long term. They have developed the ability to endure delay, accept uncertainty, and pursue a greater goal in return. From a sociological perspective, exchanging time for money is a means of keeping societies stable. It ensures that the majority remain employed, that labor is available, and that structures run reliably. But this stability is deceptive because it is based on the limitation of the individual. It turns people into cogs in a machine whose value is measured in hours. The two percent break this pattern by no longer viewing their time as a commodity, but as capital that can only be invested in freedom. From a philosophical perspective, this pattern reveals an existential tragedy. People who sell their time are selling the only thing they truly possess.

They sacrifice their life hours for symbols that promise them security or status. But the time they give away never returns. The two percent have understood that if you want to be free, you must not sell your time. Time is the foundation of life, and it should only be invested in things that last: in ideas, in structures, in relationships, in developments that extend beyond the moment. From a spiritual perspective, exchanging time for money is one of the greatest illusions of human existence. It makes people believe they can buy security, when in reality they are losing their freedom. Every hour they sell is an hour they will never get back. The two percent live in a different reality: they accept uncertainty today in order to gain freedom tomorrow. They know that true security does not lie in money itself, but in the ability to freely organize their own time. At the end of this chapter, it becomes clear: the main pattern of the 98% is not poverty, not lack of education, not lack of intelligence. It is the exchange of time for money. As long as this pattern remains unbroken, the average person remains trapped. The two percent are free because they have learned to break out of this pattern. They don't sell their time, they invest it. And that is precisely what makes them independent.

Notes:

Notes:

Chapter 10: Wealth instead of income – How the 2% build capital

There is a fundamental difference between the thinking of the majority and the thinking of the minority who belong to the two percent: the average person strives for income, the two percent strive for wealth. This difference is not just a question of income level, but a question of attitude, perspective, and overall approach to life. Earnings are short-term, wealth is long-term. Earnings are exhausted in the moment, wealth unfolds its effect over years and decades. Those who live in earnings mode remain dependent on their constant performance. Those who live in wealth mode free themselves from this dependence because they build structures that exist independently of their daily presence. Psychologically speaking, this difference can be explained by the way people perceive time and energy. The average person focuses on immediate results. They work, they receive a wage, they consume. Their thinking is short-term, they live from month to month, sometimes even from week to week. The two percent, on the other hand, think in cycles, in generations, in chains of cause and effect that extend far beyond the moment. They see money not only as a medium of exchange, but as a seed. Earnings are fruit that can be eaten immediately. Wealth is a tree that bears new fruit again and again.

Economically, this difference is reflected in the distinction between income and capital. Income is the flow that comes from work. Capital is the substance that generates income again and again. The average person focuses on the flow, the two percent on the source. Those who only use the flow remain dependent on the river. Those who own the source have power over the river. That is why the top two percent invest in capital: in real estate, in companies, in knowledge, in networks.

The average person, on the other hand, consumes their income as if there were no tomorrow and wonders why they never become free. The psychology of reward plays a decisive role here. Earnings are immediately noticeable. They give a feeling of success, control, and security. Wealth, on the other hand, requires patience. It grows slowly, often invisibly, often unnoticed. Those who think in terms of earnings cannot stand this slowness. They want immediate satisfaction, immediate reward. That is why they remain trapped in the cycle of work and consumption. The two percent, on the other hand, have learned to seek joy not only in the present, but also in building. They find satisfaction in seeing structures grow, even if the reward only becomes visible later. This ability to delay gratification is one of the decisive factors that distinguishes the average from the independent. From a sociological perspective, the focus on earnings is a tool for keeping the majority in motion. Those who live from their earnings remain dependent on their employer, the market, and the next job. They must constantly perform, constantly sell their time, and constantly expend energy.

This keeps them controllable and predictable. Those who build wealth, on the other hand, escape this control. They create their own structures, their own networks, their own systems that make them more independent. That is why the idea of building wealth meets with resistance in many cultures. It is considered elitist, immoral, deviant. But it is precisely this resistance that protects the system that keeps the average person in earnings mode. Philosophically speaking, this difference contains a profound truth about life. Earnings are transient. They are part of the flow of everyday life; they come and go. Wealth, on the other hand, is substance, it is structure, it is foundation. Those who live in the mode of earning live constantly in the flow of transience. Those who live in the mode of wealth build something that lasts. The two percent have recognized this truth and organize their lives accordingly.

They don't ask, "How much will I earn today?" but rather, "What am I building that will still have an impact tomorrow?"From a spiritual perspective, the difference is also clear here. Earnings are a symbol of the fear of the average person. They want to hold something in their hands immediately, they want to feel security immediately, they want instant gratification. Wealth, on the other hand, is an expression of trust. Those who think in terms of wealth trust that the future will bear fruit, that what is sown today will bear fruit tomorrow. This trust is not naive, but the basis of all true freedom. So, at the end of this first section, it becomes clear: the difference between earnings and wealth is the difference between short-term dependence and long-term freedom. The average person remains trapped in the mode of earnings because they seek immediate reward. The two percent are free because they build wealth that works independently of their daily performance. If you take a closer look at the life of the average person, you will see that it is characterized by a constant cycle of earning and spending. People go to work, they receive their wages, and they spend them again. At the end of the month, the same cycle begins anew. This pattern repeats itself year after year until it becomes the norm. It seems like a functioning system, but in reality it is a trap. This cycle leaves no room for real growth. It produces income, but not wealth.

Income disappears, wealth remains. Income is the stream, wealth is the source. As long as the average person considers the stream to be the source, they remain trapped in dependency. From a psychological perspective, the focus on earning is understandable. People love the feeling of immediate reward. Those who work want to see something, feel something, hold something in their hands. Earnings satisfy precisely this need. They provide quick feedback that the effort was worthwhile. But this satisfaction is deceptive because it only calms the moment, it does not shape the future. It acts like a short-term painkiller: it takes away the restlessness, but it does not heal. The two percent have recognized that long-term peace of mind can only be achieved by building wealth. Wealth means creating structures that will continue to support you in the future, regardless of your current efforts. Economically speaking, wealth is more than just accumulated money. It is capital that works. Capital is not passive, it is active. It can be invested, it can generate returns, it can create new streams of income. The average person usually sees money as something you either have or don't have, something you spend or save. The two percent, on the other hand, see money as energy that must be moved to create new structures. They invest in real estate, in companies, in knowledge, in networks. In this way, they create systems that generate income even when they themselves are not present.

The psychology of the masses keeps the average person trapped in the mode of earning. It inextricably links value and performance. Only those who work are allowed to earn. Only those who make an effort have "earned" it. This way of thinking is so deeply rooted that it almost seems moral. Those who earn income from capital are viewed with suspicion, sometimes even condemned. "Everyone must work" is the unspoken rule. But this rule is not natural, it is culturally conditioned. It serves to keep the majority in a system that controls their energy. The two percent have the courage to break this rule. They know that value is not only created by hours, but by structures that work independently of hours. Neuroscience explains this difference by the principle of delayed gratification. The average person wants immediate reward—they want their paycheck at the end of the month, they want to consume, they want to enjoy. The two percent have learned to delay gratification. They sacrifice today in order to have more freedom tomorrow. They experience satisfaction not in rapid consumption, but in the growth of structures that give them independence. This ability to delay gratification is one of the key factors for long-term success.

It allows them to build wealth while the average person consumes their earnings. From a sociological perspective, the difference between earnings and wealth is also a question of belonging. The average person lives in a culture that glorifies consumption. Those who earn a lot show it by spending a lot. Cars, houses, vacations, clothes—they are all symbols of earnings. But they are not symbols of wealth. Wealth is often invisible. It is not the car in the driveway, but the shares in a company. It is not the clothes on your back, but the capital that works quietly. That is why the difference often remains hidden. The average person sees wealth as consumption, the two percent see wealth as substance. Philosophically speaking, this reveals a profound truth about freedom. Those who live on their earnings live from hand to mouth – even if the hand is large.

They remain dependent on the next paycheck, the next month, the next salary. Those who live off their assets live off structures that endure beyond the moment. They are no longer slaves to the present, but masters of their future. The two percent have recognized this truth and organize their lives accordingly. From a spiritual perspective, the difference between income and assets is a question of consciousness. Earnings are a symbol of the fear of the average person. They want to hold something in their hands immediately in order to feel secure. Wealth, on the other hand, is an expression of trust. Those who build wealth trust in the future, in growth, in the flow of life. This trust is not naive, but rather a prerequisite for freedom. Because only those who let go of the need to have everything immediately can create something greater. At the end of this section, it becomes clear that the difference between income and wealth is not only economic, but existential. The average person remains trapped in the mode of income because they seek quick rewards. The two percent are free because they build wealth that is independent of their current performance. This is the key to why some remain dependent and others become free.

One of the greatest delusions of modern life is that people believe that as their earnings increase, their wealth will automatically grow. At first glance, this seems plausible: those who earn more should have more left over and thus be able to build wealth. But reality paints a different picture. Countless people with high incomes still live from month to month, often even in debt. Their consumption grows at the same rate as their income, and so their wealth remains zero. The illusion that income equals wealth keeps them trapped in a cycle of working, earning, and consuming—without ever becoming free. Psychologically, this behavior can be explained by the so-called "hedonic treadmill principle." People quickly get used to new standards of living. Those who double their income usually also double their consumption. The bigger house, the more expensive car, the more exclusive trips – they all swallow up the extra money. After a short time, this new standard becomes a habit, and the feeling of satisfaction disappears.

People find themselves back at square one, only at a higher level of consumption. Wealth remains elusive, even though earnings have increased. The two percent have recognized this principle and consciously break with it. They know that rising earnings only lead to growing wealth if you control your consumption and invest the surplus. They use every increase in income not for status symbols, but to build capital. While the average person turns their additional income into transitory things, the two percent turn it into structures that generate new income. This is precisely the difference between external wealth and inner freedom. From an economic perspective, wealth is not the result of high income, but of capital formation. Capital formation means that money is not consumed, but invested. Investments create new value, generate returns, and build systems that generate income independently of one's own work. The average person confuses saving with wealth creation.

They put money in accounts where it is eroded by inflation. The two percent know that money only becomes wealth when it is put into motion. They invest in real estate, in companies, in knowledge, in networks. In this way, they transform income into capital – and capital into freedom. However, the psychology of the average person prevents them from taking this step. They fear the risk. Investments seem uncertain to them, while consumption brings immediate satisfaction. They cling to the illusion that possessions provide security, even though these possessions are really just a burden.

An expensive car loses value, a big house generates costs, luxury goods tie up capital without increasing it. The average person confuses possessions with wealth. But possessions that do not work are not freedom, but a burden. The two percent have learned to consider only those things that generate income or create value as wealth. Neuroscience explains this behavior by the way the reward system responds to consumption. Purchases trigger the release of dopamine, which causes short-term feelings of happiness. Investments, on the other hand, do not initially generate a rush. They require patience, and the reward lies in the future. This is more difficult for the brain to process because it is programmed for immediate gratification. The average person therefore remains trapped in consumption mode. The two percent have learned to reprogram their reward system. They do not derive pleasure from rapid consumption, but from building structures that provide long-term freedom. From a sociological perspective, the difference between income and wealth is also evident in the role of status.

The average person uses income to buy recognition. They display their success through symbols designed to impress others. The two percent, on the other hand, use wealth to create independence. Their recognition comes not from outside, but from within. They measure their worth not by symbols, but by freedom. This difference changes their entire lives. From a philosophical perspective, this reveals a profound truth about human beings. Those who live in earnings mode remain tied to the present. They live for the moment, they consume, they show off, they prove themselves. But they do not build anything that lasts beyond the moment. Those who live in wealth mode live in a different time logic. They think about the future, they sow today to reap tomorrow, they build structures that can have an impact beyond their own lives. Wealth is not just riches, it is permanence. From a spiritual perspective, building wealth means trust. Trust in the future, trust in one's own actions, trust in the flow of life. Those who trust can let go, can do without, can be patient. The average person does not trust. They fear that tomorrow is uncertain and therefore consume today.

But this behavior creates precisely the uncertainty they want to avoid. The two percent act differently: they accept uncertainty and thereby create the basis for freedom. At the end of this section, it becomes clear: the difference between earnings and wealth is one of the biggest divides between the average and the independent. The average person consumes their income and confuses possession with security. The two percent invest their income, build up capital, and create structures that exist independently of their daily efforts. This difference is not only economic, but existential. It determines whether a person remains in the cycle of dependence or crosses the threshold to freedom. The decisive difference between earnings and wealth is evident not only in economic figures, but above all in the inner attitude with which people shape their lives. The average person sees money as something they can receive and spend. They work, they earn, they consume. Their relationship with money is short-term and reactive. The two percent, on the other hand, see money as energy that they consciously direct.

They don't think in terms of months, but in terms of decades; not in terms of consumption, but in terms of structures; not in terms of wages, but in terms of capital. This attitude changes not only their finances, but their entire existence. Psychologically speaking, the average person is caught in a constant cycle of performance and reward. They work to gain recognition and money, and they consume to feel satisfaction. But both forms of reward are fleeting. They calm them for a moment, but soon they need new input to renew their sense of security and success. This pattern resembles an addiction: work and consumption become a drug that calms the nervous system in the short term but weakens it in the long term.

The two percent have seen through this dynamic. They replace the short-term thrill with long-term stability. They know that joy lies not only in having, but in building, not in consumption, but in growth. Economically speaking, building wealth means using money in such a way that it generates more money. But this requires a different way of thinking than the average person is accustomed to. The average person thinks in terms of income, the two percent in terms of returns. Income is the reward for work, returns are the reward for capital. Those who earn income remain in the hamster wheel of effort. Those who earn returns disconnect themselves from this hamster wheel. The transition from thinking in terms of income to thinking in terms of returns is one of the crucial thresholds that mark the difference between the average and independence. The psychology of delayed gratification plays a central role here. Building wealth often means giving up something today in order to have more tomorrow. This requires patience, discipline, and trust. The average person rarely has this ability because they are conditioned to seek immediate gratification. Advertising, consumer culture, social comparisons – all of these reinforce the urge to live in the moment. The two percent resist this pressure. They invest in the future, even if today seems less promising.

But this is precisely how they create a tomorrow that is independent. Sociologically speaking, the average person lives in a culture that rewards consumption. Those who earn a lot are measured by what they show, not by what they build. Status symbols, lifestyle, possessions – these are all visible markers that bring recognition. But they are not lasting. Wealth, on the other hand, is often invisible. It is not evident in conspicuous symbols, but in quiet structures: in capital investments, in company holdings, in networks, in knowledge. That is why the difference between earnings and wealth remains hidden to many. They see consumption and consider it wealth, while true wealth grows invisibly. Philosophically speaking, there is a profound truth about freedom here. People who are fixated on earnings live in the present – but not in the liberating form of presence, but in the captive form of dependence.

They live for the now because they are afraid of tomorrow. People who build wealth live in an expanded present that includes the future. They think not only of the moment, but of what the moment can bring. They do not live in fear of the future, but with confidence in it. From a spiritual perspective, wealth means keeping energy flowing. It is not the hoarding of possessions, but the conscious directing of resources so that they bear fruit. Those who build wealth create structures that can have an impact beyond their own lives. It is an act of trust, an act of creativity, an act of self-empowerment. The average person remains in fear, the two percent act out of trust. At the end of this section, it becomes clear that the difference between earnings and wealth is not only economic, but existential.

The average person lives on income that is transient. The top two percent live on wealth that remains. They have learned to build capital instead of consuming earnings. This is precisely where the threshold to freedom lies – and the reason why some remain dependent and others become independent. When you compare the life of the average person with that of the top two percent, you realize that the decisive difference lies not in talent, not in background, and not even in opportunities, but in the understanding of money. The average person thinks in terms of earnings, while the top two percent think in terms of wealth. This difference may seem semantic, but it changes everything. It determines whether a person remains dependent or becomes free, whether they sell their time or build structures, whether they start over again and again or whether they lay foundations that will sustain them. Psychologically speaking, the mode of earning is the mode of immediate reward. People work, they receive money, they consume. This pattern satisfies the need for security, control, and recognition.

But it is a cycle that can never create freedom. It ties people to the present and robs them of their future. The two percent have learned to break out of this pattern. They defer rewards, they invest instead of consuming, they build instead of using up. In doing so, they shift their satisfaction: they find joy not in quick possession, but in slow growth. From an economic perspective, the difference is even more striking. Earnings are linear, wealth is exponential. Those who earn are dependent on their own time and energy. Those who build wealth use capital as leverage that works independently of their own time. Income can dry up at any time, but wealth creates new sources. The average person remains trapped in a linear cycle because they believe that income means security. The two percent know that only capital offers security because it generates income again and again – even when you are no longer working. Neuroscience explains the difference by the programming of the reward system. The average person seeks the quick dopamine kick: the paycheck, the purchase, the consumption. The two percent, on the other hand, have retrained their reward system. They derive pleasure from processes that only yield returns later on. They have learned to endure the unease of waiting, to accept the uncertainty of investing, and yet to remain confident. This ability to derive pleasure from building rather than consuming is one of the key differences that enables wealth.

From a sociological perspective, the focus on earnings is a tool that controls the majority. Those who live on earnings remain dependent on their employer, the market, and external factors. They are predictable, calculable, and replaceable. Those who build wealth escape this control. They become more independent, more difficult to control, and more self-determined. That is why the idea of wealth building is often not part of the social narrative. Schools teach earnings, but not wealth. Universities teach specialist knowledge, but not capital formation. Culture rewards consumption, not investment. The two percent have freed themselves from this narrative and found their own ways to create structures that give them freedom. From a philosophical perspective, the difference between earnings and wealth is the difference between transience and permanence. Earnings are the stream that flows and dries up. Wealth is the source that constantly produces new streams. Those who live on earnings live constantly in the flow of transience. Those who live on wealth have a foundation that lasts beyond the moment. This difference reveals a deeper truth: freedom does not come from what you earn today, but from what you build for tomorrow. From a spiritual perspective, wealth is an expression of trust in the future. Those who build wealth believe that it makes sense to sow today, even if the harvest will only come in years to come. They live not out of fear, but out of trust. The average person lives in a state of fear: they consume immediately because they fear that tomorrow is uncertain. But this is precisely what creates the uncertainty they want to avoid. The two percent have learned that trust is not naive, but the foundation of freedom. They accept the uncertainty of life and yet build structures that support them. At the end of this chapter, it becomes clear that the difference between earnings and wealth is one of the most fundamental differences between the average and independence. The average person remains trapped in the cycle of work and consumption because they equate earnings with security. The two percent are free because they build wealth that generates income regardless of their presence. They have understood that freedom does not lie in earnings, but in capital that remains.

Notes:

Notes:

Chapter 11: Failure and Risk – Why Average People Are Afraid and the 2% See Opportunities

When you look at how most people think, you repeatedly encounter the same deep-seated fear: the fear of failure. This fear permeates their decisions, shapes their actions, and steers their lives in directions that seem safe but in reality mean stagnation. Average people view risk as a threatening animal that must be avoided at all costs. They believe that failure is a flaw, a sign of weakness, a label that will follow them forever. And so they remain within the narrow confines of what is predictable and familiar. They avoid the new, the uncertain, the unknown – and in doing so, they prevent their own growth. The two percent, on the other hand, have a completely different relationship with risk and failure. For them, these are not the end, but the beginning. They know that no progress, no innovation, no fortune is possible without risk. They understand that failure is not the opposite of success, but part of it.

They do not see setbacks as final defeats, but as learning processes that bring them closer to their goal. While the average person experiences failure as something personal, as an attack on their value, the two percent see it as neutral feedback: as an indication of what works and what doesn't. Psychologically, this difference can be explained by the way people process fear. The brain is programmed for survival. It seeks safety, avoids danger, and wants predictability. In evolution, this made sense: those who avoided risks had a better chance of surviving. But in the modern world, this program is often a hindrance. Most risks are not life-threatening, but merely psychologically uncomfortable. A failed business deal, a lost investment, a rejected idea—none of these threaten life, only the ego. But the ego fears precisely that: hurt, rejection, loss of face. That's why the average person avoids anything that could cause them to fail. The two percent have learned to see through these mechanisms. They know that fear is often a bad advisor. They distinguish between real dangers and imagined threats. They have trained themselves to deal with uncertainty and accept that failure is part of the game. From a neuroscientific point of view, this means that they have realigned their reward system. While the average person only sees reward in security, the two percent see reward in risk because it opens up opportunities. Their brains interpret uncertainty not only as a danger, but also as an opportunity.

Economically speaking, the difference is fundamental. The average person avoids risk and therefore remains in linear, secure income structures. They rely on a steady job, a stable salary, and seemingly risk-free savings. But this security is deceptive. Inflation eats away at savings, companies lay off employees, markets change. Those who want to avoid risk often choose the most uncertain path precisely because it creates dependency. The two percent, on the other hand, consciously accept risks. They invest, they start businesses, they take chances. Not every risk bears fruit, but every risk teaches a lesson. And it is only through taking risks that opportunities arise that enable freedom. From a sociological perspective, culture also plays a role. Average societies condemn failure. Those who fail are considered losers. Those who succeed are admired.

This black-and-white logic prevents people from even getting started. They fear the judgment of others more than the actual loss. The two percent escape this judgment. They do not define their value by the opinion of the masses, but by their own development. That is why they can fail without breaking down. For them, failure is a natural part of the journey, not the end of it. From a philosophical point of view, this reveals a profound truth is revealed: life is risk. Every breath, every step, every encounter is uncertain. The attempt to avoid this uncertainty is an illusion. The average person tries to gain control through security, but loses freedom. The two percent accept uncertainty and find in it the real security: the inner strength to deal with whatever happens. Failure thus becomes not an enemy, but a teacher. Risk becomes not a threat, but an invitation. From a spiritual perspective, the fear of failure is an expression of attachment to the ego. The ego wants to win, to be recognized, to shine. It fears nothing more than defeat. But the self, which lies deeper than the ego, knows no defeat. It knows only experience. The two percent act from this deeper consciousness. They see risk not through the lens of the ego, but through the lens of growth. Failure does not threaten them, but expands them. That is why they can take paths that seem impossible to the average person. At the end of this first section, it becomes clear: the difference between the average and the two percent is not the absence of failure, but how they deal with it.

The average fears it and stands still. The two percent accept it and move on. This approach to risk and failure determines who remains dependent and who becomes free. The fear of failure is so deeply rooted in most people that it lies like an invisible grid over their entire lives. It determines which paths they take, which decisions they make, which opportunities they don't even consider. While this fear protects them at first glance, in the long run it robs them of exactly what they seek most: security, freedom, and fulfillment. In their inner logic, failure is equated with danger, risk with threat. However, this equation is a mistake that nips the potential of countless people in the bud. From a psychological perspective, the fear of failure often arises in childhood. Children learn very early on that mistakes are associated with punishment, shame, or disappointment. A bad grade, a failed attempt, inappropriate behavior—all of these things elicit negative reactions from parents, teachers, or classmates. As a result, children internalize the belief that mistakes are bad and that failure must be avoided in order to maintain recognition and belonging. This conditioning accompanies them into adulthood. It is reinforced at school and consolidated at work. The result is a culture in which perfection is sought and risk is avoided. But perfection is an illusion, and risk is inevitable. Those who believe they can control both find themselves in an endless spiral of fear and self-restraint. The two percent have recognized and broken this cycle. They have understood that mistakes are not the opposite of success, but a necessary condition for it.

They know that every mastery is based on countless failed attempts. No one learns without making mistakes, no one grows without setbacks, no one achieves anything new without leaving the old behind. For them, failure is not a stigma, but a tool. They do not see it as personal failure, but as information: as feedback on what works and what does not. This attitude transforms fear into curiosity, stagnation into movement, risk into opportunity. Economically speaking, the fear of failure is the main reason why the average person remains dependent. They don't dare to start a business because they fear the risk of failure. They don't invest because they are afraid of losing money. They remain in "safe" structures that actually make them insecure because they believe that this will help them avoid failure. But failure cannot be avoided.

Even a "secure" job can be lost, and even a "secure" investment can lose value. Those who avoid risk are not choosing security, but dependence. The two percent consciously accept risk, not because they are reckless, but because they know that opportunity lies in risk. They diversify their investments, they plan their steps, but they accept that loss is part of the game. And that is precisely why they win in the long run. From a neuroscientific perspective, the fear of failure is an overreaction of the limbic system, especially the amygdala, which amplifies danger signals. It is programmed for survival in a world where risks were life-threatening. But in the modern world, most risks are psychological or social in nature. A failed business does not threaten life, but self-image. A failed presentation does not destroy one's existence, but it does scratch the ego.

Nevertheless, the brain reacts as if it were a matter of survival. The two percent have learned to put this reaction into perspective. They train their nervous system to deal with uncertainty and shift the meaning of risk: not danger, but opportunity; not the end, but the beginning. From a sociological perspective, the fear of failure is perpetuated by society. In many cultures, failure is considered a flaw that diminishes a person's value. Those who fail lose prestige, belonging, and sometimes even support. That is why people avoid anything that could cause them to fail. But this attitude prevents innovation. Societies that stigmatize failure produce mediocrity, not pioneers. Societies that accept failure as part of learning produce progress. The two percent live in an inner culture that is independent of the outer one. They do not give failure the power to destroy their identity, but use it to sharpen their direction.

Philosophically speaking, failure is a mirror of life itself. Life means trial and error, becoming and passing away, rise and fall. Those who want to avoid failure try to avoid life itself. But life cannot be avoided. It demands risk, it demands commitment, it offers no guarantees. The two percent have accepted that certainty is an illusion. They know that failure is not the end, but a transition, a necessary step on the path to something greater. From a spiritual perspective, the fear of failure means that people place their ego above their self. The ego fears rejection, ridicule, defeat. But the self knows that no experience is wasted. Every mistake is a lesson, every defeat an expansion, every risk a gateway to deeper insight.

The two percent live from this awareness. They do not fear failure because they do not see it as a threat, but as an encounter with the truth. And the truth is always a teacher. At the end of this section, it becomes clear that average people remain trapped because they fear failure and avoid risk. The two percent are free because they accept failure and see risk as an opportunity. This difference is not only economic, but existential. It determines whether a person lives in fear or in freedom, whether they remain average or dare to take the leap into the extraordinary. Attitude toward risk is one of the clearest dividing lines between the 98% and the 2%. While the average person associates risk with danger, uncertainty, and loss, the two percent see it as an opportunity for growth and freedom. The difference is not that the 2% are fearless, but that they have found a different way of dealing with it. Fear is universal, but what you do with it is what distinguishes the average from the independent. Psychologically speaking, fear is often understood as a warning signal that must be blindly followed. Those who feel fear withdraw, avoid, postpone, or refrain from making decisions. This keeps them within the narrow confines of what is familiar. But this familiar framework is rarely the place where growth occurs. It is a cage that pretends to offer security but creates stagnation. The two percent use fear as an indication of where development is possible.

They know that where fear is greatest, the greatest breakthrough often awaits. They do not learn to avoid fear, but to embrace it and use it as a guide. From an economic perspective, risk is the source of all returns. No fortune, no innovation, no company is created without risk. The average person, who avoids risk, remains in structures that are supposedly stable but are in fact fragile. They rely on a secure job, a secure investment, a secure routine. But in a dynamic world, these certainties are illusions. Jobs disappear, markets collapse, technologies become obsolete. Those who believe they can avoid risk are in fact choosing a form of dependency that makes them vulnerable. The two percent, on the other hand, accept that risk is unavoidable and make it their ally. They calculate, they examine, they weigh things up – but they act. Neuroscience explains the difference by how the brain works. The limbic system, especially the amygdala, reacts to uncertainty with stress signals.

For the average person, this means avoidance. But the prefrontal cortex, the seat of planning and reflection, can regulate these signals. The two percent have learned not to take the impulses of fear as an end point, but as a starting point. They use their ability to self-regulate to act despite their fear. In doing so, they learn that behind fear lies not doom, but expansion. This experience changes the nervous system in the long term: it learns to interpret risk not as a threat, but as a challenge. Sociologically speaking, the difference becomes even clearer. The average person lives in a culture that stigmatizes failure and morally devalues risk. Those who take risks and lose are ridiculed or criticized. Those who take no risks are considered sensible. This creates a society of caution that keeps its members in mediocrity. The two percent escape this norm. They seek communities where risk is considered normal and failure is understood as a learning process. In such environments, perceptions shift: risk becomes not a stigma, but a measure of courage.

Philosophically speaking, risk is the price of life. Every decision is risky, every day is uncertain, every encounter can turn out differently than planned. Those who believe they can avoid risk misunderstand the nature of existence. Life itself is a risk: to be born, to love, to act, to trust. The two percent have accepted this. They know that risk is not the enemy, but the space in which freedom arises. Those who avoid risk avoid life itself. Those who accept risk accept life. From a spiritual perspective, risk is an expression of trust. Trust means letting go, accepting that you cannot control everything, being willing to dance with the unknown. The average person does not trust. They hold on, they cling, they seek guarantees. But these guarantees do not exist. They are illusions that bind them. The two percent live in a different consciousness. They accept uncertainty as part of existence and find peace in it. They know that failure does not mean loss, but experience, that risk is not danger, but opportunity. At the end of this section, it becomes clear that risk is not what destroys the average person, but what could liberate them—if they had the courage to accept it.

But they remain trapped because they fear risk and avoid failure. The two percent, on the other hand, see risk as the path to freedom and failure as the teacher that allows them to grow. This difference in attitude turns the same situations into completely different paths in life. One sees danger and stops, the other sees opportunity and moves on. If you take a closer look at the concept of failure, you realize that, in people's perception, it says much more about their inner attitude than about external reality. The actual event – an investment that doesn't pay off, a project that fails, an idea that doesn't resonate – is always just a moment, a point in time. But the interpretation of this moment determines whether it paralyzes or liberates, whether it destroys or builds. Average people see this point as an end. They experience failure as a final defeat that calls their value into question. The two percent see the same point as a transition, as feedback, as a necessary stop on the way to greater success. From a psychological perspective, this difference can be explained by what is known as “attribution style.” The average person tends to interpret failure as internal, stable, and global. Internal means they blame themselves. Stable means they believe the failure is permanent. Global means that they apply it to all areas of their lives. Thus, a failure in one project becomes a narrative of general incompetence. This pattern leads to fear, resignation, and avoidance. The two percent, on the other hand, interpret failure as external, variable, and specific. External means that they see circumstances and contexts, not just their own person. Variable means that they understand failure as changeable. Specific means that they limit it to the one area in which it occurred. This keeps their identity intact, their motivation intact, and their courage alive. From an economic perspective, these differences are of enormous significance. The average person avoids investments or entrepreneurial steps because they fear failure as a personal disaster.

They remain in secure structures that tie them to income but never give them freedom. The two percent factor in failure. They know that not every investment will succeed, that not every project will bear fruit. But they spread their risks, learn from losses, and grow from setbacks. And in the long term, it is precisely these setbacks that enable them to achieve greater profits. From a neuroscientific perspective, it is the ability to cognitively reevaluate that makes the difference. The average person experiences failure and remains stuck in the emotional response: shame, fear, withdrawal. The two percent, on the other hand, activate the prefrontal cortex to reinterpret the situation. They ask: "What have I learned? What can I change? How do I move forward?" In doing so, they not only regulate their emotions, but also train their brains to be resilient.

With each of these reassessments, the nervous system becomes more flexible, fear diminishes, and the capacity for action increases. Sociologically speaking, the fear of failure is reinforced by social narratives. Stories of success are glorified, stories of failure are hushed up. The media reports on winners, not on learning processes. Schools reward correct answers, not courageous attempts. Families praise security, not risk-taking. In this environment, failure seems like a flaw. But the two percent live in a different narrative. They tell themselves and others different stories. They see role models who have failed and yet achieved great things. They know that every successful pioneer has countless defeats behind them.

In this way, they create a culture in which failure is not a stigma, but a prerequisite. From a philosophical point of view, the way we deal with failure reveals our attitude to life itself. Those who avoid failure avoid life. Because life means change, trial and error, becoming. Those who accept failure accept life. They recognize that failure is not a deviation from the path, but part of the path. They understand that every fall is also a rise, that every loss holds a lesson, that every defeat is a chapter, not the book. With this attitude, failure is no longer feared, but accepted as an inevitable companion. From a spiritual perspective, failure is an act of liberation. It breaks down the ego, which considers itself untouchable. It reveals the limits of control and confronts us with the truth of uncertainty.

Those who embrace it experience humility—and humility is the foundation for growth. The average person avoids this experience because they want to protect their ego. The two percent allow it and thereby gain depth, breadth, and freedom. They see risk as a dance with the unknown and failure as a teacher that guides them beyond the ego. At the end of this section, it becomes clear that failure and risk are not enemies, but necessary forces in life. The average person fears them and remains in a false sense of security. The two percent accept them and find in them the source of their freedom. The difference lies not in circumstances, but in attitude.

And this attitude determines whether one remains average or opens up the space of possibilities that only the courageous enter.

When you look at the essence of life, you realize that without risk there can be no development, without failure there can be no progress, and without uncertainty there can be no freedom. And yet this is precisely the point where the paths of average people and the two percent diverge. The average person avoids risk because they believe it prevents loss. The two percent embrace risk because they know that only where there is something to lose is there also the possibility of gaining more than they ever thought possible. Psychologically speaking, this division is a question of inner perspective. The average person views the future through the lens of fear. They ask, "What could go wrong?" and remain trapped in that thought. Every idea, every possibility, every dream is immediately reduced to its dangers. The result is passivity, procrastination, stagnation. The two percent, on the other hand, view the future through the lens of opportunity. They ask, "What could succeed?" and let that guide them. They know that not everything will succeed, but that every success opens up new space that would never be accessible without risk. This difference in the question—fear or opportunity—changes their entire lives. From an economic perspective, this attitude means that the average person relies on security that is not really security. They save money in accounts that are devalued by inflation. They cling to jobs that could be lost at any time. They avoid investments that could multiply their capital because they fear losses. As a result, they remain trapped in structures that appear to protect them but in reality increase their dependence. The two percent invest even if they could lose.

They start businesses even if they could fail. They dare to take new steps even if they are ridiculed. They accept losses because they know that the greater loss lies in not daring to take any risks. From a neuroscientific point of view, this difference is reflected in the way the brain processes uncertainty. The average person remains trapped in the activity of the amygdala, which reacts to danger. Their nervous system triggers stress, and they immediately seek avoidance. The two percent, on the other hand, activate the prefrontal cortex, reflect, reevaluate, and shift their focus. Their brains learn to see uncertainty not only as a danger, but as a space for learning. With every experience of risk-taking, they train their nervous system to remain flexible and resilient. This creates an inner strength that allows them not only to endure risks, but to use them as a driving force for their development. From a sociological perspective, the fear of risk is reinforced by social norms. Those who fail are ridiculed. Those who dare are criticized. Those who act differently are questioned. This culture of mistrust keeps the majority in check. But the two percent have freed themselves internally from this judgment. They do not seek recognition in consensus, but freedom in difference. They know that they do not need everyone's approval, but only the clarity of their own attitude. This creates an independence that goes far beyond finances: independence in thinking, feeling, and acting. From a philosophical point of view, risk is an expression of the truth that life itself offers no guarantees.

Every breath is uncertain, every encounter unpredictable, every step a potential mistake. Those who avoid this uncertainty avoid life itself. The average person seeks guarantees and finds only illusions. The two percent accept the absence of guarantees and find strength in it. For them, failure is not an enemy, but a friend who shows them the way. For them, risk is not an abyss, but a gate that opens only to those who have the courage to walk through it. From a spiritual perspective, this means that the fear of failure is an expression of the ego clinging to control. The ego wants to remain intact, wants to shine, does not want to lose. But the self, which lies deeper than the ego, knows no defeat. It knows only experience, expansion, growth. The two percent act from this deeper self. They let the ego fail and thereby gain freedom. They know that losses are not the end, but a transition, that failure is not a break, but a step. This attitude gives them an inner peace that the average person never achieves as long as they remain under the spell of their fear. At the end of this chapter, it becomes crystal clear: average people remain trapped because they fear failure and avoid risk. The two percent are free because they accept failure and see risk as an opportunity. This difference is not only economic, but existential. It determines whether a person lives in fear or in freedom, whether they avoid life or embrace it. Failure and risk are not obstacles, but gateways. The average person stops at the gate, while the two percent walk through it. And that is precisely why they belong to the two percent – because they have understood that the path to freedom always leads through the valley of risk.

Notes:

Notes:

Chapter 12: Mental Independence – Inner Freedom as a Prerequisite for Outer Freedom

When you ask why so few people achieve true freedom, you inevitably come across an invisible foundation that is often overlooked: mental independence. Without it, any outer freedom remains a fragile construct. Wealth can be built up, status can be gained, security can be created – but as long as a person remains internally dependent, the external remains uncertain. Mental independence is the invisible root from which everything else grows. It is the silent foundation that determines whether external freedom lasts or not. The average person lives in a state of permanent mental dependence. They base their thinking on expectations, social norms, and external evaluations. Their self-worth depends on how others see them, how they compare to others, and what recognition they receive. They are internally bound to judgments, opinions, and norms that they have not chosen themselves. These bonds are often invisible, but they guide their entire lives. They work not only to earn money, but also to belong. They consume not only to satisfy needs, but also to impress others. They strive not only for security, but also for the feeling of being right. Thus, their inner world is controlled by the outside world, and their outer freedom remains only a shadow. From a psychological point of view, this dependence manifests itself in the conditioning of the self-image.

People link their value to external parameters. They feel successful when they receive recognition and worthless when they do not. These mechanisms are already shaped in childhood: through praise and criticism, through grades and comparisons, through expectations and punishments. Children learn that they are loved when they do the right thing and less loved when they fail. This conditioning becomes deeply ingrained in the nervous system and accompanies the adult. The average person reproduces this pattern without questioning it. They live in dependence on external voices that determine their inner self. The two percent have recognized and broken through these mechanisms. They know that external freedom is only possible if inner freedom is attained first.

They do not work primarily on their wealth, but on their consciousness. They train their thinking, their emotions, their reactions. They break the bonds that tie their self-image to others. They accept that they make mistakes without diminishing their value. They accept rejection without their identity being shattered. They accept uncertainty without losing their inner peace. This mental independence makes them unshakable. And it is precisely this that enables them to build structures that support external freedom. From an economic perspective, mental independence is crucial because it determines how we deal with money, risk, and opportunities. The average person makes decisions out of fear. They fear loss, avoid risk, and seek security. This attitude limits them because it prevents them from seizing opportunities. Mental dependence blinds them to possibilities. The two percent do not make decisions out of fear, but out of clarity. They are inwardly free enough to recognize opportunities, consciously take risks, and accept failure.

This allows them to act more flexibly, courageously, and with greater foresight. Mental freedom becomes the basis for economic freedom. Neuroscience shows this difference in the prefrontal cortex, which is responsible for self-control, reflection, and conscious decisions. The average person often reacts impulsively, driven by fear or a need for recognition. The two percent consciously regulate their emotions. They do not allow themselves to be paralyzed by fear, seduced by praise, or destroyed by criticism. They train their nervous system so that they can remain calm in the face of uncertainty. This ability to maintain inner peace amid external turmoil is the foundation of their mental independence. Sociologically speaking, mental dependence is the norm. Societies consist of networks of expectations, norms, and roles that steer individuals in certain directions. Those who do not conform to these expectations risk exclusion. That is why most people live in consensus, even if it makes them unfree. The two percent, however, accept this dynamic but do not bow to it. They do not live against society, but within it—yet they do not allow themselves to be determined by it internally. They remain free enough to think differently, act differently, and decide differently. This makes them creators, while the average person remains a follower. From a philosophical perspective, mental independence means that people recognize the source of their value within themselves. They understand that they do not become valuable through external successes, possessions, or recognition, but that their value exists independently of these things. This realization frees them from the slavery of comparison.

It frees them from the pursuit of recognition. It gives them peace in the midst of a world that constantly demands performance. The two percent live out of this peace. They build structures not to prove themselves, but to create freedom. From a spiritual perspective, mental independence is the realization that the self does not depend on external circumstances. It is the awareness that who you are lies deeper than any role, any opinion, any success. This awareness gives you an inner freedom that no external power can destroy. Those who have found this freedom can lose everything and still remain unbroken. The average person fears loss because they believe it means losing their self. The two percent know that they cannot lose what they truly are. At the end of this first section, it becomes clear that mental independence is the invisible prerequisite for external freedom. Without it, wealth remains fragile, success empty, security deceptive. The average person remains trapped because they are internally dependent. The two percent are free because they have learned to belong to themselves. This inner freedom is the key that opens all external doors. True independence does not begin on the outside, but on the inside. Those who do not belong to themselves, who do not control their thoughts, who do not understand their feelings, will always be determined by forces beyond their control. Mental dependence is subtle but powerful. It manifests itself in the constant search for validation, in the fear of rejection, in the need to conform. The average person lives in this dependence without being aware of it.

They consider their thoughts to be free, but they are shaped by the expectations of others. They believe their decisions are independent, but they are influenced by norms that they have adopted without questioning them. From a psychological perspective, this external control manifests itself in a tendency toward social conformity. People orient themselves toward the behavior and opinions of their group. They conform in order to secure belonging. This conformity made sense in evolutionary terms: those who resisted the group risked exclusion and thus danger. But in the modern world, it leads to a subtle lack of freedom. The average person bases their thinking on what is accepted, not on what is true. They make decisions based on what seems safe, not on what truly liberates them.

The two percent have learned to recognize this dynamic and to detach themselves from it internally. They know that belonging is important, but never at the expense of their own freedom. Economically speaking, this mental dependence has far-reaching consequences. The average person stays in secure jobs, even if they make them unhappy, because they are afraid of being different. They avoid entrepreneurship because they fear being ridiculed or condemned if they fail. They do not invest because they are afraid of being considered reckless by others. Thus, the opinions of others determine their financial future. The two percent, on the other hand, act out of inner clarity. They make decisions not to gain recognition, but to create freedom. In doing so, they take paths that remain unimaginable to the average person. From a neuroscientific perspective, mental independence is closely linked to the ability to self-regulate. The limbic system reacts automatically to social stimuli: praise activates reward centers, criticism activates stress responses. The average person remains at the mercy of these impulses. Their nervous system is dependent on external reactions. The two percent, on the other hand, train their prefrontal cortex to regulate these impulses. They do not allow themselves to be destroyed by criticism or seduced by praise. They remain in a state of inner balance that allows them to make decisions independently of external influences. This ability makes them resilient and unshakeable. From a sociological perspective, mental independence is rare because societies depend on conformity.

Norms, rules, and expectations hold the masses together. They create stability, but they also create mediocrity. Those who break away from these norms are often considered outsiders. But it is precisely these outsiders who open up new paths. The two percent accept the existence of social norms, but they do not allow themselves to be determined by them internally. They can live within society without being dependent on it. This ability makes them creators rather than followers. From a philosophical point of view, mental independence means that people find the source of their truth within themselves. They recognize that external voices have no more power than they give them. They understand that freedom does not lie in pleasing everyone, but in remaining true to themselves. Mental independence is the ability to stand alone without feeling lonely. It is the art of swimming against the tide without losing your footing. It is the inner certainty that your own value is non-negotiable. From a spiritual perspective, mental independence is a return to one's core. It means that a person recognizes that their value does not depend on successes, roles, or opinions. They are independent of all these things because they are free in their deepest essence. This realization brings a peace that no external power can destroy. The average person lives in fear because they believe they could lose what defines them. The two percent are free because they know they cannot lose what they truly are.

At the end of this section, it becomes clear that mental independence is not a luxury, but a prerequisite. Without it, external freedom remains fragile, dependent on opinions, norms, and circumstances. The average person remains trapped because they allow themselves to be controlled internally. The two percent are free because they have learned to control their thoughts, feelings, and decisions themselves. Inner freedom is the foundation of external freedom—and only those who attain it can become truly independent. If you examine the mechanisms of inner dependence more closely, you will see that they are often invisible in nature. It is not chains of steel that bind people, but thought patterns that wrap themselves around their consciousness like fine threads. They are barely noticeable, but they have a powerful effect. The average person lives within these patterns without questioning them.

They believe their thoughts are free, but in reality they are shaped by family, school, media, culture, and society. These influences determine what they believe is possible, what they fear, and what they strive for. Mental dependence is so dangerous because it makes people believe that they are acting freely—when in reality they are only repeating what has been instilled in them. From a psychological perspective, inner dependence arises from the tendency to place external authorities above one's own inner voice. This pattern is practiced as early as childhood. Children learn that parents, teachers, or other adults know better what is right and wrong. They learn to conform in order to gain approval. Later in life, they continue this pattern by replacing their parents with bosses, partners, society, or trends. They continue to conform, even when they believe they are acting independently. The average person confuses conformity with reason and conformity with truth. The two percent have broken through this mechanism. They hear the outside voices, but they don't let them be louder than their own. Economically speaking, this mental dependence has far-reaching consequences. Those who believe they are only allowed to follow paths that are accepted by the majority will never take extraordinary paths. The average person opts for a secure job, a familiar career, and trusted investments—not because they want to, but because they fear being wrong otherwise. They adhere to norms because they believe that security lies only in the masses.

But the masses do not create freedom, only mediocrity. The two percent act differently: they know that security does not lie in the majority, but in their own clarity. They are willing to act against convention if it serves their freedom. And that is precisely how wealth, innovation, and new paths are created. Neuroscience explains this difference in terms of how the brain deals with social pressure. For the average person, social pressure is a signal to conform. Praise activates the reward center, criticism triggers stress. That is why they constantly seek confirmation and avoid rejection. The two percent, on the other hand, have learned to regulate these reactions. They find praise pleasant, but not decisive. They see criticism as information, not as a threat. Their nervous system is flexible enough to maintain inner peace, even when the outside world contradicts them. This flexibility is the foundation of their mental independence. Sociologically speaking, the difference is evident in how people define their identity. The average person derives it from external factors: their role at work, their social status, the expectations of their culture. The two percent define it from within: their values, their vision, their consciousness. This makes them less susceptible to manipulation and pressure. They can live within society without being controlled by it. This attitude makes them more resilient, courageous, and independent. From a philosophical point of view, mental dependence is a form of self-alienation.

People no longer live from their own center, but from external control. They lose contact with their inner source and believe that their value depends on external factors. Mental independence means regaining this contact. It means recognizing that one's own being does not depend on roles, successes, or opinions. This realization sets one free. For those who know that they are valuable regardless of external circumstances become unshakeable. From a spiritual perspective, mental independence is a return to one's own origins. It means that people recognize that they are not their thoughts, their roles, or their stories. They are more than that – they are a consciousness that is free from external definitions.

This consciousness gives them an inner peace that no external power can destroy. The average person lives in fear because they believe that their value is fragile. The two percent live in freedom because they know that their value cannot be lost. At the end of this section, it becomes clear that mental dependence is the invisible chain that binds the average person. It keeps them in patterns they did not choose for themselves. Mental independence is the invisible force that liberates the two percent. It allows them to make decisions based on clarity rather than fear. It allows them to swim against the tide without losing their footing. It allows them to build external freedom because they already possess internal freedom. Mental independence is not a one-time decision, but an ongoing process. It is not something you achieve in a day and possess forever, but an attitude that must be practiced, consolidated, and deepened again and again. The average person underestimates this dimension. They believe that independence is a question of circumstances: more money, a secure job, a bigger house.

But these are external conditions that can change at any time. True independence lies in the ability to remain free even when external securities disappear. And that can only be achieved through mental freedom. From a psychological point of view, this means that people learn to observe their own thoughts instead of being controlled by them. The average person identifies completely with their thoughts. When they think a worry, they feel worried. When they think a fear, they feel threatened. When they think a judgment, they believe it to be the truth. Thus, they live in an inner automatism that makes them dependent. The two percent develop distance from their thoughts. They know that a thought is just a thought—not reality. They observe it, examine it, and consciously decide whether to follow it or not. This ability transforms them from driven individuals into creators. From an economic perspective, mental independence changes the entire approach to opportunities and risks. The average person makes decisions out of fear.

They fear loss, seek security, and remain within the familiar. Their mental dependence blinds them to possibilities that lie outside their comfort zone. The two percent make decisions based on clarity. They view risks soberly, do not allow themselves to be paralyzed by fear, and do not allow themselves to be seduced by greed. Their inner freedom allows them to act rationally and courageously at the same time. As a result, they make decisions that lead to long-term freedom, while the average person remains stuck in a circle of security that is not security at all. Neuroscientifically, this difference can be explained by the functioning of the nervous system. The average person often remains trapped in the dominance of the limbic system, which is programmed for short-term rewards and quick threat avoidance. The two percent make greater use of the prefrontal cortex, which is responsible for reflection, planning, and conscious control. Mental independence therefore also means that the brain learns to regulate emotional impulses instead of blindly following them. With every conscious decision made against automatic fear, the neural network of independence is strengthened. From a sociological perspective, mental independence manifests itself in the ability not to be carried away by collective moods. Societies fluctuate between euphoria and panic, between trends and taboos, between approval and rejection. The average person follows these waves because they want to belong.

Their inner dependence makes them susceptible to mass movements. The two percent remain independent because they live according to their own inner standards. They perceive trends, but they do not allow themselves to be determined by them. They hear the voices of the majority, but they do not make decisions based on them. This inner independence allows them to stand firm even when the masses waver. From a philosophical point of view, mental independence means that people become aware of their own freedom. They recognize that they always have a choice, even when external circumstances are limited. Even in difficult situations, even in uncertainty, even in loss, they can choose how they think, how they feel, how they act. This realization is the core of all freedom. The average person does not recognize this choice. They believe they are victims of circumstance. The two percent recognize that they are the creators of their attitude. And this attitude determines more than any external condition. From a spiritual point of view, mental independence is an awakening.

It is the awareness that human beings are more than their thoughts, more than their roles, more than their stories. It is the realization that true freedom does not come from outside, but from within. The average person seeks liberation through external changes, while the two percent find liberation in their consciousness. They know that inner freedom cannot be taken away because it does not depend on external things. At the end of this section, it becomes clear that mental independence is not a theoretical concept, but a daily practice. It is the art of controlling oneself instead of being controlled. It is the ability to remain internally free amid external uncertainty. It is the foundation on which all external freedom grows. The average person remains trapped because they avoid this inner work. The two percent are free because they do it every day. There is a reason why mental independence is considered a prerequisite for external freedom: it is the foundation without which everything else remains fragile. Those who are not free on the inside will repeatedly create structures on the outside that reflect this inner lack of freedom. They will choose jobs that give them a false sense of security but create dependency.

They will have relationships that give them a sense of belonging but curtail their freedom. They will engage in consumption that satisfies them in the short term but binds them in the long term. The life of the average person is a mirror of their inner lack of freedom.

They seek freedom externally without ever finding it because they do not possess it internally. Psychologically speaking, this dynamic is a cycle. Those who are internally dependent react to external uncertainty with fear. Out of fear, they choose structures that appear to offer security. However, these structures reinforce their dependence because they bind them ever more deeply to external conditions. This creates a vicious circle in which internal lack of freedom reinforces external dependence and external dependence confirms internal lack of freedom. The two percent have broken this cycle. They start from within. They create an attitude that is free from dependence, that is self-sufficient, that is not determined by praise or criticism. From this attitude, they create external structures that reflect their freedom. Economically speaking, this difference is particularly clear. The average person seeks security in a steady salary, in a supposedly stable job, in familiar paths.

But this security is fragile. Companies change, markets collapse, securities disappear. Those who remain internally dependent are shaken by every external change. The two percent, on the other hand, create wealth, companies, and investments not because they need security, but because they want to shape freedom. They are internally free enough to take risks, cope with setbacks, and break new ground. That is why they can create structures that make not only themselves but also others independent. From a neuroscientific point of view, mental independence means that the nervous system has learned to create a distance between external stimuli and internal reactions. The average person reacts automatically: a loss causes panic, criticism causes shame, risk causes avoidance. The two percent have developed the ability to consciously process these stimuli. They create a pause between stimulus and response. This pause is where their freedom lies. It is where they decide how they want to think, how they want to feel, how they want to act. This conscious shaping of their internal responses makes them unshakable in the face of external fluctuations.

From a sociological perspective, mental independence is evident in the fact that the two percent retain the ability to think differently in a world full of conformity. They are not dependent on the judgment of the masses, on trends, or on the approval of others. They move within societies, but they do not allow themselves to be defined by them. They can live within the norm without being subject to it internally. This independence makes them creators. The average person remains a follower because they are internally dependent. The two percent become pioneers because they are internally free. From a philosophical perspective, mental independence reveals the true essence of freedom: that it is not given, but taken. Freedom is not a gift that someone receives. It is an attitude that one chooses. Those who choose inner freedom will also be able to shape it externally. Those who do not choose it remain unfree, even if they are materially secure. Mental independence is the ability to determine one's own thoughts, feelings, and actions from within oneself. It is the foundation without which no external freedom can endure. From a spiritual perspective, mental independence means that a person recognizes that they are not the sum of their external circumstances. They are not their job, their possessions, or their status. They are consciousness that remains independent of all these things. This consciousness makes them free.

The average person lives in fear because they identify with external things. When they lose these things, they believe they are losing themselves. The two percent know that they cannot lose what they are at their core. This realization makes them unshakeable. At the end of this chapter, it becomes abundantly clear: external freedom is only stable when it is based on inner freedom. The average person remains in a cycle of dependency because they do not recognize this connection. They seek freedom externally and lose it again and again. The two percent start from within. They create mental independence, and from this grows external freedom. That is why they are free, while the average person remains trapped.

Notes:

Notes:

Chapter 13: The Role of Habits – Why Success Is Shaped Every Day

When you ask about the deeper reasons why so few people find their way to true independence, self-determination, and prosperity, you inevitably come across an inconspicuous but powerful principle: habit. It is not big decisions, nor even dramatic turning points, that shape a person's life as much as the small actions they repeat day after day. Habits are the invisible architects of our destiny. They shape our thoughts, they shape our emotions, they determine our actions – and thus our entire lives. The average person underestimates the power of habits. They regard them as trivial, as minor quirks of everyday life. They think that it is major events that determine their lives: completing an education, choosing a career, deciding for or against a relationship, buying a house. These things are undoubtedly important, but they are rare. Habits, on the other hand, are everyday occurrences. And because they are everyday occurrences, they seem insignificant. But that is precisely where their power lies: they add up. Every small action that is repeated daily carves deep grooves into the nervous system, the body, and the consciousness. These grooves shape the course of a life.

The two percent know this. They have realized that success does not come from rare highlights, but from inconspicuous repetition. They understand that wealth, freedom, clarity, and strength are not the result of one-time decisions, but of daily habits that act like a silent engine. For them, every day is a building block, every hour an investment, every habit a lever. They see everyday life as the source of their success, while the average person considers everyday life to be incidental and only has their eye on the big events. Psychologically speaking, habits are stored programs. The brain loves efficiency. It wants to save energy, it wants repetition, it wants patterns. That is why repeated actions become automatic.

They no longer happen consciously, but unconsciously. The average person thus lives most of their day according to old, unconscious programs. They don't think about why they act the way they do, they simply repeat what they are used to. If these patterns were beneficial, it would help them get ahead. But often they are patterns of convenience, fear, or conformity. So day after day, they repeat what keeps them average. The two percent, on the other hand, consciously intervene in this mechanism. They understand that their brains are malleable. They use the plasticity of the nervous system to imprint beneficial patterns. They reprogram themselves by consciously choosing which habits to build and which to discard. Economically speaking, habits are crucial because they shape how we deal with money, work, and opportunities.

The average person develops habits that keep them dependent in the long term: they consume more than they earn. They save, but without a strategy. They work, but without consciously investing in their development. They plan for the short term, but not for the long term. These habits seem harmless, but they add up to a reality of life that binds them. The two percent develop different habits. They invest regularly, even in small amounts. They educate themselves every day. They use every opportunity to network, learn, and grow. These seemingly small routines act as invisible multipliers that create enormous differences over years and decades. From a neuroscientific perspective, habits are an expression of neuroplasticity. Every repetition strengthens neural connections.

The more often a thought is thought or an action is performed, the stronger the synaptic pathways become. This creates a kind of highway in the brain that automatically guides actions. The average person builds highways that keep them in comfort and conformity. They reinforce their fears, their doubts, their passivity through daily repetition. The two percent build highways in the opposite direction: toward courage, clarity, and the power to act. They consciously use repetition to shape themselves. From a sociological perspective, habits are also socially embedded. People adopt routines that they observe in their environment. The average person surrounds themselves with people who cultivate similar patterns: television instead of learning, consumption instead of investment, comfort instead of growth. These social habits reinforce each other. The two percent consciously choose their environments.

They seek out people who cultivate similar beneficial habits, thereby reinforcing each other in a culture of growth. Philosophically speaking, habits reveal the truth that freedom is not achieved in big moments, but in small, daily choices. Every person has the freedom to decide how to shape their day. But because this freedom is inconspicuous, the average person does not perceive it. They believe that big moments are decisive and overlook the fact that big moments are only the result of small daily decisions. The two percent understand that greatness does not arise all at once, but accumulates. They consciously live in repetition, and freedom grows out of this repetition. From a spiritual perspective, habits are an expression of one's inner state of consciousness. The average person lives in habits of unconsciousness. They act without really being present. Their routines are an expression of sleep.

The two percent live in habits of consciousness. They use everyday life as an exercise, as an opportunity to deepen their inner clarity. Every action becomes an opportunity to cultivate awareness. That is why they not only perform different external habits, but also live in a different inner state. At the end of this section, it becomes clear that success does not come from big leaps, but from small steps that are repeated every day. Habits are the invisible forces that shape our lives. The average person underestimates them and remains trapped. The two percent use them consciously and become free. Those who change their habits change their lives – not at some point in the future, but every day. If you want to understand the essence of success, you have to shift your gaze from the big moments that everyone can see to the inconspicuous habits that work behind the scenes. Because the truth is: success is not born in moments of jubilation, but in the quiet hours of repetition, in the daily routines that no one notices. The average person lives under the illusion that life is determined by a few big decisions. They tell themselves that happiness, wealth, and freedom are the result of a single bold step, a sudden opportunity, or an extraordinary talent. But in reality, it is the small, seemingly insignificant actions that make the difference. The two percent know this and live their lives accordingly. Psychologically speaking, the power of habits lies in the fact that they structure our thinking. Every repeated action reinforces not only physical patterns, but also mental ones.

Those who dwell on negative thoughts every day train their brains to see the world through these lenses. Those who engage in constructive thoughts on a daily basis train themselves to see solutions and opportunities. The average person thinks that their mood is the result of their circumstances. In reality, their mood is the result of their repeated thoughts. Habits in thinking are just as powerful as habits in action. They shape self-image, expectations, and perception. That is why the difference between the average and the two percent is not only external, but also internal: one repeats doubt, the other repeats confidence. From an economic perspective, the effect of habits becomes apparent over long periods of time. The average person thinks and acts in the short term. They repeatedly choose what is pleasant now, even if it will be expensive later. They do not save, they do not invest, they do not educate themselves further, because the effort involved is greater than the benefit at the moment. But these decisions add up. One day of convenience makes no difference, but a thousand days shape a life.

The two percent act differently. They repeat small decisions that seem insignificant at first, but have an exponential effect over the years. Those who invest a small amount every day build long-term wealth. Those who read every day build knowledge that sets them apart from others. Those who act every day instead of just dreaming achieve results that add up. Neuroscience shows that this process can be seen in the functioning of synapses. Each repetition strengthens the efficiency of neural networks. The brain builds pathways that become stronger through use. This makes a thought that is often thought easier to think. An action that is often performed becomes easier to perform. Habits are nothing more than these reinforced pathways. The average person reinforces pathways that keep them passive through repetition. The two percent reinforce pathways that keep them active. And because the brain responds to repetition, what you do often eventually becomes second nature. Sociologically speaking, habits shape not only individuals but entire cultures. Communities are formed through shared routines. The average person lives in environments where comfort, entertainment, and conformity have become the norm. These habits shape their perception of normality. Those who don't participate seem strange. The two percent create different norms.

They seek out environments where learning, growing, and acting are habits. There, progress is considered normal, not stagnation. These environments in turn reinforce their individual patterns, creating a culture of freedom. Philosophically speaking, this reveals a profound truth: a person is not what they do occasionally, but what they do regularly. Virtue, character, success, freedom—none of these arise in exceptional situations, but through repetition. The average person hopes for that one moment that will change everything. The two percent know that this moment will never come unless a thousand small steps are taken first. Habits are the silent proof that freedom is not a sudden gift, but a work shaped daily.

From a spiritual perspective, habits are a practice of self-realization. The average person sleeps in their routines because they live them unconsciously. They lose themselves in processes that distance them from their essence. The two percent use habits to become more conscious. Every action becomes an opportunity to practice mindfulness, deepen presence, and strengthen inner clarity. In this way, routine becomes not a cage, but a path to liberation. Those who live consciously can use every repetition to penetrate deeper into their own being. At the end of this section, it becomes clear that success is not a gift or a stroke of luck. It is the inevitable result of habits that are cultivated every day. The average person lives in habits that bind them. The two percent live in habits that liberate them. Those who understand the power of repetition realize that every small action has meaning. Because it shapes not only the day, but the whole of life. When you look at the structure of human development, it becomes clear that habits are the invisible framework in which everything unfolds.

No matter how big your dreams are, how clear your plans are, or how impressive your goals are, if your daily actions don't match those goals, everything remains theory. The average person lives precisely in this contradiction. They talk about change, but their days remain the same. They want progress, but they repeat patterns that keep them stuck. They long for freedom, but their habits bind them to dependence. The two percent have understood that the invisible power of habits determines victory or defeat. Psychologically speaking, habits are an expression of the so-called "automatic self." This concept describes how humans do not consciously control a large part of their actions, but rather carry them out based on stored patterns. The average person believes they are free in their decisions, but in reality, they act largely on autopilot. This autopilot is filled with the routines of their past: thought patterns they have never questioned, reactions they have become accustomed to, actions they repeat over and over again. If these patterns are not conducive to their success, they remain stuck in a cycle that blocks them. The two percent have become aware of this autopilot. They examine which patterns they carry and which ones bind them. They overwrite old programs with new ones by consciously choosing which actions they repeat every day. From an economic perspective, the power of habits is particularly evident.

Prosperity does not come from luck or individual major successes, but from consistent routines in dealing with money, time, and energy. The average person spends more than they earn, not because they are unreasonable, but because their habits are shaped that way. They consume when they are frustrated, they save when they feel under pressure, and they never invest regularly. These patterns keep them dependent. The two percent, on the other hand, have adopted different habits: conscious investing, controlled consumption, continuous education. Over the years, these routines act like invisible levers. They create freedom where others experience captivity. Neuroscience explains this through the processes of myelination. Each repetition not only strengthens synaptic connections, but also the insulation of nerve pathways. This means that actions that are repeated often become not only easier, but also faster and more efficient. In other words, the brain builds an infrastructure for what you do regularly. The average person builds an infrastructure of comfort, fear, and passivity through repetition.

The two percent build an infrastructure of clarity, discipline, and courage. That's why they can seemingly effortlessly do things that are unimaginable to the average person. From a sociological perspective, habits shape entire systems. Societies are not made up of theories, but of routines that are shared collectively. The average person lives in cultures where entertainment, consumption, and conformity have become the norm. These collective habits reinforce their individual patterns. They adapt without realizing it and unconsciously adopt the behavior of the majority. The two percent live in a different culture—not necessarily geographically, but internally. They create environments where different rules apply: learning instead of distraction, action instead of hesitation, investing instead of consuming. These social spaces reinforce their beneficial habits, so that they remain not just individuals, but form entire networks of growth. From a philosophical perspective, habits show that freedom is not an abstract ideal, but a lived practice.

No one becomes free by merely thinking about freedom. Freedom is earned – through daily decisions that promote inner and outer independence. The average person remains unfree because they make daily decisions that reinforce their dependence. They think freedom is a goal that will be achieved at some point. The two percent understand that freedom is a habit—a way of living that is formed day by day. From a spiritual perspective, habits are a mirror of the state of consciousness. The average person lives in routines that keep them asleep. They repeat actions without being aware of it and thus remain trapped in an inner dream. The two percent use habits as a practice of mindfulness. They see every repeated action as an opportunity to become more present, clearer, and more conscious. In this way, even the everyday becomes a path to liberation. For them, routine is not mechanical, but meditative. At the end of this section, it becomes clear: habits are the silent force that determines life. The average person remains trapped because they unconsciously repeat old patterns. The two percent become free because they consciously choose new patterns. Success is not the result of luck or exception, but of daily habits that add up over years. Those who change their habits change their lives – not at some point in the future, but every day, with every repetition. When you study the biographies of successful people, you quickly realize that their success was not the result of sudden luck or a one-time moment, but the inevitable consequence of their habits.

These habits are not random quirks, but conscious decisions that have been repeated until they have become second nature. The average person only sees the visible results – wealth, status, independence – and believes they are the result of talent or external circumstances. But the two percent know that it is the invisible power of habits that forms the foundation of all these results. Psychologically speaking, this means that habits shape identity itself. People become what they do repeatedly. Those who think every day that they are incapable program their self-image accordingly. Those who think every day that they can seize opportunities form a self-image of competence and confidence. Habits are not just actions, they are also thought patterns that become deeply ingrained in the subconscious. The average person lives in habits of self-limitation: doubt, fear, procrastination. These patterns repeat themselves day after day until they become a fixed identity.

The two percent live in habits of self-empowerment: clarity, courage, decisiveness. These patterns also repeat themselves until they become identity. Economically speaking, the difference between the average and the two percent is obvious over years and decades. A person who consumes daily without investing will experience dependency after years. A person who invests small amounts daily will experience freedom after years. The difference lies not in a single moment, but in repetition. The average person underestimates the power of compound interest—not only in money, but in life. Small habits add up to big results. The two percent consciously take advantage of this. They know that every daily action is an investment that multiplies over time. From a neuroscientific perspective, habits are an expression of learning. The brain changes with every repetition. Neural pathways are strengthened or weakened depending on how often they are used. The average person lives in a comfort zone. They reinforce networks that keep them in the status quo. The two percent live in paths of development. They reinforce networks that promote courage, clarity, and discipline. Over time, what initially takes effort becomes easy. That's why the two percent seem effortless, while the average person believes they are extraordinary. In truth, they have simply laid different paths.

From a sociological perspective, habits are the invisible laws that shape communities. The average person moves in circles where stagnation has become the norm. They unconsciously adopt the patterns of their environment: the same conversations, the same routines, the same expectations. The two percent create different environments for themselves. They seek out people whose habits promote growth. In this way, they reinforce each other and form cultures of freedom. Success is not only individual, but also collective, a result of shared habits. From a philosophical perspective, habits are the bridge between potential and reality. Every person has infinite potential, but only daily actions determine whether it becomes reality. The average person dreams, but does not act. The two percent dream and act every day in accordance with that dream. They know that freedom does not come from one-off actions, but from the quiet perseverance that creates habits. This perseverance is the real strength that transforms life. From a spiritual perspective, habits are a mirror of inner consciousness. The average person lives unconsciously and repeats old patterns that bind them. The two percent live consciously and create new patterns that set them free. Every action becomes an opportunity to become more present, clearer, more alert. In this way, everyday life itself becomes a path to liberation. Success is then not only external, but also internal: a state of clarity, calm, freedom. At the end of this chapter, it becomes abundantly clear: Success is not shaped by exceptional situations, but by everyday habits. The average person underestimates their power and remains stuck in their old patterns. The two percent use them consciously and thereby create freedom. Every day is a decision, and every habit is a building block. Those who recognize the power of habits and consciously shape them hold the key to a life that far exceeds the average.

Notes:

Notes:

Chapter 14: The Psychology of the 2% – How Thinking Differently Leads to Different Results

There is an invisible difference that separates the two percent from the remaining ninety-eight percent – and this difference does not begin in external actions, but in thinking. Psychology is the foundation of every action, and every action shapes life. So if you want to understand why the two percent achieve results that seem unimaginable to the average person, you have to study their thinking. Because thinking is not neutral. It is the silent force that determines whether someone remains dependent or sets out in freedom. The average person believes that external circumstances are the key to success: education, background, contacts, luck. They explain their situation with factors beyond their control. When they fail, they look for external culprits. When they don't achieve success, they explain it away with a lack of opportunities. This attitude relieves them in the short term because it shifts responsibility. But in the long term, it robs them of the power to change their lives. Those who believe that external circumstances determine their fate relinquish their creative power. The two percent think differently.

They recognize that external circumstances have an influence, but they do not see them as decisive. They understand that it is their inner attitude that makes the difference. The same obstacle that seems insurmountable to the average person becomes a challenge for them that makes them stronger. The same risk that paralyzes the average person becomes an opportunity for them to seize. The same failure that destroys the average person becomes a lesson for them to grow from. They have internalized that they always have choices—not about the circumstances themselves, but about their interpretation and their response. Psychologically speaking, the core of this difference lies in what is known as locus of control.

The average person has an "external locus of control." They believe that their life is determined by factors beyond their control: politics, the economy, bosses, markets, fate. This attitude breeds passivity. The two percent have an "internal locus of control."

They are convinced that they themselves are the architects of their lives – not by controlling everything, but by always having influence over their attitude and actions. This inner conviction generates responsibility, courage, and the ability to act. Economically, this difference leads to completely different results. The average person sees risks and retreats. They say, "That's not possible because the circumstances are bad." The two percent see risks and ask, "How can I use them?" They find ways where others find excuses. They see opportunities where others see obstacles. And because they act while the average person waits, they create opportunities that make a difference. From a neuroscientific point of view, this difference is visible in the brain. Those who live with an external locus of control activate fear centers more frequently. Their nervous system reacts passively, their stress levels rise, and their ability to act declines. Those who live with an internal locus of control activate the prefrontal cortex, the area responsible for planning, problem solving, and self-control, more frequently. Their nervous system remains more flexible, their stress levels decrease, and their ability to act increases. In other words, thinking literally shapes the brain, and the brain shapes action. From a sociological perspective, the psychology of the majority leads them to remain in systems that make them unfree. Those who believe they have no power stay in secure jobs, even if they make them unhappy.

They stick to consumption patterns, even if they put them into debt. They remain in structures that bind them because they believe there is no other way. The two percent free themselves from these structures because they think differently. They do not see systems as givens, but as constructs that can be used or abandoned. They do not blindly conform, but question and shape.

Philosophically speaking, this reveals a fundamental question: Does man live as a victim or as a creator? The average person consciously or unconsciously chooses the role of victim. They relinquish responsibility, they relinquish power, they relinquish freedom. The two percent choose the role of creator. They take responsibility, even when it is inconvenient. They bear the burden of their decisions, but also reap the rewards. They recognize that freedom always comes with responsibility. From a spiritual perspective, the difference lies in how the two percent interpret life.

The average person sees chaos, chance, and injustice. The two percent see meaning, opportunity, and development. They trust that every event, even the difficult ones, has something to offer them. They do not live in resignation, but in confidence. This attitude gives them both peace and courage. At the end of this first section, it is clear that the psychology of the two percent differs radically from the psychology of the average. They do not think in terms of limitations, but in terms of possibilities. They do not look for culprits, but for solutions. They do not live as victims, but as creators.

And because their thinking is different, their results are also different. When you examine a person's inner world, it quickly becomes clear that their thoughts are not merely fleeting phenomena, but form stable structures that shape their lives. Every thought is like a seed that, if thought often enough, grows into a tree. These trees of thought cast shadows or provide light – depending on which thoughts have been nurtured. The average person nurtures doubt, fear, and limitation. The two percent nurture confidence, clarity, and possibilities. These differences in thinking are invisible, but they inevitably materialize in the outside world. From a psychological perspective, the difference between the average and the two percent arises from what is known as cognitive attitude. The average person lives with a deficit mindset. They ask: "What am I missing? What could go wrong? What don't I have?" Their attention is focused on scarcity, and their actions follow this focus.

The two percent live with an abundance mindset. They ask: "What is possible? What do I have? What can I make of it?" Their focus is on resources and opportunities. This makes them act more creatively, courageously, and constructively. These differences in thinking create completely different life paths. From an economic perspective, this attitude leads to different decisions. The average person sees obstacles and retreats. They see a risk and avoid it. They see a crisis and panic. The two percent see obstacles and look for ways to overcome them. They see a risk and ask how it can be managed. They see a crisis and recognize the hidden opportunities.

That is why they take advantage of opportunities that remain invisible to the average person. Their thinking opens doors that appear closed to others. Neuroscientifically, this difference can be understood in terms of the interaction between the limbic system and the prefrontal cortex. The average person remains trapped in the dominance of the limbic system. Their thoughts revolve around danger, uncertainty, and possible losses. This puts their nervous system into a state of stress and avoidance. The two percent consciously activate the prefrontal cortex by controlling their thoughts. They focus their attention on solutions instead of problems, on possibilities instead of obstacles. In this way, they change not only their thinking, but also the biochemical states of their bodies. Their brains work toward creativity and action, while the average person remains blocked in a state of fear. From a sociological perspective, the difference is evident in the way people react to collective moods. The average person is swept up in the panic and euphoria of the masses. When others are afraid, they are afraid too. When others are enthusiastic, they are enthusiastic too. They follow the thought currents of society. The two percent remain independent. They observe the masses, but they do not let themselves be determined by them. They think for themselves, they reevaluate, they remain calm where others waver. This ability makes them resistant to collective hysteria. From a philosophical point of view, the psychology of the two percent reveals a deeper understanding of freedom. The average person thinks that freedom lies outside: in better circumstances, in more resources, in greater security. The two percent understand that freedom lies within: in the ability to think clearly regardless of circumstances. This freedom of mind is the true source of all external freedom.

It allows them to see opportunities where others see dangers. It allows them to take paths that others consider impossible. From a spiritual perspective, the psychology of the two percent is an expression of expanded consciousness. The average person lives in a mindset of separation: separated from possibilities, separated from power, separated from trust. The two percent live in a mindset of connection: connected to their potential, connected to opportunities, connected to a deeper meaning. This attitude gives them serenity, courage, and confidence that sustain them even in difficult times. At the end of this section, it becomes clear that psychology determines life. The average person thinks small and lives small. The two percent think big and live big. The difference is not in talent, not in origin, not in luck—it is in the way of thinking. Those who think differently get different results. That is why the psychology of the two percent is the invisible key that enables their external freedom. When you focus on how much thinking shapes reality, it becomes clear that a person's external circumstances are not random, but largely the result of their inner beliefs and patterns. The psychology of the two percent differs fundamentally from that of the average person because it is rooted in a different mental foundation. The average person lives with thoughts of limitation. They say to themselves: "That's not possible," "That's too difficult," "I'm not cut out for that." Such statements are not just harmless phrases, but self-reinforcing programs that control behavior and determine results. The two percent, on the other hand, have developed a psychology that is characterized by openness, possibility, and creative drive. They ask themselves: "How can it be done?", "What can I learn?" "What path is there that I haven't seen yet?" Simply by asking these different questions, they open doors that remain closed to others. Psychologically speaking, this is referred to as "self-efficacy expectation." The average person has low self-efficacy expectations: they don't really believe that their actions make a decisive difference. That's why they try less, dare less, and give up more quickly. The two percent have high self-efficacy expectations. They trust that their actions will have an effect—not always immediately, not always without setbacks, but in the long term. This attitude makes them more persistent, courageous, and creative. Self-efficacy is a psychological key that explains why some people seem to cross boundaries effortlessly, while others stop at the same boundaries. Economically, this inner attitude leads to significantly different strategies. Those who believe that their actions have little effect will avoid risks, rely on certainties, and remain within structures that set guidelines for them. They will not invest their energy in their own projects because they do not believe that they can succeed. Those who are convinced that their actions make a difference, on the other hand, will seize opportunities, make investments, and try new things. This attitude opens up markets, creates innovation, and generates wealth. Not because the two percent have more resources, but because they make different decisions—decisions based on their psychology. Neuroscience shows this in the functioning of neural networks. Thoughts are not merely immaterial phenomena; they leave traces in the brain. Repeated thoughts strengthen synaptic connections.

Those who repeatedly think, "I can't do this," build a stable neural network of helplessness. Those who think, "I'll find a way," build a network of creativity and problem solving. These networks determine how quickly and efficiently the brain works in certain ways. The average person unconsciously programs themselves for limitation through their thoughts. The two percent consciously program themselves for expansion. Over time, this programming becomes second nature—and is reflected in the results. From a sociological perspective, the psychology of the two percent is evident in the fact that they do not allow themselves to be infected by collective resignation. In many societies, there is a mindset of scarcity:

"That's just the way it is," "You can't change anything," "It's pointless." These collective beliefs reinforce each other until they act like an invisible law. The average person adopts this mindset and reproduces it in their everyday life. The two percent set themselves apart from this. They create subcultures of courage and possibility. They seek out interaction with people who also think differently, thereby reinforcing their own attitude. This creates a psychological immunity to the resignation of the masses. From a philosophical perspective, this difference touches on the question of the nature of reality. Is the world fixed and unchangeable, or can it be shaped? The average person believes in a rigid world. They see boundaries as insurmountable and circumstances as given. That is why they remain passive. The two percent believe in an open world.

They see boundaries as challenges, circumstances as changeable, reality as malleable. This belief enables them to act. It is not naive optimism, but an existential decision that radically changes their own lives. From a spiritual perspective, the psychology of the two percent means that they live in trust rather than fear. The average person trusts in external securities and yet loses them again and again. That is why they live with a basic feeling of threat. The two percent trust in their own consciousness, in their inner strength, in the greater field of life. They do not see themselves as victims of a random universe, but as part of a creative process. This trust makes them more fearless, more relaxed, and at the same time more determined. At the end of this section, it becomes clear that the psychology of the two percent is not innate, but learned. It is the result of decisions, awareness, and practice. Anyone could develop it—but most people remain trapped in a mindset of scarcity. The two percent break out because they have learned to think differently. And because they think differently, they create different results.

A visible key that enables their external freedom. Most people underestimate how strongly their thoughts guide their lives like invisible threads. They believe that thinking is a neutral side effect, a kind of inner commentary on life. In reality, however, it is the main architect. Those who think small build small spaces. Those who think big create big horizons. The average person has never learned to consciously direct their thinking. They let it drift like a boat without a rudder, determined by currents. These currents are the opinions of others, social norms, memories, and fears. This results in thinking that is not free, but determined by others. The two percent, on the other hand, actively take control of the wheel. They know that thoughts can not only be reflected, but also shaped. They are aware that every thought has a power that becomes action, and every action leaves a trace that shapes results. From a psychological perspective, the difference lies in the ability to engage in cognitive self-management. The average person thinks automatically, while the two percent think consciously. The average person repeats old beliefs that they have adopted from childhood, school, or their environment. These beliefs run like programs in the background and determine what they believe they can or cannot do. They think, “I'm not good enough,” “I have no choice,” “I mustn't make any mistakes.” These sentences are invisible barriers.

The two percent recognize these barriers and overcome them. They replace old programs with new ones that expand their thinking instead of limiting it. They tell themselves: “I can learn,” “I will find a way,” “I am allowed to make mistakes because they teach me.” This new self-management not only changes their thinking, but also their entire lives. Economically, the power of psychology is particularly evident in crises. The average person reacts to crises with fear. They withdraw, they save themselves into poverty, they cling to securities that are not really securities at all. Their psychology leads them into a narrow mindset. The two percent see opportunities in crises. They know that every crisis is not only a danger, but also an opportunity. They act while others hesitate.

They invest while others retreat. Their psychology allows them to recognize that moments of uncertainty offer opportunities that make the biggest difference. That is why they seize opportunities that the average person misses. Neuroscientifically, this difference can be seen in how the brain reacts to stress. When faced with uncertainty, the average person experiences overactivity in the amygdala. This triggers fear, which blocks the prefrontal cortex. As a result, they lose the ability to think clearly, remain creative, and find solutions. The two percent train their nervous system to regulate such stress reactions. Through breathing, mindfulness, or other mental techniques, they create the opportunity to keep the prefrontal cortex active. This allows them to remain solution-oriented while others become blocked. Their psychology is not just a way of thinking, but a trained ability to keep the brain in a state of clarity. From a sociological perspective, the psychology of the two percent is evident in their distance from the masses. The average person is guided by opinions, trends, and collective moods. They think like the majority thinks and act like the majority acts. This conformity provides short-term security, but long-term mediocrity. The two percent have learned to think independently. They examine opinions instead of blindly accepting them. They observe trends, but they do not let themselves be driven by them. They have the courage to think for themselves, even if the masses do not understand them. In doing so, they create paths that others only recognize much later. Philosophically speaking, the core question is whether humans own their thinking or are possessed by it.

The average person is possessed by their thoughts. They believe that what they think is automatically true. The two percent own their thinking. They examine it, they shape it, they use it consciously. This gives them distance from their thoughts, which creates freedom. Because freedom does not begin on the outside, but on the inside, in the space between thought and action. Those who do not know this space are prisoners of their thoughts. Those who know it are the architects of their own lives. From a spiritual perspective, the psychology of the two percent is an expression of an expanded consciousness that transcends the ego. The ego always thinks in terms of gain and loss, evaluation and comparison. It seeks confirmation and fears rejection. The average person lives in this ego-based thinking and makes it the basis of their identity. The two percent see through this game. They recognize that true thinking does not have to be controlled by the ego, but by a greater consciousness. They do not think in order to protect their ego, but to open up possibilities. That is why they are capable of taking courageous steps that seem impossible to the average person. It becomes clearer: psychology is the invisible lever that determines whether a person remains average or belongs to the two percent.

The difference lies not in external circumstances, but in inner attitude. The average person thinks automatically, the two percent think consciously. The average person sees limits, the two percent see possibilities. The average person allows themselves to be guided, while the top two percent guide themselves. And this difference in thinking shapes worlds that are hardly comparable. If we understand thinking as the root of all results, it becomes clear that the differences between the average and the top two percent are not random or external, but deeply rooted in the psychological structure. The psychology of the majority is characterized by fear, conformity, and a longing for security. The psychology of the two percent, on the other hand, is characterized by courage, independence, and a longing for freedom. This inner orientation acts like an invisible compass that guides every decision, even if it seems insignificant at the moment. That is why life paths are so different.

From a psychological point of view, the decisive difference lies in the attitude toward the unknown. The average person perceives the unknown as a threat. New paths seem risky, uncertainty creates fear, and this fear leads to withdrawal. The two percent do not primarily see danger in the unknown, but opportunity. For them, uncertainty is not an obstacle, but the field in which new things can emerge. This attitude changes everything: while the average person stops at the first sign of resistance, the two percent keep going. While the average person remains in their comfort zone, the two percent grow beyond themselves. Economically, this difference is easily visible. The average person hardly invests in themselves because they fear it will not pay off. They remain in safe but narrow structures because they believe that risk means loss. The two percent consciously invest in knowledge, experience, and networks because they understand that risk can mean not only loss but also gain. They act while others hesitate. That is why they build wealth, while the average person hardly builds up any reserves. Their psychology allows them to seize opportunities that remain hidden to others because they are too preoccupied with their fears. Neuroscientifically, this is reflected in the difference between a stress-driven and a growth-oriented brain. The average person trains their nervous system to go into alarm mode when faced with uncertainty. As a result, they repeatedly switch to fight-or-flight responses that block clear thinking. The two percent train their nervous system for resilience. They learn to remain calm even in uncertain situations, so that their prefrontal cortex remains active.

This allows them to develop creative solutions while others freeze up. Over time, this resilience becomes a kind of natural state that makes them unshakable. From a sociological perspective, the psychology of the two percent is also an attitude toward collective thinking. The average person adapts to the beliefs of those around them. If the masses say something is impossible, they believe it. If the masses are afraid, they are afraid. If the masses consume, they consume too. The two percent, on the other hand, develop a psychological distance from the masses. They listen, but they decide for themselves. They take opinions into account, but they examine them critically. They have the courage to think against the grain. This courage sometimes isolates them, but in the long run it gives them the freedom to go their own way. From a philosophical point of view, the psychology of the two percent reflects the realization that thinking itself is not absolute. The average person confuses thoughts with truth. They believe that what they think is automatically real. The two percent have realized that thoughts are tools.

They are useful, but not absolute. They can be examined, changed, replaced. This freedom in dealing with one's own thinking is a philosophical breakthrough: it transforms people from prisoners of their thoughts to creators of their consciousness. Finally, spiritually, it becomes clear that the psychology of the two percent is based on trust. The average person lives with a basic feeling of fear that limits them. The two percent live with a basic feeling of trust—in themselves, in their abilities, in life as a whole. This trust gives them a serenity that sets them free. They don't act because they're afraid of losing something, but because they enjoy creating something. That is why they experience setbacks differently: not as defeats, but as part of a larger process. At the end of this chapter, it becomes clear that psychology is the decisive difference. The average person lives in thoughts that keep them small, while the two percent live in thoughts that make them great. This difference is not visible as long as you only look at external results. But it becomes obvious when you understand that every external reality begins internally. Those who think differently live differently. Those who think consciously live consciously. And those who embrace the psychology of the two percent can free themselves from the average and create a life characterized by freedom.

Notes:

Notes:

Chapter 15: Social dynamics – How environment and culture cement mediocrity

When you ask why most people remain average despite good intentions, numerous opportunities, and many chances, you inevitably come across the power of the social environment. Hardly any other factor shapes how a person thinks, feels, and acts as much as the culture in which they live and the people they surround themselves with. Individuals often believe they are free and independent, but in reality, their thoughts and actions are deeply interwoven with the invisible threads of social dynamics. The environment can be a source of inspiration and growth, but it can also be a cage that cements mediocrity and stagnation. From a psychological perspective, humans have a deep, evolutionarily shaped longing for belonging. In early times, the survival of the individual was only possible within the group. Being excluded meant danger to life and limb. This ancient pattern continues to have an effect today: We adapt because we want to belong. We adopt opinions, even if we don't share them, because we don't want to isolate ourselves.

We follow habits that harm us simply because they make us feel part of the community. The average person underestimates this dynamic and lives under the illusion that their decisions are autonomous. But in fact, many of their decisions are imitations of the majority. The two percent have seen through this mechanism. They know that belonging is a basic need, but that blindly living for belonging becomes a prison. That is why they consciously choose their environments. Economically, it can be observed that poverty, prosperity, and freedom do not depend solely on individual abilities, but to a large extent on the social environment. Those who live in a culture where consumption, debt, and short-term thinking are normal unconsciously adopt these patterns. Those who live in a culture where investment, learning, and long-term action are normal also adopt these patterns. The environment acts like an invisible law that dictates what is "normal." The average person adheres to this norm because deviation requires courage.

The two percent create a different "normal" for themselves. They move in environments where growth, freedom, and personal responsibility are taken for granted. This reinforces beneficial patterns and weakens hindering ones. Neuroscience explains the power of social dynamics through mirror neurons. The brain is designed to automatically mirror the emotions, attitudes, and actions of others. Those who constantly see people who are passive, fearful, or resigned begin to unconsciously adopt these states. Those who experience people who act courageously, clearly, and creatively also reflect these qualities. The average person does not understand this mechanism and believes they can remain independent, even if they live in an environment that constantly weakens them. But the brain is not neutral. It is shaped by observation. That is why it is no coincidence that the two percent choose carefully with whom they spend their time. They know that every encounter is a form of imprinting. From a sociological perspective, culture is a powerful amplifier. It determines what is considered success in a society, what is considered normal and what is considered deviant.

The average person adapts to the unwritten laws of culture. They adopt its definitions of status, success, and security. They follow trends because they want to belong. They strive for symbols that have been defined by culture as desirable, even if they leave them feeling empty inside. In this way, culture becomes an invisible force that stabilizes mediocrity. The two percent break out of this dynamic. They do not perceive culture as an immutable law, but as a construct that they can question and overcome. While the average person is a prisoner of culture, the two percent become creators of their own culture. Philosophically speaking, this touches on the question of freedom. Is a person free when they conform, or do they lose their freedom in the process? The average person believes that freedom is compatible with security—with a steady job, a secure income, a status that others recognize. But in reality, they are trapped in these securities. The two percent understand that freedom always comes at a price: the courage to deviate. Those who want to be free must have the courage to think differently, act differently, live differently—even if culture disapproves. True freedom begins where belonging is no longer based on conformity, but on conscious choice. From a spiritual perspective, the power of the environment is evident in the way it shapes the individual's state of consciousness. The average person lives in fields of unconsciousness created by constant distraction, consumption, and conformity. These fields keep them in a state of sleep. The two percent seek or create fields of consciousness. They surround themselves with people who are awake, who ask questions, who look deeper.

This also makes their own consciousness clearer. In this way, the environment affects not only thoughts and actions, but also the depth of being. At the end of this section, it becomes clear that social dynamics are not a minor issue, but a decisive one. They shape what is considered normal, they shape identity, they reinforce patterns. The average remains mediocre because it unconsciously follows the laws of culture. The two percent free themselves because they recognize, question, and transcend these laws. If you really want to be free, you must have the courage to change not only your own thoughts, but also your environment and the culture in which you live. If you seriously examine the influence of the environment on a person's life, you realize that no individual really exists in isolation. Every person is like a node in a network, crisscrossed by influences, expectations, and unwritten rules. This network is not static, but alive—it reacts, reinforces, punishes, and rewards. For the average person, this means that their behavior is primarily determined by conformity. They orient themselves to what others do because they instinctively sense that deviation can have social costs. The two percent have learned to consciously see through this network and forge new connections that support them instead of shackling them. From a psychological perspective, the principle of social proof is at work in this process. People conclude what is right or wrong based on the behavior of others.

When everyone in a group makes a decision, it feels dangerous for individuals to act differently. The average person therefore prefers to follow the majority, even if that majority leads them astray. They tell themselves, "If everyone is doing it, it must be right." The two percent ask the crucial question: "Just because everyone does it, does that mean it's right?" This question alone sets them apart from the mediocre. Because as soon as you start to view social norms not as truth but as convention, a space of freedom emerges. Economically speaking, this mechanism is particularly powerful. Consumer societies thrive on people buying what others buy, striving for what others strive for, admiring what others admire. Status symbols are nothing more than cultural markers that signal belonging. The average person acquires them to feel secure, to avoid standing out from the crowd. But in doing so, they reinforce systems that keep them dependent. The two percent recognize this mechanism and free themselves from it. They don't invest in symbols, but in substance. They don't measure their worth by what others see, but by the freedom they feel inside and in their reality. Neuroscience explains this process through the functioning of mirror neurons. Humans are biologically predisposed to imitate behavior. This ability was once essential for survival: those who learned what was safe within the group survived. Today, however, this same ability has become a trap. Those who constantly observe people living mediocre lives unconsciously adopt their patterns.

The average person believes they are making free choices, but their brain mirrors what it sees. The two percent consciously use this knowledge. They surround themselves with role models who are further ahead than they are. They know that the brain automatically adapts, and so they create an environment that forces them to grow. From a sociological perspective, the power of social dynamics is evident in the way norms function. Norms are the invisible laws of a community. They determine what is permitted, what is considered successful, and what is considered failure. The average person considers these norms to be natural. They adapt to them, even if they make them unhappy. The two percent understand norms as human constructs. They recognize that norms are changeable and have the courage to break them. In this way, they leave the circle of conformity and enter spaces where new possibilities arise. From a philosophical point of view, there is a deeper question hidden here: What is truth—what the majority believes, or what proves itself in life? The average person confuses majority opinion with truth. They believe that if everyone says it, it must be true. The two percent separate majority opinion from truth.

They check for themselves, they experience for themselves, they trust their experience more than the echo of the masses. This attitude makes them independent and gives them the strength to go their own way. From a spiritual point of view, this means that the environment has a vibration that either supports or weakens the individual. The average person lives in fields of heaviness that are fed by fear, envy, and competition. They wonder why they are tired, blocked, or empty, but do not realize that they are unconsciously absorbing the energy of their environment. The two percent choose fields of clarity. They surround themselves with people who radiate hope, trust, and strength. This changes not only their thinking, but also their inner state. Spiritually speaking, the environment is a mirror—and those who consciously choose what they reflect change their being. At the end of this section, it becomes clear that social dynamics are not only external conditions, but also internal forces. They shape what a person believes, thinks, feels, and does. The average person remains mediocre because they unconsciously follow the laws of the masses. The two percent rise above this because they consciously choose which dynamics they allow to shape them. Freedom begins when you realize that belonging does not require blind conformity, but conscious choice.

If you take a closer look at why so many people remain average despite good intentions and numerous opportunities, you realize that social dynamics are not just an external influence, but deeply affect the structure of identity. Every person grows up in a culture that instills certain values, norms, and expectations in them. These are not perceived as mere opinions, but as apparent reality. The average person confuses culture with truth. They believe that what everyone else does is right, that what everyone else strives for is also desirable. This blinds them to alternatives. The two percent, on the other hand, see through this deception. They know that culture is always a construct – and that every construct can be changed. From a psychological perspective, identity is created through a process of mirroring. People learn who they are by receiving feedback from others. A child is shaped by the praise and criticism of its parents, by the expectations of school, by the norms of society. This mirroring leads many people to base their identity on what others think of them. The average person remains trapped in this dependency. They do not live from their own center, but from adapting to the image that others reflect back to them.

The two percent break this mirror. They recognize that identity does not have to be an echo of their surroundings, but a conscious decision. They define themselves independently of how the majority sees them. Economically, this has far-reaching consequences. The average person strives for status symbols that are defined as valuable by the culture. They buy what others buy, they work how others work, they live how others live – not because it fulfills them, but because it brings them recognition. But this recognition is deceptive. It binds them to systems that keep them dependent. The two percent, on the other hand, base their actions not on external status, but on inner value. They invest in freedom rather than symbols, in knowledge rather than recognition, in substance rather than appearance. These decisions have a long-term effect, even if they have to swim against the tide in the short term. Neuroscience explains the power of these dynamics through the brain's reward system. Social recognition activates the same system as material rewards. When others nod in approval, when you receive praise or feel like you belong, dopamine is released. This biochemical feedback reinforces the behavior. The average person lives in constant dependence on this mechanism. They repeat actions that ensure they belong, even if they take them further away from freedom.

The two percent learn to reprogram their reward system. They do not seek short-term recognition, but train their brains to experience long-term freedom as a reward. This enables them to make decisions that are unpopular in the moment but lead to extraordinary results in the long term. From a sociological perspective, cultures are designed to maintain stability. Every culture develops mechanisms to sanction deviation. Those who think differently risk exclusion. Those who act differently are criticized. Those who live by different values are questioned. These mechanisms keep the average person in line. They fear sanctions and therefore conform.

The two percent accept these tensions. They are willing to endure criticism, accept exclusion, and put up with incomprehension. Because they know that conformity is not worth the price of freedom. From a philosophical point of view, this raises the question of what truth really is. Is truth what the majority lives by, or what endures, even if it is unpopular? The average person confuses majority opinion with truth. They believe that if many people do it, it cannot be wrong. But history shows that majorities can be wrong, that cultures change, that norms pass away. The two percent do not seek truth in consensus, but in experience, in depth, in inner coherence. They are willing to stand alone if it means living in harmony with themselves. From a spiritual point of view, the power of the environment is evident in the way it colors the inner state. Those who live in fields of fear, envy, and competition inevitably take on these vibrations. The average person does not notice how much this blocks them internally. The two percent choose their fields consciously. They seek out places, people, and cultures that radiate clarity, trust, and openness. This changes not only their thinking, but also their being. Spiritually speaking, this is the key:

You become what you connect with. At the end of this section, it becomes very clear: the environment and culture are not just a backdrop, but actively shape our lives. The average person remains mediocre because they unconsciously adopt its rules. The two percent break these rules and create their own. Social dynamics can be restrictive or liberating – depending on whether you live them unconsciously or shape them consciously. When analyzing the hidden forces that keep people average, one inevitably encounters the subtle mechanisms of social conformity. These mechanisms are so deeply embedded in everyday life that most people are not even aware of them. They do not act like chains that can be immediately recognized, but like fine threads that slowly but steadily spin a web around the individual. Once caught in this web, it is almost impossible to move freely. The average person does not recognize this web—they consider it normal. The two percent, on the other hand, see behind the surface and understand the invisible dynamics that prevent people from realizing their potential. From a psychological perspective, several processes are at work here simultaneously.

One of them is social conditioning: from an early age, people learn that reward and punishment are regulated by conformity. A child who behaves conformingly receives praise. A child who deviates receives reprimands. These patterns are repeated at school, at work, and among friends. This creates an internal program that says, "If you want to belong, then be like the others." The average person internalizes this program and repeats it throughout their life. The two percent, on the other hand, break with this pattern. They understand that belonging at the price of self-sacrifice is not true belonging. They do not seek conformity, but authentic community. Economically, this is of central importance. Many people base their financial life decisions on what others do. They go into debt because everyone else does. They buy things that symbolize status because culture demands it. They work in structures that exchange their time for money because this is the social norm.

These collective patterns cement mediocrity. The two percent understand that financial advancement cannot be achieved by copying the majority, but by consciously deviating from it. They recognize that prosperity comes from consciously going against the grain: not consuming when others consume, but investing; not seeking security when others are afraid, but seizing opportunities. Neuroscience explains the power of social dynamics through the mechanism of reward expectation. The brain responds not only to real rewards, but also to the prospect of social recognition. When someone expects their behavior to generate approval, their brain releases dopamine. This creates motivation. The average person is bound to this biochemical loop: they constantly seek recognition and base their actions on it. The two percent break this loop.

They shift the source of reward from outside to inside. They train their brains to enjoy self-determination, freedom, and real progress—regardless of whether the majority applauds or not. From a sociological perspective, this dynamic is particularly evident in the tendency of cultures to reward conformity and sanction deviation. Societies function stably when many people share similar values and behave in similar ways. That is why mechanisms such as peer pressure, social ostracism, or subtle exclusion are effective. The average person fears these mechanisms so much that they voluntarily remain within the bounds of expectations. The two percent accept being looked at askance, criticized, or misunderstood.

They accept the price of difference because they know that freedom is never free. This courage is what separates the mediocre from the extraordinary. Philosophically speaking, this issue touches on the question of whether a life of conformity is truly an authentic life. The average person sacrifices authenticity in favor of belonging. They live as culture expects them to and lose their own identity in the process. The two percent live according to their inner truth, even if that means experiencing less approval. For them, authenticity means that their lives are shaped from their own center, not from the expectations of others. This is not an easy path, but it is the only one that leads to true freedom. From a spiritual perspective, the power of social dynamics is even more subtle. Every environment radiates a certain energy. In fields of fear, competition, and conformity, consciousness becomes narrower, heavier, and less clear. In fields of trust, courage, and openness, it becomes wider, lighter, and clearer. The average person unconsciously moves in fields that limit their consciousness. The two percent consciously choose their fields. They opt for spaces where growth is possible, for relationships that strengthen freedom, for cultures that allow questions. Spiritually speaking, this is an act of purification: letting go of fields that bind and entering fields that liberate.

At the end of this section, it becomes clear that social dynamics are not background noise, but the invisible architects of life. The average person remains mediocre because they do not recognize these forces and blindly follow them. The two percent rise above this because they see through the dynamics, make conscious choices, and have the courage to live against the invisible laws of the masses. Those who want to be free must understand that freedom is not only an internal decision, but also an external one: the choice of environment and the willingness to escape the silent forces of social conformity. When you look at the interplay between the individual, their environment, and culture in all its depth, it becomes clear that most people do not fail because of a lack of knowledge or skills, but because of the invisible laws of their social world.

These laws are stronger than many believe because they work unconsciously. The average person does not act because they have made a rational decision, but because they unconsciously follow the expectations that their environment places on them. They live according to a social script that was not written by them, but by the culture into which they were born. The two percent differ in that they question this script and have the courage to rewrite it. From a psychological perspective, this reveals the power of social identity. To a large extent, every person defines themselves by the group to which they belong. The average person clings to this belonging because it gives them security. But this security comes at a price: it binds them to the boundaries of the group. They live as is customary "among us," they think as is thought "among us," they strive for what is considered success "among us." The two percent, on the other hand, understand that social identity is a choice.

They do not seek belonging at any price, but rather belonging that strengthens them. They consciously decide which circles they move in, which cultures they live in, which voices they give meaning to. In doing so, they create an identity that is not characterized by mediocrity, but by freedom. Economically, this dynamic means that prosperity and poverty often cannot be explained by individual talent, but rather by cultural patterns. Those who live in an environment where consumption is normal will imitate consumption. Those who live in an environment where investment is normal will imitate investment. The average person underestimates how much this imitation determines their life. They believe they are free, but their behavior is an echo of their environment. The two percent break this cycle by changing their environment or consciously redesigning it. They know that if you want different results, you have to move in different social circles. Neuroscience explains this through the influence of habit networks, which are shaped not only individually but also collectively. The brain is designed to seek out and adopt patterns. These patterns are not only personal routines but also cultural codes. Language, values, symbols—all of these form neural structures that determine our thinking. The average person adopts the codes of their culture without questioning them. The two percent question and choose. They lay new neural pathways that enable them to act differently from the majority.

Over time, these different connections become the basis of their freedom. From a sociological perspective, it is clear that cultures are stabilized primarily by their invisible taboos. There are things that are said and things that are not said. There are paths that are taken and paths that are not taken. These taboos are more powerful than laws because they remain unspoken. The average person conforms to them because they are afraid of being excluded. The two percent break taboos. They say what must not be said, they do what is not expected, they take paths that lie outside the norm. This makes them disruptive factors in the system – but it is precisely this that creates new opportunities. From a philosophical point of view, this raises the question of whether conformity can ever lead to true fulfillment. The average person lives a life that is accepted by others, but often remains empty inside. They fulfill roles that others assign to them and lose their own identity in the process. The two percent forego external acceptance in order to gain inner harmony. They understand that a life that pleases society but contradicts their own heart is a wasted life. Freedom means leaving the voice of culture behind and following one's own inner truth. From a spiritual perspective, social dynamics create fields of energy that either weaken or strengthen the individual.

Those who live in fields characterized by fear, competition, and conformity unconsciously feel heaviness, constriction, and exhaustion. Those who live in fields that are supported by trust, courage, and authenticity feel expansiveness, lightness, and strength. The average person does not notice this difference and wonders why they feel burned out or blocked. The two percent perceive these subtle differences and consciously choose their fields. Spiritually speaking, this is one of the deepest keys to freedom: recognizing that you are not a victim of culture, but a co-creator. At the end of this section, and thus also at the end of this chapter, it becomes abundantly clear: mediocrity is not a coincidence, but a product of social dynamics. It is created by cultures, reinforced by environments, and unconsciously reproduced by people. Those who remain average do so not because they are incapable, but because they are prisoners of these invisible laws. The two percent break out because they have the courage to question, break, and rewrite these laws. Freedom is never just individual, but always social as well. It begins where one has the courage not only to change one's own thinking, but also the field in which that thinking arises.

Notes:

Notes:

Chapter 16: Self-deception and justification – Why 98% defend their pattern

When you ask why so many people remain average despite all the opportunities available to them and do not move toward the top 2%, you encounter a mechanism that is deeper and more subtle than mere fear or complacency: self-deception. Humans are masters at telling themselves stories that prevent them from seeing the uncomfortable truth. These stories are not just superficial excuses. They are complex psychological constructs that protect one's own identity. Those who sugarcoat their lives preserve a sense of stability, even if they remain trapped in reality. The average person not only unconsciously defends their mediocrity, they actively justify it. They construct systems of arguments that explain and legitimize their behavior. In doing so, they protect themselves from the realization that they could do more, dare more, change more.

From a psychological perspective, the core of this phenomenon lies in what are known as defense mechanisms. Sigmund Freud already described how the ego develops strategies to protect itself from unpleasant truths. Rationalization, projection, repression—all these mechanisms serve to keep the self-image stable. The average person uses them extensively to justify their life. They say to themselves: "I don't have time," "It's too late for me," "Others were luckier." These statements are not random, but rather an expression of deep-rooted defense. They prevent the ego from acknowledging the painful truth: that it could achieve different results by thinking and acting differently. From an economic perspective, self-deception is evident in the way the average person handles money. Many people get into debt and justify this with statements such as: "Everyone does it," "You only live once," "The house is an investment, even if it ties me down." These justifications obscure the fact that these decisions make them unfree in the long term. Those who consume instead of investing have to explain to themselves why this is okay. Self-deception serves to avoid cognitive dissonance—the uncomfortable feeling of doing something that you know deep down is not wise. The two percent recognize these mechanisms and refrain from this deception. They clearly see that every decision has a consequence and consciously accept it instead of glossing over it. Neuroscience explains this phenomenon through the functioning of the limbic system. When the brain is confronted with a truth that threatens its self-image, it reacts with stress. This activation is experienced as pain – not only emotionally, but also physically. To avoid this pain, the brain resorts to cognitive strategies: it changes perception, distorts reality, and ignores facts. Thus, self-deception arises not from malice, but from a protective mechanism. The average person remains stuck in this protection.

They live in an inner bubble where uncomfortable truths are softened or reinterpreted. The two percent consciously break through this protection. They face the unpleasant truth and train their nervous system to endure the pain associated with true self-awareness. From a sociological perspective, these illusions stabilize in groups. People confirm each other's justifications. Those who say, “It's normal to be in debt,” receive approval from others who are also in debt. Those who say, “It's normal to hate your job,” receive confirmation from others who are experiencing the same thing. This creates collective illusions that reinforce each other. The average person lives in such echo chambers of self-deception. The two percent leave these spaces. They seek out people who speak the truth, even when it is uncomfortable, thereby reinforcing a culture of clarity rather than a culture of justification. From a philosophical perspective, self-deception raises the question of how much truth a person can bear. The average person unconsciously chooses to endure less truth in order to maintain stability. They prefer to live in an illusion that protects them rather than in a truth that challenges them. The two percent choose the more difficult path.

They see truth as liberating, even if it hurts. For them, a life of illusion is not a life, but a shadow. That is why they are willing to take off the masks of self-deception and bear the pain of realization in order to gain freedom. Spiritually speaking, self-deception is a form of separation from one's own being. Those who lie to themselves distance themselves from their essence. They live in stories that lead them away from their core. The average person lives in this separation, often without realizing it. The two percent strive for unity between the inner and outer worlds. They want their lives to correspond to the truth they feel inside. That is why they are willing to expose themselves, to see their own lies and break their own masks. Spiritually, this is the decisive step: to realize that liberation is only possible if one gives up the delusions one tells oneself.

At the end of this first section, it becomes clear that self-deception and justification are the silent guardians of mediocrity. They keep the 98 percent trapped in their patterns because they prevent them from becoming aware of the uncomfortable truth. Only those who have the courage to recognize and endure these deceptions can break out of the circle of mediocrity. The two percent have this courage—and that is precisely why they are among the few who are free. If you want to understand why people cling to patterns that harm them, you encounter a peculiar mixture of psychology, biology, and culture. It is not enough to say that people are comfortable or afraid. The mechanism is deeper: it is the mind's ability to construct a reality that appears consistent, even if it is based on illusions. The average person lives in this construction and defends it because it gives them security. The two percent recognize that these constructions have a stabilizing effect, but ultimately make them unfree. From a psychological point of view, the principle of cognitive dissonance is at work here. Whenever a person performs an action that is not in line with their inner convictions, a state of tension arises. This tension is unpleasant and must be resolved.

The average person resolves it not through change, but through reinterpretation. They justify their behavior until it feels consistent again. They don't say, "I consume too much and need to change my behavior," but rather, "You don't treat yourself to anything else." They don't say, "I'm afraid of change," but rather, "It's reasonable to be cautious." Justification transforms contradictions into apparent harmony – but at the price of truth. Economically, this attitude leads many people to remain in structures that bind them. They work for decades in jobs that make them unhappy and say, "That's just how life is." They go into debt for consumer goods and say, "I want to make my family happy." They miss opportunities and say, "It would have been too risky anyway." These statements are not objective truths, but self-deceptions that serve to avoid pain. If you repeat them often enough, you will eventually believe them.

The average person then no longer lives only within external limitations, but also within an internal logic that makes these limitations seem right. Neuroscience explains this phenomenon through the brain's reward and protection mechanisms. Unpleasant truths activate stress networks. Self-deception, on the other hand, is calming. When people tell themselves a story that justifies their actions, the brain releases reward chemicals that provide short-term relief. This is why self-deception is so attractive: it reduces inner tension without requiring a change in behavior. But in the long term, it reinforces neural patterns that lead to stagnation. The brain becomes accustomed to mistaking illusions for reality. The two percent train their nervous system differently. They learn to endure the tension of cognitive dissonance and resolve it through change rather than self-deception. That's why they keep moving while others stand still. Sociologically speaking, self-deception is stabilized by collective narratives. Societies create stories that explain why things are the way they are. "You need a secure job."

"You shouldn't stand out." "You mustn't make mistakes." These statements are not truths, but cultural constructs that ensure stability. The average person accepts them because they make them feel like they are doing the right thing. The two percent recognize that these are stories – and that stories can be changed. That's why they leave the cultural script behind and write their own. From a philosophical perspective, the question arises as to whether truth is sought at all or whether stability is more important. The average person often unconsciously chooses stability. Truth could force them to change their life—and that change would be exhausting, risky, painful. That's why they reject truth, even when it reveals itself. They ignore it, twist it, wrap it up in stories that are easier to bear. The two percent see truth as a prerequisite for freedom. They accept that truth is sometimes painful, but they know that only truth paves the way for real change. From a spiritual perspective, self-deception is a veil that obscures the true self. The average person lives in this veil and confuses it with their identity.

They say, "That's just how I am," without realizing that they are only repeating stories. The two percent are willing to lift this veil. They want to see who they are beyond the delusions. They accept the pain because they know that freedom awaits behind the illusion. Spiritually speaking, every self-deception is an obstacle on the path to unity, and every recognition of deception is a step toward truth. This shows precisely that the 98 percent do not defend their pattern because they are malicious, but because their minds are wired to avoid unpleasant tensions. But this defense keeps them trapped. Those who want to be free must stop telling themselves stories that are comforting and begin to see truths that are challenging. The two percent have taken this step—and that is precisely what sets them apart from the rest. When one considers the depth of self-deception, it becomes clear that it is not just an individual weakness, but a collective structure that sustains entire societies. People tell themselves stories to justify their decisions, and these stories weave together to form a web that creates normality.

The average person lives in this web without noticing it. For them, it is reality. But reality is not what is, but what is believed and repeated. That is why the average person defends their patterns so passionately: they are defending not only habits, but an entire worldview built on illusions. From a psychological perspective, this behavior can be explained by the need for consistency. People want to experience themselves as rational and coherent. When their behavior and beliefs diverge, an inner rift arises. The average person cannot bear this rift, so they shift the truth. Instead of changing their behavior, they change their narrative. They say, "I never wanted that anyway" when they don't achieve something. They say, "It was fate" when they fail. They say, "It's better this way" when they don't take advantage of opportunities.

These statements are band-aids on deep wounds. They prevent healing because they cover up the wound instead of opening it up. The two percent dare to feel the rift. They endure the tension without immediately smoothing it out. This creates space for real change. Economically, self-deception leads to a fatal spiral. Those who believe that their financial situation is unchangeable, that prosperity is reserved for only a few, that investing is too risky, will confirm these beliefs. They make decisions that reinforce their delusions: they stay in their secure jobs, they consume instead of investing, they avoid risks and thus confirm that they have no opportunities. It is a self-reinforcing system that keeps them in mediocrity. The two percent have a different attitude: they realize that they sometimes make mistakes, that not every investment is successful, that not every step leads to immediate success.

But they don't need deception to justify this. They accept reality, learn from it, and move on. Neuroscience shows that self-deception is closely linked to the brain's reward system. Truth can cause pain—it activates networks associated with threat. Deception, on the other hand, is reassuring because it creates illusions of security. The brain releases calming neurotransmitters when reality is reinterpreted in such a way that it appears less threatening. That is why self-deception feels pleasant. It is a kind of internal anesthetic. But like any anesthetic, it prevents healing. The two percent consciously forego this anesthetic. They choose the pain of truth because they know that only it can bring long-term liberation.

From a sociological perspective, groups reinforce these patterns by cultivating common justifications. Entire societies are based on self-deception: that prosperity comes from consumption, that security comes from conformity, that happiness can be achieved through status symbols. These narratives are repeated so often that they seem like laws of nature. The average person defends them because they find comfort in them. Those who question them are marginalized. The two percent risk this marginalization. They break with collective narratives and thereby create new spaces for freedom. From a philosophical perspective, self-deception raises the question of how much illusion humans need in order to live. Is truth always bearable? The average person chooses illusion, albeit unconsciously, because it is easier to bear. But this ease is deceptive. It prevents growth and freedom. The two percent believe that truth, however difficult it may be, is the only way to true life.

They see deception not as protection, but as a prison. That is why they choose truth, even if it hurts. From a spiritual perspective, self-deception is a veil that obscures consciousness. It prevents people from recognizing their true nature. The average person lives in this veil and defends it because they believe it to be reality. The two percent tear away the veil. They see through their own illusions and accept that they are not always pleasant. But it is precisely this insight that leads them to greater clarity, to a state of inner truth that is independent of external circumstances. Here it becomes clear: the 98 percent defend their patterns not out of reason, but out of fear. They deceive themselves in order to avoid pain, thereby creating a life that is stable but narrow. The two percent, on the other hand, accept pain in order to gain truth, thereby creating a life that seems riskier but is broad. The difference lies not in circumstances, but in the courage to let go of illusions. One of the most remarkable characteristics of human beings is their ability to shape their own reality in such a way that it remains bearable for them – even if it actually limits them. This ability to tell themselves stories that alleviate pain and shift responsibility is deeply rooted in the human psyche. The average person uses it instinctively, almost reflexively, to see their life in a way that makes sense, even if it keeps them dependent. In doing so, they defend their patterns not only unconsciously, but consciously.

They become advocates for their own limitations, fighting for the walls of their prison because they believe those walls offer protection. The two percent recognize this paradox. They know that walls promise security, but in reality prevent freedom. Psychologically, this phenomenon can be explained by the so-called confirmation bias. People seek information that confirms their beliefs and ignore information that questions them. The average person is a master at this. They read articles that prove them right, surround themselves with like-minded people, and interpret events in a way that supports their view. In this way, they build a fortress of self-deception. The two percent, on the other hand, specifically seek out information that challenges them. They question their beliefs, examine their own ways of thinking, and are willing to recognize mistakes. That is why they grow, while the average person stagnates. Economically, this defense of the pattern leads to decisions that are harmful in the long term. The average person stays in jobs that make them unhappy because they tell themselves, "Security is more important than freedom." They go into debt for consumption because they believe, "You only live once." They don't invest because they are convinced, "That's only for rich people."

These statements are not truths, but protective narratives. They prevent them from realizing that they themselves could achieve different results by making different decisions. The two percent do without these narratives. They clearly see that job security often means dependence, that consumption rarely brings real joy, and that investing is possible even with little capital. Their clear vision enables them to take paths that remain closed to the average person. From a neuroscientific perspective, defending patterns can be explained by the way the reward system works. The brain loves predictability. Familiar patterns activate a feeling of security. Unfamiliar patterns trigger stress. That's why old behavior feels "right," even if it's harmful, while new behavior feels "wrong," even if it would be liberating. The average person confuses this feeling with truth. They believe, "Because it feels familiar, it must be right." The two percent see through this deception. They know that familiarity is not a measure of truth, but only a sign of repetition. That's why they train their brains to tolerate the unknown until it becomes familiar. From a sociological perspective, the group stabilizes the patterns of the individual. Those who question something risk rejection. That is why the average person defends not only their own beliefs, but also the beliefs of the group to which they belong.

They say, "That's how it's done," because they feel that deviation would isolate them. The two percent accept this isolation. They know that true freedom does not come from the approval of the group, but from loyalty to their own truth. That is why they can let go of what the group considers indispensable. Philosophically speaking, this reveals the profound paradox of human existence: people often defend precisely what makes them unfree. They cling to chains because they are familiar. They fight for boundaries because they promise security. They sacrifice freedom because responsibility frightens them. The average person lives in this paradox and does not recognize it. The two percent see it clearly and decide to let go of the familiar, even if it means uncertainty. They understand that freedom always carries uncertainty—and that this uncertainty is the price one pays for an authentic life. From a spiritual perspective, defending patterns is a form of identification.

People confuse their patterns with their identity. They say, "That's just the way I am." They believe that their fears, doubts, and limitations are part of their essence. That's why they defend them as if they were defending themselves. The two percent realize that patterns are not the true self. They see them as conditioning that can be let go of. Their essence lies deeper—beyond patterns and stories. By seeing through this illusion, they find a freedom that the average person cannot even imagine. What can I take away from this: The 98 percent defend their patterns passionately because they consider them to be their self. They justify their limitations because they believe they protect them. But in truth, they only protect their captivity. The two percent have the courage to break through this deception. They see that freedom comes not from defense, but from letting go. This is the core of their difference.

If you follow the dynamics of self-deception to its ultimate cause, you realize that it is not merely a weakness, but a deeply rooted principle of human life. People defend their patterns because these patterns give them a sense of identity, belonging, and security. The average person lives under the illusion that their life, as it is, is the only one possible. They defend this illusion because its collapse would trigger an existential crisis. The two percent are willing to risk this crisis. They understand that the collapse of an illusion is painful, but at the same time the beginning of a new freedom. Psychologically speaking, this means that the 98 percent are not simply lazy, but that they live in a complex defense system. This system protects their self-image from collapse. It explains defeats in a way that makes them bearable, reinterprets failures, and relativizes shortcomings. This system prevents people from having to confront the truth in all its depth. The average person says to themselves, "I did my best" – even if they hardly tried.

They say, "Others were luckier" – even if they didn't take advantage of opportunities. They say, "It wasn't meant to be" – even if they themselves were responsible. These statements are like shields that protect the ego. The two percent do without these shields. They allow themselves to feel the full harshness of reality. That is why they are not unbreakable, but vulnerable – yet it is precisely this vulnerability that sets them free. From an economic perspective, it is clear that these patterns of justification not only shape individual lives, but also stabilize entire systems. Consumer societies thrive on people justifying why they spend money on things they don't need. Labor markets thrive on people justifying why they stay in jobs that make them unhappy. Financial systems thrive on people justifying why they consider debt to be normal. The average person keeps these systems alive by defending them. The two percent break with this logic. They recognize that many of these structures are only stable through illusion and withdraw from them. They do not live for consumption, security, or status—but for freedom. From a neuroscientific perspective, justification acts like a drug. It calms the nervous system, alleviates the pain of cognitive dissonance, and provides short-term peace. But like any drug, it demands repetition. The more often a person deceives themselves, the stronger the neural connections that support this deception become. Over time, they believe their own lies.

The average person lives in this vicious circle: they repeat their stories so often that they become "truth." The two percent have the courage to break this cycle. They recognize their own stories and take away their power by no longer repeating them. They train their brains to endure tension without calming it with illusion. Sociologically speaking, justifications are the cement that holds the culture of mediocrity together. Everyone justifies themselves with similar phrases, and thus a collective narrative emerges: "It's normal not to be free." "It's normal to keep a low profile." "It's normal to endure your life." These phrases form the foundation of mediocrity. They are so deeply ingrained that hardly anyone questions them. The two percent do. They withdraw from this collective narrative and write a new one. That is why they often seem like provocateurs to the average person. But in truth, they are harbingers of another possibility. From a philosophical perspective, it becomes clear that self-deception is not simply an individual problem, but a question of the relationship between truth and life. The average person chooses to live in illusion because they believe that truth is too difficult. The two percent choose truth, even if it is difficult, because they know that illusions ultimately kill—not the body, but the spirit. Only a life lived in truth is truly alive. Everything else is a form of twilight. From a spiritual perspective, self-deception is the deepest separation from the self. Those who lie to themselves lose touch with their innermost core. They live in layers of stories that distance them from their essence. The average person lives in this separation and does not realize how much it weakens them. The two percent choose the path back. They dissolve the layers of deception until they recognize the truth of their being. Spiritually speaking, this is a return to the origin—to the unity that has always been there but was hidden. At the end of this section, and thus at the end of this chapter, it becomes crystal clear: the 98 percent defend their patterns because they believe that otherwise they would collapse. They cling to delusions because they believe they cannot live without them. But these delusions are their prison. The two percent realize that the collapse of the illusion is the beginning of freedom. That is why they dare to do what others avoid: they let the deception die in order to truly live.

Notes:

Notes:

Chapter 17: Vision and Long-Term Thinking – How the 2% Think About Decades

When you examine the mindset of those few people who belong to the two percent who are financially, mentally, and existentially independent, you encounter a pattern that radically distinguishes them from the average: their ability to think in terms of decades. The average person lives to the rhythm of short-term needs, day-to-day problems, and immediate desires. They base their actions on what will provide them with security or satisfaction in the coming weeks or months. The two percent, on the other hand, develop an inner attitude that goes far beyond the present. They do not live for the moment alone, but for a horizon that spans years and decades. This ability to think long-term is one of the biggest differences between a mediocre life and an extraordinary one. From a psychological perspective, this ability is rare because the human brain is evolutionarily programmed for short-term rewards. In early times, it was essential for survival to grab food immediately when it was available and to act immediately when danger threatened.

To this day, the brain's reward system reacts strongly to immediate gratification. That is why the average person finds it so difficult to consistently pursue long-term plans. They prefer the obvious – quick consumption, immediate recognition, immediate security. The two percent have recognized this neural programming and consciously overwritten it. They train their minds to be able to tolerate delayed gratification. They postpone satisfaction in favor of greater goals; they give up today in order to be free tomorrow. Economically speaking, this is a fundamental difference. The average person saves, if at all, in the short term, or consumes immediately as soon as money is available. They live in a cycle of income and expenditure that keeps them dependent. The two percent, on the other hand, think in terms of decades. They build structures that are not designed for immediate gratification, but for sustainability. They invest capital that does not yield a profit today, but in ten or twenty years. They think in terms of generations, not months. This long-term view allows them to build wealth, while the average person repeatedly loses themselves in the cycle of consumption. Neuroscience explains the difference by the function of the prefrontal cortex, the region of the brain responsible for planning, foresight, and self-control. The average person hardly uses these abilities.

Their thinking revolves around the obvious, and they justify this with statements such as, "You have to live in the moment." But in reality, it is not "living in the moment" but being trapped in the short term. The two percent train their prefrontal cortex by consciously pursuing long-term goals, even if this causes discomfort in the short term. They experience reward not in quick enjoyment, but in the idea of long-term success. Sociologically speaking, this difference is reflected in the way cultures perceive time. In Western consumer societies, the short term dominates. Everything is geared toward speed, immediacy, and instant gratification. People order online and want next-day delivery. They expect quick profits, quick careers, quick results. The average person adapts to this culture and adopts its logic of time. The two percent, on the other hand, escape this dictate. They create their own culture of time, which is not oriented toward the pace of the masses, but toward the rhythm of their vision. They plan decades ahead, while others can barely see beyond the next month. From a philosophical perspective, this touches on the question of the meaning of life.

Do you live for today or for tomorrow? The average person answers this question unconsciously by constantly satisfying short-term desires. They escape into consumption, distractions, and the feeling of having something now. But they pay with emptiness when the future arrives and there is no substance. The two percent recognize that today only makes sense if it is part of a larger whole. They build their lives in such a way that each day is a building block in a vision that extends beyond their own lives. This is where their quiet strength lies. From a spiritual perspective, the ability to think in decades is a form of trust. Those who think in the short term live in fear: fear of missing out, fear of missing something, fear that tomorrow is uncertain. Those who think long-term live in trust: trust that tomorrow will bear fruit, trust that patience will be rewarded, trust that their own decisions will stand the test of time. The two percent live in this trust. Their thinking in decades is not only economically wise, but spiritually profound. It means seeing through the illusion of immediacy and fitting into the flow of time without being rushed by it. At the end of this first section, it becomes clear that vision and long-term thinking are not mere strategies, but an attitude that makes the difference between the average and the exceptional. The average defends its short-term thinking because it is easier, more comfortable, more familiar. But the two percent choose the more difficult path: they forego quick happiness in order to reap great happiness. They sacrifice the moment to gain decades. This is precisely what sets them apart from the masses. When comparing the mindsets of the average person with those of the two percent, it is particularly striking how much the perspective on time determines the difference. The average person thinks in cycles that are narrowly defined: the next paycheck, the next vacation, the coming months until the end of the year. Their thinking is short-sighted because they link their decisions to immediate needs. The top two percent, on the other hand, don't think in terms of months or years, but in terms of decades. They view their lives as a long-term project that doesn't depend on the mood of the day, but on a clear vision that they pursue over long periods of time. From a psychological perspective, this ability to think long-term is related to the concept of "delayed gratification." Experiments such as the famous marshmallow test have shown that children who are able to overcome short-term temptations in order to receive a greater reward later are more successful in the long term. The average person often remains trapped in the inability to delay gratification. They want immediate pleasure, immediate security, immediate recognition. But every time they give in to this temptation, they weaken their ability to achieve long-term goals. The two percent, on the other hand, consciously train their ability to delay gratification. They know that true fulfillment does not lie in quick consumption, but in building a foundation that will last for decades. Economically, this difference is reflected in how people invest – not only financially, but also in terms of energy, time, and emotion.

The average person invests their time in short-term distractions, their money in consumption, and their energy in tasks that bring immediate gratification. The two percent invest their capital where it will bear fruit over years and decades. They invest in education, in networks, in projects that only yield returns after a long time. This difference in how they deal with time and resources is crucial: it separates those who remain in the cycle of dependency from those who gain freedom. From a neuroscientific perspective, this difference is deeply rooted in the brain. The average person lives out of the limbic system – the part of the brain that controls emotions and short-term needs. It reacts to stimuli, seeks quick gratification, and avoids discomfort. The two percent activate their prefrontal cortex more strongly—the center for planning, self-control, and long-term thinking. They are able to control their impulses and not let themselves be ruled by the urges of the moment. This ability can be trained, but it requires discipline and awareness. This is precisely what sets the two percent apart: they take training their minds as seriously as others take training their bodies. From a sociological perspective, cultures differ in their perception of time.

Consumer societies promote short-termism by providing constant incentives: advertising, discounts, instant gratification. Those who live in such a culture are unconsciously programmed to act in the moment and neglect the future. The average person adapts to this culture and adopts its pace. The two percent, however, escape this compulsion. They build a counterculture in which patience, planning, and long-term thinking are more important than speed. They recognize that culture is powerful, but not without alternatives. That is why they create their own understanding of time that is not bound to the illusion of immediacy. From a philosophical point of view, long-term thinking is an expression of a deep understanding of transience. Those who think in the short term live under the illusion that life is secured by immediate gratification. But in reality, time slips away from them as they try to hold on to it. The two percent recognize that time is a stream that can only be used meaningfully if it is directed in a direction that has meaning beyond the moment. They understand that true freedom comes when you see today as a building block for tomorrow, not as an isolated event.

From a spiritual perspective, long-term thinking is an act of trust in life itself. Those who live only in the present, out of fear of tomorrow, live in a state of scarcity. They believe that they must take now because tomorrow there may be nothing left. Those who live for the long term live in a consciousness of abundance. They know that there is enough time, enough opportunities, enough resources if they use them wisely. This trust makes the two percent independent of fear. They can wait patiently because they are anchored in abundance, not scarcity. It becomes clear that vision and long-term thinking are not strategies that can be applied superficially, but deeply rooted attitudes that shape the way we think, feel, and act.

The average person remains in a short-term cycle because they do not control their impulses and the culture confirms this. The two percent escape this pull and create a mindset that spans decades. They know that those who focus on decades gain freedom, while those who focus only on the moment remain trapped. The ability to think long-term is not a coincidence, but a consciously developed skill that differs fundamentally from the habit of short-term orientation. The average person lives in a rhythm determined by external circumstances, cultural expectations, and immediate needs. They react instead of creating. The two percent, on the other hand, have an inner standard that extends far beyond the urgencies of the day. They do not live in reaction mode, but in vision mode. Their decisions are not improvised responses to coincidences, but conscious building blocks of a larger plan that is intended to last for decades. From a psychological perspective, the concept of future projection plays a role here. The average person projects their future from the present, believing that the next few years will be a repeat of what they already know. They do not think in terms of new possibilities, but in terms of repetitions.

That is why risks seem threatening to them: they could interrupt their familiar continuity. The two percent, on the other hand, use their ability to imagine. They create images of a future that may be radically different from the present. These images are not mere dreams, but visions that structure their actions. They know that the future does not have to be derived from the past, but that it is shaped by decisions. Economically, this difference is particularly evident. The average person sees money as a means of satisfying short-term needs. They think in terms of expenditure, not investment. They ask, "What can I afford now?" The two percent, on the other hand, ask, "What will bear fruit in ten or twenty years?"

This difference may seem subtle, but it leads to radically different results. The average person consumes their future, while the two percent build it. Over decades, this difference adds up to a gap that is almost impossible to bridge. In neuroscience, the ability to maintain visions over long periods of time is closely linked to what is known as mental simulation. The brain can play out the future in the mind as if it were real. The average person rarely uses this ability—usually to amplify worries or fears. They simulate disasters, risks, dangers. The two percent use it to imagine opportunities, developments, and long-term effects. This trains their brains for growth and patience, not fear and avoidance. Long-term thinking is not just a mindset here, but a practiced mental state that strengthens neural networks that enable patience, self-control, and foresight. From a sociological perspective, the difference between short-term and long-term thinking is also determined by the stories a culture tells about success. In societies that glorify short-term consumption, quick success is considered the ideal.

Those who get rich quickly are admired. Those who consistently build up their wealth over decades go unnoticed. The average person adopts these cultural stories and bases their life on them. The two percent see through the stories and create their own. They know that true success does not come from a flurry of flashbulbs, but from decades of quiet work. That is why they resist cultural pressure and remain true to their long-term path. Philosophically speaking, vision is an attitude toward time. The average person lives as if time were an enemy running away from them. They fight against transience by trying to hold on to the moment. But the more they hold on, the faster time slips away. The two percent, on the other hand, see time as an ally. They know that decades are their capital, that slowness creates depth, and that patience means strength. They do not view their lives as a sequence of moments that are lost, but as a continuum that unfolds meaning when consciously shaped. From a spiritual perspective, long-term thinking means freeing oneself from the spell of fear. Fear lives in the short term. It says, "Secure yourself now, enjoy now, avoid pain now."

Trust lives in the long term. It says, "Trust that the seeds you sow today will bear fruit tomorrow." The average person lives under the spell of fear and justifies this as realism. The two percent live in trust and see this as the true reality. Their long-term perspective is not just a strategy, but an expression of a deeper spiritual attitude: the conviction that life will sustain you if you consciously entrust yourself to it. It becomes clear that the difference between the 98 percent and the two percent lies not only in how they make decisions, but in how they understand time. The average person lives as if there were only today, and thus loses tomorrow. The two percent live as if today were the seed of tomorrow, and thus gain decades. This attitude changes everything—and it is the key to why so few become independent, while so many remain trapped in the cycle of mediocrity. If you really want to understand how the top 2% think, you have to realize that vision and long-term thinking are not just external strategies, but an inner attitude that permeates every area of their lives. While the average person lives in a world dominated by short-term goals, instant solutions, and immediate gratification, the top 2% have a different relationship with time.

They are able to view their entire existence as a mosaic in which each piece does not have to shine individually, but rather forms a picture when viewed as a whole. They see this picture, while others only recognize fragments. From a psychological perspective, this reveals a pattern that is deeply rooted in the structure of human consciousness. The average person lives in a mental confinement created by the constant pressure of immediate needs. They think about what they need to do now to avoid pain or gain pleasure.

This short-term thinking is relieving because it avoids complex decisions. But it comes at the price of stagnation. The two percent, on the other hand, have learned to live with this complexity. They accept ambiguity and uncertainty because they know that long-term clarity will emerge from them. Their vision allows them to endure the pain of the present without losing their direction. Economically speaking, this is the difference between consumption and investment, between short-term survival and long-term development. The average person sees money as a means to satisfy immediate needs. That is why they live in a cycle in which every income is quickly turned into expenditure. They justify this with statements such as, “You have to treat yourself sometimes.” But in reality, they are robbing themselves of their future. The two percent see money as energy that can be shaped. They invest it where it will bear fruit in decades to come – not because they avoid enjoyment, but because they know that deeper enjoyment comes from freedom, not consumption. From a neuroscientific perspective, the difference can be explained by the ability to self-regulate.

The average person quickly gives in to impulses because their brain is programmed for quick rewards through the release of dopamine. They buy because they feel like it, they eat because they crave it, they act because they want to feel better in the short term. The two percent train their brains not to act on these impulses immediately. They create structures that delay rewards and thus enable greater effects. This training changes neural networks so that long-term thinking no longer seems tedious, but becomes a habit. From a sociological perspective, the difference becomes particularly clear when analyzing the role of cultures. Consumer societies promote short-termism by constantly persuading people that they have new needs. Advertising, media, social comparisons—all of this keeps the average person in a state of constant unrest. They believe that they must buy now, act now, keep up now. The two percent stand against this cultural tide. They create their own culture of waiting, building, and patience. They do not put themselves under pressure to show immediate results, but trust that the results will come in their own time. From a philosophical point of view, this is an expression of a deep understanding of time and being. The average person lives in a state of mind that could be described as "chronological captivity": they see time as a sequence of moments that are lost. That is why they try to fill as many of these moments as possible with pleasure before they disappear. But the more they do so, the emptier these moments become.

The two percent live in a different relationship with time. They do not see it as an enemy, but as a partner. They understand that the value of a moment lies not in its intensity, but in its embedding in a larger whole. From a spiritual perspective, this means that long-term thinking is a form of devotion. The average person lives in resistance to transience. They fight against the passage of time by trying to preserve the moment. The two percent, on the other hand, surrender to the flow. They trust that their vision will take shape over time. They live in the certainty that life itself will work with them if they remain true to it. This devotion gives them serenity. They don't have to have everything right away because they know they will achieve everything in due course. Here, too, it becomes clear that vision and long-term thinking are not merely tools, but an attitude toward life that enables freedom. The average person remains imprisoned by short-term thinking because they allow themselves to be ruled by their impulses, their culture, and their fears. The two percent, on the other hand, live from an inner clarity that allows them to keep their eyes on the decades ahead without being distracted by the pressures of the moment.

They know that time is not working against them, but for them – as long as they are willing to use it wisely. To understand the true power of vision and long-term thinking, one must recognize that it is not just about planning, investing, or rational strategies, but about a way of being. The average person remains trapped in a cycle of short-term worries and desires because they constantly tie their thoughts, feelings, and actions to the here and now. They believe that they are acting freely, but in reality they are prisoners of their impulses and their culture. The two percent, on the other hand, live from an inner perspective that understands time in a different way. For them, every day is part of a decades-long project. They experience their lives not as a series of coincidences, but as the unfolding of a vision that is greater than themselves. Psychologically speaking, this is the highest form of self-leadership.

The average person feels that external circumstances determine their life. They say, "I couldn't help it, the situation required it." The two percent, on the other hand, take radical responsibility. They understand that every step they take today is a seed for the future. They are able to evaluate actions not by their short-term effect, but by their long-term impact. This perspective gives them a calmness that the average person lacks. While the average person is immediately shaken by setbacks, the two percent see failure as just one moment in a larger process. Economically, this means that they think in terms of generations rather than years. The average person saves for their next vacation or car. The two percent build structures that will benefit their children and grandchildren. They create values that are not consumed immediately, but passed on.

This difference shows why they are not only materially but also existentially more independent. Those who think long-term build a foundation that can withstand storms. Those who live in the short term build on sand. Neuroscience shows the power of the "mental time horizon" here. Studies have shown that people who are able to imagine their future in detail act less impulsively and make better decisions. The average person has a short time horizon: they see the next week, the next month, maybe the next year. The two percent have a broad time horizon: they imagine where they want to be in twenty or thirty years and base their actions on that.

This broad horizon not only changes their decisions, but also their biochemistry. It calms the stress system and strengthens the feeling of control and meaning. From a sociological perspective, long-term thinking also means freeing oneself from society's short-term expectations. The average person lives as culture dictates: fast career, fast consumption, fast status. The two percent escape this pace. They know that true value takes time to mature. They resist the pressure to show immediate results and accept that their path sometimes remains invisible. But it is precisely this invisibility that protects them from distractions. While the average person is lost in the noise of the moment, they quietly work on a project that will last for decades. From a philosophical perspective, vision means not seeing one's own life as an endless repetition of the same thing, but as a meaningful movement toward a goal. The average person lives as if every day were a burden that must be borne. The two percent live as if every day were a building block that forms a bigger picture. This attitude transforms the experience of time. What seems grueling to the average person is fulfilling for them because they see meaning in everything that extends beyond today. Ultimately, the ability to think in decades is an expression of inner freedom. Those who live in the short term live in fear: fear of missing out, fear that tomorrow is uncertain, fear of not getting enough. Those who live in the long term live in trust: trust that life will sustain them, that time is an ally, that patience will bear fruit. The two percent embody this trust. They do not live in scarcity, but in abundance, because they know that they are part of a larger process that does not end in the moment. At the end of this chapter, it becomes clear that vision and long-term thinking are perhaps the strongest forces that make the difference between the average and the exceptional. The average remains mediocre because it lives in the prison of the moment. The two percent free themselves because they have the courage to think in terms of decades. They live with an inner horizon that allows them to weather crises, seize opportunities, and create works that endure. The difference between mediocrity and freedom is ultimately a question of time horizon. Those who only see the moment lose the future. Those who have decades in view gain life.

Notes:

Notes:

Chapter 18: From consumer to producer – value creation instead of consumption

When you look at the paths people take in life, you quickly realize that the majority of society remains stuck in a role that has been made almost self-evident by culture: the role of the consumer. The average person is defined by what they consume – by the things they buy, the services they use, the experiences they consume. This attitude is not just an individual pattern, but an expression of a society that systematically programs people to be consumers. But the two percent have a different relationship with the world. They do not see themselves primarily as consumers, but as creators.

They produce value, they create structures, they shape realities. This reversal from consumer to producer is one of the key reasons why they rise above the average. From a psychological perspective, consumption is convenient because it provides instant gratification. Buying something, experiencing something, owning something – all of this activates the brain's reward system and provides short-term pleasure. But this pleasure is fleeting. It creates no substance, it leaves no foundation. The average person lives in this cycle of short-term satisfaction followed by emptiness. They constantly need new stimuli to fill this emptiness, and thus become dependent on consumption. The two percent see through this mechanism. They recognize that true fulfillment lies not in constant taking, but in giving, in creating, in producing. Psychologically speaking, their identity transforms from that of a dependent taker to an independent creator. Economically, this difference is particularly clear. Consumers are the foundation of every economy—their consumption keeps the machinery running. But the real power lies not with the consumer, but with the producer. Those who create something that others consume gain influence, freedom, and prosperity. The average person limits themselves to buying other people's products and services, thus remaining dependent.

The two percent, on the other hand, ask: "What can I create that will serve others?" They build companies, develop ideas, write books, create art, invent technologies. They do not live off what they consume, but off what they create. From a neuroscientific perspective, the step from consumer to producer is a change in the reward system. Consumption activates the limbic system on a superficial level. Production, on the other hand, activates deeper networks associated with creativity, meaning, and self-efficacy. Those who create something experience a different quality of joy—one that lasts longer and strengthens the self. The average person is always looking for new stimuli because their satisfaction quickly fades. The two percent find satisfaction in the slowness of creation because they know that the joy of something they have created themselves is deeper and more lasting than any consumed distraction. From a sociological perspective, the role of the consumer is also a cultural assignment. Modern societies educate people from an early age to consume. Advertising, media, education systems—they all convey the message that a person's value lies in what they can afford. The average person unconsciously accepts this message. They measure their status by the brands they wear, the things they own, the trips they take. The two percent reject this narrative.

For them, value lies not in consumption, but in creation. They do not measure themselves by what they own, but by what they produce. In doing so, they escape the cultural programming that keeps millions trapped in the cycle of consumption. Philosophically speaking, this difference touches on the question of the meaning of human existence. Are humans here to consume or to create? The average person lives as if consumption were the meaning of life—they work to earn money and spend that money to buy things. Their life revolves in a cycle of work and consumption that repeats endlessly. The two percent see meaning in creation. They believe that humans should not only take, but also contribute.

Their lives are an expression of this attitude: Every day is an opportunity to leave something behind that has meaning beyond the moment. From a spiritual perspective, the shift from consumer to producer ultimately means a return to one's own creative core. Humans are creative beings by nature. Children playfully create worlds before they are turned into consumers. But culture overlays this creative power and directs it toward consumption. The average person loses touch with their inner creativity over the course of their life. The two percent consciously cultivate it. For them, every creative act—whether it's developing an idea, building a project, or shaping a new reality—is an expression of their inner being.

Spiritually speaking, they live in harmony with their nature, while the average person is alienated from it. Let's be clear: the difference between the 98 percent and the two percent often begins with a seemingly simple question: am I a consumer or a producer? The average person remains trapped in the role of consumer because they believe there is no alternative. The two percent, however, choose to create value. They know that those who produce gain freedom. Those who only consume remain dependent. When you think more deeply about why the average person remains in the role of consumer, you realize that it is not just convenience or ignorance, but a deeply ingrained cultural narrative. People grow up in a system that conditions them from an early age to derive their value not from what they create, but from what they consume. Advertising, society, and even the education system act like an invisible program that leads individuals into an attitude of taking. Thus, consumption becomes not just an action, but part of one's identity. The two percent have the courage to escape this programming. They recognize that true identity lies not in consumption but in creation—and that freedom only begins when people shift from the role of pure consumers to that of producers.

Psychologically speaking, the urge to consume is rooted in an interplay of emotions and neural reward. The brain is designed to respond to immediate stimuli with feelings of pleasure. Buying a product, experiencing a moment of pleasure, consuming a commodity—all of these trigger a dopamine response that provides short-term satisfaction. But this satisfaction is not lasting. It demands repetition. The average person lives in this endless loop of stimulus and reward without ever finding true fulfillment. The two percent understand that this loop is a trap. They shift their sources of pleasure away from consumption and toward creation. As a result, they experience joy not in quick purchases, but in slow building, not in quick rewards, but in the deep experience of self-efficacy. From an economic perspective, producers are the drivers of value creation. They are the ones who transform ideas into products, knowledge into services, creativity into culture, and visions into businesses. Consumers, on the other hand, are the drivers of demand. They secure the market, but they do not determine it.

Those who produce shape the playing field; those who consume play by the rules of others. The average person is content to be a consumer and believes that this is where they find freedom. But in reality, they live dependent on what others have created. The two percent create what others depend on. They shift the balance of power by becoming creators themselves. Neuroscience shows the difference in the way the brain constructs meaning. Meaning does not arise through passive consumption, but through active creation. Studies show that people who create something—be it a work of art, a business, a garden, or a thought—experience a deeper form of satisfaction than those who only consume. This satisfaction is not linked to external stimuli, but to the feeling of having influence, making a difference, leaving a mark. The average person deprives themselves of this form of meaning because they channel their energy into consumption. The two percent experience it every day because they know that value creation is the foundation of true fulfillment. From a sociological perspective, the consumer is a figure that has been deliberately shaped by culture.

Modern societies increasingly define identity through consumption: what clothes you wear, what car you drive, what devices you use, what experiences you buy. The average person adopts this definition and makes it their truth. Their self-worth is determined by external factors, by the symbols they buy. The two percent break this mechanism. They define themselves not by symbols, but by substance. Their value lies not in what they possess, but in what they produce. As a result, they are not at the mercy of culture, but stand above it. From a philosophical point of view, this leads to a fundamental question: Do you live to take, or do you live to give? The average person chooses, mostly unconsciously, to take.

They see life as a resource to be consumed. The two percent see it as a stage on which they can contribute something. For them, humans are not consumers, but creators. This change in perspective changes everything: their view of work, time, relationships, their own existence. From a spiritual point of view, the path from consumer to producer ultimately means a return to the original nature of humans. Humans are creative from birth. Children paint, build, invent, and create worlds. It is culture that turns them into passive consumers by devaluing creativity and glorifying consumption. The average person thus loses touch with their inner creator. The two percent preserve or reactivate it. For them, every day is a creative act – not only in material terms, but also in spiritual terms.

They produce thoughts, experiences, possibilities. Spiritually speaking, they live in harmony with the creative principle of life, while the average person remains in the illusion of consumption. Here, too, it becomes clear that the separation between consumer and producer is not only economic, but also existential. Those who consume remain dependent because they live off what others create. Those who produce become free because they generate value from within themselves. The average person remains a consumer because it is convenient and culturally accepted. The two percent choose the harder but liberating path of the producer – and that is precisely why they do not belong to the average. If you look at the path from consumer to producer in depth, you realize that it is not purely an economic decision, but an inner transformation that affects all levels of human existence. The average person lives in a state of dependence. They focus their lives on what they receive from outside and thus lose awareness of their own creative power.

Consumption becomes their identity: they believe that they are what they own, what they consume, what they show. The two percent, on the other hand, break this pattern. They understand that true identity lies not in taking but in giving, not in consumption but in creation. They do not live in dependence but in self-efficacy. From a psychological perspective, this step is so difficult because it involves a reordering of inner values. Consumers seek recognition and fulfillment through external things. They measure themselves by symbols: clothing, technology, status objects. But these symbols quickly fade, and with them, inner stability. That's why they constantly have to keep adding more. The two percent break free from this spiral by anchoring their value not in having, but in being and doing. They experience joy in creating something, regardless of whether it receives immediate applause or not. This joy is more stable because it does not depend on the approval of others, but arises from their own actions. From an economic perspective, the difference is dramatic. Consumers contribute to the functioning of the economy, but they do not determine it. They respond to offers, prices, and advertising. Producers, on the other hand, set the rules.

They create products that others buy, services that others use, ideas that shape others. This gives them influence and freedom. The average person spends their entire life spending money on what others create and remains dependent on wages, prices, and markets. The two percent create themselves and thereby shift the balance of power. They build structures that serve not only themselves but also others. From a neuroscientific perspective, the difference can be seen in the activation of different networks in the brain. Consumption primarily stimulates the reward system, which generates short-term pleasure but quickly fades away. Production, on the other hand, activates the network for self-efficacy and meaning. Those who create something experience not only joy, but also a deep sense of meaning. This feeling has a stabilizing effect on the entire nervous system. It gives life direction and anchors the self. The average person deprives themselves of this feeling because they lose their energy in consumption. The two percent experience it because they channel their energy into creation.

From a sociological perspective, the fixation on consumption leads to a culture that alienates people. Advertising and the media create the image that happiness can be bought. But behind this image lies a void that demands ever more consumption without ever being fulfilled. The average person lives in this void and defends it because it is familiar. The two percent break the cycle by asking not "What can I buy?" but "What can I contribute?" This change in perspective changes their position in society. They are no longer driven, but creators. Philosophically speaking, this touches on the question of the meaning of life. Is life a stage on which one consumes, or a workshop in which one creates? The average person lives as if life were a series of consumer experiences. They work to buy things and buy things to forget that they are unhappy. The two percent see life as an opportunity to leave their mark.

They know that in the end, you are not measured by what you have owned, but by what you have created. From a spiritual perspective, the path from consumer to producer ultimately means a return to the creative essence of human beings. Every person has the ability to create—ideas, works, relationships, realities. But this ability is buried by the culture of consumption. The average person loses access to it because they direct their energy outward. The two percent cultivate this access. For them, every creative act is an expression of their connection with life itself. They experience themselves as part of a larger creative movement that does not end in consumption, but in constant renewal. Here, too, it becomes clear that the difference between consumer and producer is not only a difference in action, but in being. Those who consume live in dependence because they live off what others have created.

Those who produce live in freedom because they generate value from within themselves. The average person remains trapped in the pattern of consumption because they do not want to see the emptiness behind it. The two percent recognize this emptiness and choose the path of creation—even if it is more difficult. But it is precisely this path that gives them the independence that most people are denied. If we take a closer look at the relationship between consumption and production, it becomes clear that this is not just an economic distinction, but a fundamental question of power and freedom. Consumers are always in the position of receiving. They wait for others to offer them something; they react to markets, advertising, and trends. Their role is passive. Producers, on the other hand, are active creators. They create what others will consume, they set trends, they define markets. Their role is active and creative. The average person remains trapped in the passive role, while the two percent choose the active role. This choice changes their entire lives because they are no longer dependent on external circumstances, but create circumstances themselves. From a psychological perspective, the passive role of the consumer is comfortable because it offers the illusion of security. Those who consume do not have to bear the risk of something going wrong. They buy what works, they use what is available, they live in systems that others have built. But this security is deceptive.

It deprives people of the experience of self-efficacy. The average person sacrifices freedom for convenience and does not realize that this makes them increasingly dependent. The two percent are willing to endure the uncertainty of production. They know that every creative endeavor involves risk—that a project can fail, that an idea may not work out. But they accept this uncertainty because they know that only it enables true freedom. From an economic perspective, the difference is evident in the distribution of wealth. Consumers spend money, producers earn money. Consumers finance the dreams of others, producers realize their own. The average person lives their life according to the logic: "I earn to buy." The two percent live according to the logic: "I create to multiply." This shifts the balance of power. Those who consume work for the prosperity of others. Those who produce work for their own prosperity and that of many others. Over years and decades, this difference adds up to a gap that is almost impossible to close. From a neuroscientific point of view, producing is associated with a stronger sense of meaning because it puts the brain into a different mode of functioning. Consumption activates the limbic system, which generates short-term pleasure. Production activates the prefrontal cortex and the dopaminergic reward system in a more sustainable way. Those who produce experience meaning because they are not just reacting, but creating. This feeling is not fleeting, but deeply rooted. The average person deprives themselves of this feeling because they waste their energy on constant consumption. The two percent experience it because they invest their energy in creating new value. Sociologically speaking, the difference means that consumers support society as it is, while producers change societies. Consumers keep existing systems running. They buy what is offered, they adapt, they reinforce trends. Producers, on the other hand, break patterns. They bring new things into the world, they create alternatives, they change structures. The average keeps the world stable, the two percent change it. It is this power of change that gives them not only freedom but also influence.

From a philosophical point of view, this difference touches on the question of autonomy. Is a person free when they consume what they want? Or are they only free when they create what they themselves consider meaningful? The average person confuses consumer choice with freedom. They believe they are free because they can choose between products. But this choice is in fact an illusion, because it only takes place within the limits set by others. The two percent see that freedom does not lie in choosing from what is on offer, but in creating offers themselves. They know that true freedom lies not in consumption, but in creation. From a spiritual perspective, production is an expression of the creative nature of human beings. Consumption separates people from their essence because it makes them dependent on external things.

Production connects them with their essence because it is an expression of their inner creativity. The average person lives in separation, the two percent in connection. Production means coming into harmony with the creative principle of life. It is an act of unity with something greater than oneself. Here, too, it becomes clear that the difference between consumer and producer is not only economic, but existential. Those who consume live in dependence. Those who produce live in freedom. The average person defends their role as a consumer because it is comfortable and familiar. But this role is their prison. The two percent choose the more difficult but more liberating role of producer—and that is precisely what makes them the few who do not remain average. The transformation from consumer to producer is one of the most profound changes a person can make, and it explains why the two percent of the population live and think so differently from the 98 percent. The average person remains in the role of consumer because they do not realize that this role keeps them dependent. They believe that consumption means freedom because they can seemingly choose what they buy, where they travel, and what services they use. But this choice is not real freedom, but an illusion.

For as long as they only consume, they live within the boundaries that others have created for them. True freedom only arises when they themselves create—when they generate value that goes beyond their own consumption. From a psychological perspective, this step means that a person reprograms their reward system. Consumers live in a cycle of instant gratification: buy, enjoy, lose interest, desire again. This loop keeps them trapped and weakens their ability to be self-effective. Producers, on the other hand, train their psyche to derive joy from the process of creation. The two percent experience their greatest satisfaction not in buying, but in creating. They know that the path is longer, that reward comes later, that failure is part of the process. But it is precisely this delay that makes the joy deeper, because it is rooted in the act of creation itself and does not depend on external stimuli. Economically, producing means changing sides – from the demand side to the supply side. Consumers react to markets, producers shape them.

Those who consume are constantly giving up resources. Those who produce attract resources. Over the years, this difference becomes more pronounced. The average person becomes the driver of demand, but remains dependent on the products that others have created. The two percent create themselves, they fill markets with new products, they set the conditions. That is why their prosperity grows, while the average barely survives despite working. From a neuroscientific point of view, producing generates a different quality of happiness. While consumption provides the quick dopamine rush of the reward loop, production activates the deeper system of meaning, purpose, and self-efficacy. This happiness lasts longer, is more stable, and less dependent on external circumstances. Those who create anchor their identity in doing, not in having. The average person deprives themselves of this experience because they lose their energy in the cycle of consumption. The two percent, on the other hand, nourish their nervous system with the power of creation, and this power makes them resilient, creative, and free.

From a sociological perspective, the producer is a figure who changes societies. Consumers secure the existing, producers create the new. The average person keeps systems stable by supporting them through their consumption. The two percent break patterns by introducing something new. Their role is revolutionary, even if it seems inconspicuous in everyday life. They change cultures, markets, and institutions by no longer just taking, but giving. Their creative power shifts the balance and opens up new possibilities for others. From a philosophical perspective, this raises a fundamental question: Do humans live to consume or to create? The average person answers this question implicitly by consuming throughout their life. They work to buy and buy to forget that they are empty. The two percent answer the question consciously: they live to create. For them, life is a stage on which they leave their mark. This attitude gives their existence meaning, depth, and direction.

Finally, from a spiritual perspective, production is an expression of unity with life itself. Life is creative. Nature constantly produces new things; growth is its principle. Consumption separates people from this principle because it reduces them to taking. Production reconnects them to it because it puts them in the role of co-creator. The average person lives in separation, the two percent in connection. Producing means understanding yourself as part of the creative force of life—and that gives you inner freedom that no amount of consumption can ever replace. At the end of this chapter, it becomes clear that the path from consumer to producer is the decisive step that separates the average from the two percent. It requires courage, patience, and a willingness to leave comfort zones. It means taking responsibility, taking risks, and accepting uncertainty. But it gives something that is priceless: freedom. The average person remains a consumer and thus dependent. The two percent become producers – and therefore independent.

Notes:

Notes:

Chapter 19: Transformation of thinking – steps to inner independence

There is a point in life when the difference between the 98 percent and the two percent can no longer be explained by external circumstances, origin, or opportunities, but exclusively by the way of thinking. Transformation does not begin in external structures, but in the inner world of the individual. Those who remain average do so because they do not change their way of thinking. They live in thought patterns that keep them dependent. Those who break free from these constraints and become one of the few who achieve true freedom undergo a transformation of thinking that goes far beyond superficial motivational slogans. It is a quiet but radical process in which one's own thinking is completely reorganized. From a psychological point of view, it is beliefs that structure thinking. The average person carries beliefs such as: “Security is the most important thing,” “I am dependent on circumstances,” “I cannot achieve more than what is given to me.” These beliefs are invisible, but they guide every decision, every action, every feeling.

They shape the reality of the average person. The two percent have learned to question and override such beliefs. They replace dependence with personal responsibility, fear with trust, limitation with possibility. This transformation is not a quick act, but a process that requires patience and awareness. But it is a prerequisite for any form of external independence. Neuroscience explains this through the plasticity of the brain. The human brain is not rigid, but malleable. Synapses strengthen where thoughts and actions are repeated over and over again. The average person thinks in the same patterns, day after day, year after year. This reinforces neural pathways that keep them dependent. The two percent, on the other hand, consciously use this plasticity. They train their brains with new thoughts, new perspectives, and new decisions. This creates new neural networks that enable different perceptions and actions in the long term. Transformation of thinking is therefore not only a psychological phenomenon, but also a biological one. From a sociological perspective, it is culture that shapes thought patterns. The average person adopts the narratives dictated by their society: that you have to work in order to consume, that security should be prioritized over freedom, that risks should be avoided because they are dangerous. These narratives are rarely consciously questioned because they are supported by the majority. The two percent question them radically. They ask: "Is that really true?", "Does this idea serve me?", "Is that a truth – or just a cultural convention?" This ability to see through collective beliefs is one of the most powerful steps towards inner independence.

From a philosophical point of view, the transformation of thinking is a return to freedom of mind. The average person lives in a mental prison whose bars are made of thoughts they never chose for themselves. They believe they are free, but they only move within the boundaries that others have set for them. The two percent realize that thoughts are not the truth, but tools. They use their thinking consciously instead of being used by it. This freedom of mind is the very core of inner independence. It means no longer being determined by inherited patterns, but consciously choosing how to think and act. Finally, from a spiritual point of view, the transformation of thinking is an opening to a deeper dimension of being. The average person identifies completely with their thoughts. They believe they are what they think. The two percent realize that they are more than their thoughts. They experience themselves as consciousness that has thoughts but is not possessed by them. This distance from their own thoughts gives them inner freedom. They can let go of old patterns because they know that they are not their thoughts, but rather the observer of those thoughts. At the end of this section, it becomes clear that transforming one's thinking is not a superficial act, but a radical reorganization of one's inner space. It means letting go of old beliefs, forming new neural pathways, seeing through cultural narratives, gaining philosophical freedom, and achieving spiritual awareness. The average person remains mediocre because they do not take this step. The two percent become free because they have the courage to fundamentally change their way of thinking. The transformation of thinking is not a sudden process, but a gradual one that takes place quietly and invisibly within, long before it becomes visible on the outside.

The average person does not recognize this because they want to measure change primarily by external results: income, possessions, status, recognition. But inner transformation cannot be immediately grasped in such categories. It begins quietly, with a change in perspective, with a shift in how the world is perceived and interpreted. This is precisely where the first crucial difference between the two percent and the rest lies: the few start with their thinking and not with external circumstances. Psychologically speaking, thinking is not neutral. Every thought carries an emotional charge that drives action. The average person repeats thoughts that generate fear, scarcity, and dependence. These thoughts form an invisible framework that determines their life. A person who believes deep down that they cannot live without security will never develop the courage to break new ground. Those who believe that prosperity is only possible through luck or inheritance will never seriously try to create prosperity. These thoughts act like self-fulfilling prophecies. The two percent break this cycle by consciously choosing their thoughts. They decide which inner beliefs they nurture and which they unlearn. In this way, they gradually free themselves from the tyranny of the unconscious.

From a neuroscientific perspective, this change involves the rewiring of neural pathways. The brain is plastic: it changes according to the thoughts and actions that a person regularly repeats. The average person reinforces old patterns through constant repetition. They think the same thoughts every day, say the same sentences, and confirm the same beliefs. Their brain thus becomes a machine that always produces the same reality. The two percent consciously use this plasticity. They train their brains with new impulses by asking different questions, taking new perspectives, and making different decisions. This gradually creates new neural networks that enable freedom instead of dependence. Sociologically, this process is reflected in the way people adopt cultural narratives. The average person believes what everyone else believes.

They adopt statements such as "You have to work hard to make ends meet" or "Security is the most important thing in life" without ever questioning them. These beliefs are so deeply rooted in culture that they seem like laws of nature. But they are not laws of nature, they are social constructs. The two percent recognize this and dare to break these constructs. They allow themselves to believe other stories—stories of freedom, of creativity, of possibilities. By telling other stories, they begin to live other realities. Philosophically speaking, this is about the difference between a deterministic and an open worldview. The average person lives as if their future is predetermined, as if their life is fixed by their background, education, social status, or external circumstances. This attitude relieves them because it takes away responsibility. But it keeps them trapped in powerlessness. The two percent understand that the future is not predetermined, but can be shaped. They see thinking not as a mirror of reality, but as a tool with which reality is shaped. This insight transforms their entire attitude. Where the average person sees limits, they see possibilities. Where the average person sees a prison, they see a door. From a spiritual perspective, the transformation of thinking is the step from identifying with thoughts to consciousness that transcends thoughts. The average person believes they are their thoughts. When they think, "I am weak," they believe they are weak. When they think, "I can't do this," they believe they are incapable. The two percent recognize that thoughts are only phenomena that come and go.

They are not the truth, but possibilities. By gaining this distance, they are free to choose which thoughts they give meaning to and which they do not. This step gives them a freedom that goes deeper than any external independence. It becomes very clear: transforming thinking means seeing through the invisible mechanisms that keep the average person dependent. It means letting go of old beliefs, establishing new neural patterns, questioning cultural narratives, gaining philosophical freedom, and developing spiritual awareness. The average person remains trapped in old patterns because they do not consciously shape their thinking. The two percent become free because they have the courage to renew their world of thought. The inner transformation of thinking is not just a theoretical idea, but a practical process that can take place at any moment. The average person believes that change is difficult and time-consuming, that it takes years of preparation, external circumstances, or extraordinary opportunities to become truly free. But in truth, change begins with a single moment: the moment when a person realizes that they no longer have to consider their thoughts to be absolute truths. This realization is the seed of inner independence. Because as soon as you understand that thoughts do not reflect reality, but create reality, a space opens up in which new possibilities become visible. From a psychological perspective, the power of this step is evident in the dissolution of old thought patterns. The average person considers their beliefs to be irrefutable. They say things like "I'm not good enough,"

"I have no choice," "It's always been this way and it will always be this way." Such thoughts act like invisible chains that restrict their freedom of action. The two percent, on the other hand, develop the ability to recognize these chains. They question whether such statements are actually true – and discover that they are just repeated thoughts that have become deeply ingrained. By refusing to continue to regard these thoughts as irrefutable, they open themselves up to new scope for action. This inner freedom radically changes their lives. From a neuroscientific point of view, this is a process of neuroplasticity. The brain is not fixed on maintaining old patterns forever. Rather, new synaptic connections are formed when a person begins to think different thoughts and have different experiences. The average person unconsciously repeats old patterns, thereby reinforcing neural pathways that steer them in the same direction over and over again. The two percent consciously take other paths. They train their brains like a muscle by consciously adopting new perspectives. This creates new neural pathways that become stronger over time, while the old ones fade away. Transformation of thinking therefore literally means rewiring the brain. From a sociological perspective, the power of this transformation is particularly evident in the fact that a person can detach themselves from the collective ways of thinking of their culture. The average person is trapped in what everyone believes.

They adopt social norms without questioning them because they are confirmed by the majority. They trust the masses more than themselves. The two percent develop the courage to think against the grain. They ask questions that others do not ask. They question what everyone else takes for granted. They know that truth does not lie in the majority, but in the clarity of their own consciousness. In this way, they free themselves from the invisible nets of cultural conditioning. Philosophically speaking, transforming one's thinking means disempowering the authority of thoughts themselves.

The average person is a prisoner of their own inner voice. This voice tells them what they can and cannot do, what is possible and what is not. They believe it blindly. The two percent, on the other hand, learn to recognize this voice as one of many influences, not as the final authority. They experience that behind the voice lies a greater consciousness that is free of judgments and limitations. This experience is the beginning of true inner freedom. For when thoughts are no longer unconscious rulers, they can serve as tools—and tools can be used purposefully. From a spiritual perspective, this process is a return to the inner observer. The average person identifies with the flow of their thoughts and is carried away by it. They have no distance from what is happening in their mind.

The two percent, on the other hand, discover that they are more than this flow. They realize that there is an inner space that remains unchanged while thoughts come and go. From this space, they can choose which thoughts have meaning and which do not. This gives them a freedom that is not bound to external circumstances. Again, a clear idea: the transformation of thinking is not an abstract ideal, but a practical path that is open to everyone. The difference between the average and the exceptional lies not in the possibilities, but in the willingness to consciously shape one's own thinking. Those who question their old beliefs, who train their brains to think in new ways, who detach themselves from cultural narratives, who philosophically remove the authority of their thoughts and spiritually discover their inner observer, become free. The average person remains in their old patterns because they do not recognize that they themselves create them. The two percent become free because they have the courage to transform the source of their thinking. The transformation of thinking is a quiet but powerful process that goes much deeper than it appears at first glance. It means not only replacing old beliefs with new ones, but fundamentally renewing the entire way you perceive yourself, other people, and the world. The average person fails at this because they try to change external circumstances without changing their thinking. They believe that they will be free if they earn more, if they have different relationships, if they are lucky.

But as long as they remain trapped in old patterns of thinking, their problems will repeat themselves in new forms. Freedom does not begin on the outside, but on the inside – in the ability to transform one's own way of thinking. From a psychological point of view, this process is closely linked to the ability to be cognitively flexible. The average person remains stuck in rigid patterns. They view the world through the same categories they have known since childhood. They think in fixed terms such as "this is right" and "this is wrong," "this works" and "this doesn't work." This rigid way of thinking provides them with orientation, but it limits their possibilities. The two percent have developed the ability to think flexibly. They can let go of old perspectives and adopt new ones. This flexibility allows them to see opportunities where others only see obstacles. They know that every situation allows for different interpretations – and they choose the interpretation that opens up freedom for them. Neuroscience explains this ability through the adaptability of the prefrontal cortex. This part of the brain is responsible for reevaluating information, inhibiting old patterns, and opening up new options for action. The average person hardly uses this ability because they unconsciously remain stuck in familiar patterns. The two percent train their prefrontal cortex by consciously trying out new ways of thinking. They expose themselves to unfamiliar situations, question old assumptions, and allow their brains to build new neural networks. In this way, transformation becomes not just a philosophical concept, but a neurological reality.

From a sociological perspective, transforming one's thinking means breaking free from the thought structures of a society that are characterized by fear and control. The average person lives by rules that keep them small. They believe that they must prioritize security over freedom, that risk should always be avoided, and that they must conform in order to be accepted. These rules are not natural, but socially constructed. The two percent see through them and dare to think differently. They ask the question: "What if these rules are not true?" This question alone is enough to lay the foundation for inner independence. From a philosophical point of view, the transformation of thinking is an act of self-liberation. The average person is a slave to their own thoughts. They believe they must follow them because they appear to be true. But truth in thinking is relative. Every thought is a lens through which one views the world—and lenses can be changed. The two percent understand that freedom does not mean having no thoughts, but being free to choose which thoughts to give meaning to. They turn their thinking into a tool instead of being at its mercy. From a spiritual point of view, this process is a return to inner silence. The average person lives in a constant stream of thoughts. They identify with this noise and lose the ability to distinguish between themselves and their thoughts. The two percent learn to step behind their thoughts, into the space of silence from which clarity arises. In this silence, they realize that they are not their thoughts, but the consciousness that perceives them. This realization is the deepest step toward inner independence. This section makes it clear that transformation of thinking is the prerequisite for all further steps. Those who think like the average will act like the average—and lead the same life as the average. However, those who have the courage to transform their thoughts change not only their actions, but their entire existence. The average remain trapped in their patterns because they do not recognize the source of their dependence. The two percent, on the other hand, become free because they have the courage to start where true change begins: in thinking. The inner transformation of thinking is only complete when a person realizes that they have the choice to no longer focus their consciousness on old patterns, but on a new reality that they actively create.

The average person does not recognize this freedom of choice. For them, their thoughts are like laws of nature: they believe they must obey them because they are so familiar and seemingly without alternative. They say, "That's just the way I am," and don't realize that they are chaining themselves to thoughts. The two percent have understood that no thought is final. They have learned to see their inner reality as a field that can be shaped—through consciousness, through attention, through decision. This step is the decisive transition from inner dependence to inner independence. Psychologically speaking, this is the highest form of self-control. While the average person thinks their emotions are the result of external circumstances, the two percent know that emotions arise from internal evaluations. A problem is never just the problem itself, but the meaning a person gives it. The average person remains trapped in meanings that keep them small: they see obstacles where there are opportunities and threats where there are chances. The two percent train themselves to consciously choose different meanings. They understand that a setback is not a failure, but an opportunity to adapt. They know that uncertainty does not mean danger, but freedom. This ability to redefine meanings is a central step in transforming the way we think. From a neuroscientific perspective, this demonstrates the power of reframing – reevaluation. Studies show that the brain does not respond to objective reality, but to the interpretation that a person gives to that reality. The average person lives in rigid interpretations that activate their stress systems and limit their possibilities. The two percent have learned to train their brains in new ways. They reevaluate situations, give them different meanings, and in doing so calm their nervous systems, expand their scope of action, and develop resilience. In this sense, transforming thinking means not changing the world, but changing the way the brain processes it. From a sociological perspective, it is also about the ability to break free from collective thinking traps. The majority interprets the world according to patterns of fear: one must play it safe, conform, follow the mainstream. These patterns are repeatedly reinforced by the media, institutions, and habits. The average person accepts them unquestioningly and believes them to be self-evident. The two percent develop the ability to see through these patterns.

They recognize that the majority opinion is rarely an expression of truth, but rather an expression of habit and fear. In doing so, they create a space for thinking that functions independently of the masses—a space of inner independence that enables them to act and live differently. From a philosophical perspective, the transformation of thinking is an act of self-determination. The average person lives in a world shaped by foreign thoughts: from parents, teachers, the media, politicians. They consider these adopted thoughts to be their own and thus lose their sovereignty. The two percent realize that they are not obliged to keep these foreign thoughts. They decide to choose their own thoughts, create their own narratives, and live their own truth. This step is the real beginning of freedom: no longer being a product of foreign ways of thinking, but a conscious creator of one's own mind. From a spiritual perspective, the complete transformation of thinking means that people no longer consider their thoughts to be the center of their identity. The average person identifies with every thought that arises and thus lives in constant unrest. The two percent realize that they are not their thoughts, but the consciousness that perceives these thoughts. This realization brings deep peace.

For when one knows that thoughts come and go without touching the true self, a freedom arises that is independent of circumstances, opinions, and external boundaries. This freedom is true inner independence. At the end of this chapter, it becomes very clear: transformation of thinking is not a question of intelligence, education, or background, but a question of choice. Every person can decide to question their thoughts, choose new meanings, let go of old patterns, and detach themselves from identifying with their thinking. The average person does not do this and remains trapped in inner dependence. The two percent consistently follow this path—and achieve inner freedom, which becomes the basis for outer freedom. Those who transform their thinking change their lives. Those who do not remain where they are.

Notes:

Notes:

Chapter 20: Breaking out of the average – How anyone can start walking the path of the 2%

For many people, the idea of breaking out of the average sounds like a distant dream, like a possibility that may be open to others, but not to themselves. For the essence of the average lies precisely in the fact that it sees itself as the norm, as an inescapable reality that defines the framework of life. But this framework is not natural, it is man-made. It arises from habits of thought, from cultural narratives, from unconscious beliefs that are passed down through generations. Those who begin to recognize these invisible threads feel for the first time the possibility of cutting them. The exit from the average does not begin with external wealth, nor with a special talent, nor with a stroke of luck—it begins with an inner decision.

This decision is perhaps the most difficult step because it means a radical departure from familiar security. The average person lives in a web of comfort and fear. Comfort, because it is easier to do what everyone else does. Fear, because any deviation from the norm means uncertainty. However, those who want to belong to the two percent who become truly independent must be prepared to leave this web. They must recognize that the supposed security of the average is in fact an invisible prison, and that freedom does not lie where everyone else is, but where only a few have the courage to take a different path. From a psychological perspective, this step is a break with the so-called social comparison logic. The average person is guided by what others do and adopts their standards. They do not ask, "What do I really want? " but "What are others doing, and how can I belong?" This orientation ensures belonging, but it comes at the cost of independence. The two percent break away from this dynamic. They begin to develop their own internal standards. They allow themselves to think differently, even if it means swimming against the tide. These internal standards are the first anchor that leads them out of the average. Neuroscientifically, this step is reflected in a change in the so-called default mode network, the neural network responsible for self-reflection and inner narratives. In the average person, this network is programmed for repetition: they think what they have always thought, they tell themselves the same stories about themselves, they confirm the same limits. The exit begins when a person starts to change these stories. When they no longer say, "I can't," but rather, "Maybe more is possible." When they no longer ask, "What if I fail?" but rather, "What if I succeed?" These small shifts in thinking change the neural architecture—and open up paths that were previously invisible. Sociologically speaking, breaking out is an act of detachment from collective expectations. Societies have invisible mechanisms with which they ensure conformity: norms, rewards, sanctions. The average person adapts to these mechanisms because they believe that deviation is dangerous. But history shows that progress has always come from those who did not remain average, but questioned the norms. Those who follow the path of the two percent must therefore be prepared to question these collective expectations. They must recognize that conformity ensures recognition but prevents freedom. From a philosophical perspective, stepping outside the norm is an act of personal responsibility.

The average person lives with the attitude that life owes them something. They wait for opportunities, for better circumstances, for outside help. But this attitude keeps them passive. The two percent take responsibility. They understand that no one will come to save them. That freedom is not given, but taken. That the first step is not to expect something, but to act themselves. This philosophical shift—from passivity to personal responsibility—is the foundation of breaking away. Finally, from a spiritual perspective, breaking away is an awakening. The average person sleeps in routines, in thought patterns, in a world they do not question. They live as if on autopilot, convinced that there is no alternative. Opting out is the awakening to the realization that they are free to start anew at any time. That they are more than their thoughts, more than their habits, more than their past. This awakening gives them an inner freedom that no external power can take away. It is the moment when a person realizes: "I am not condemned to remain average. I can choose to live differently." Clearly and unambiguously: Breaking out of the average is not a mysterious secret, but a path that is open to everyone. It begins with a decision—the decision to no longer remain within the confines of the familiar.

This decision is difficult because it means letting go: letting go of security, of conformity, of old stories. But it is the first step toward the freedom that the two percent have found. And this step is possible—at any time, for anyone who has the courage to take it. The path out of mediocrity is not a sudden leap into a completely new reality, but a slow, steady shift in inner attitude and, with it, outer decisions. Those who live an average life today already have the same potential as those who belong to the two percent. The difference lies not in innate talent, intelligence, or background. The difference lies solely in the fact that the average person leaves their potential untapped, while the two percent begin to consciously activate it. Breaking out of the average therefore does not begin with grand external deeds, but with the quiet discipline of realigning one's own thoughts, feelings, and actions. From a psychological perspective, this is primarily about the ability to perceive oneself. The average person lives in patterns that they hardly notice. They react to external impulses without realizing that they themselves are the ones who give these impulses meaning. Their thoughts run like an internal program that they have never checked. They think what they have always thought and wonder why their life remains the same. The two percent, on the other hand, develop the ability to observe themselves. They recognize when a thought is holding them back, when an emotion is paralyzing them, when an old pattern is trapping them in dependency. This self-awareness is the first step, because you can only change what you consciously recognize.

In neuroscience, this ability manifests itself in the activation of what is known as metacognition—thinking about thinking. The brain is capable of observing itself and reflecting on its own processes. The average person hardly uses this ability. They live identified with their thoughts as if they were absolute truths. The two percent consciously train their metacognition. They take a step back and view their own thought patterns from a distance. This creates an inner space in which change becomes possible. Without this space, the old patterns repeat themselves over and over again. With it, the freedom to choose something new opens up. From a sociological perspective, breaking away from the average always means breaking with the unwritten laws of the majority. Anyone who starts to go their own way will encounter resistance. Friends, family, colleagues—they all reflect the expectations of society and encourage individuals to remain average. "Be reasonable,"

"Don't take any risks," "Do what everyone else does" – such phrases are the voice of the collective that wants to keep the individual within the norm. The two percent do not meet this resistance with rebellion, but with clarity. They know that they do not have to define themselves in relation to others, but for themselves. Breaking out of the average therefore does not mean fighting the world, but detaching oneself from it internally. Philosophically speaking, this process is a step toward autonomy of the mind. The average person believes that they are only free when they enjoy external freedoms – the right to vote, to travel, to consume.

But true freedom begins within. It arises when one is no longer a slave to one's own habits, fears, and cultural narratives. Breaking away from the average means no longer allowing one's mind to be dominated by inherited patterns, but instead becoming the architect of one's own thinking. This autonomy is the core of all independence. From a spiritual perspective, stepping out of the norm is ultimately an awakening to the realization that humans are more than their role in the collective. The average person identifies with their position in the social fabric: with their work, their status, their relationships. They believe that they are only what others see in them. The two percent recognize that these roles are masks, but not the true self. They sense that there is a freedom within them that is not affected by external attributions. Those who step out of the average enter this inner space of freedom and begin to live from it. This section also makes it clear that stepping out of the average is not an external act, but an inner journey. It begins with self-awareness, with the ability to recognize one's own patterns. It requires a willingness to remain clear-headed in the face of pressure from the majority. It requires rediscovering the autonomy of the mind and shaping one's own life no longer from adopted roles, but from the depths of one's own consciousness. Every person has this possibility within them. But only those who are willing to take the quiet, uncomfortable, but liberating path will actually walk it.

The idea of following the path of the two percent initially provokes resistance in many people. It is as if an invisible protective mechanism kicks in, whispering: "This is not for you, it is only for a select few." But this mechanism is itself part of average thinking. It serves to preserve the status quo and keep the individual in their comfort zone. The truth is that the path is not reserved for the few. Every person has the potential to break out. The only difference is whether they find the courage to take the first steps. Psychologically speaking, courage is not an innate privilege, but a trainable state. The average person waits for fear to disappear before acting. But fear does not disappear by waiting, but by acting. The two percent have understood that courage is not the absence of fear, but the decision to act despite fear. They train their minds to no longer be paralyzed by the fear of uncertainty, but to understand this uncertainty as a space of freedom. Breaking out of the average therefore begins when a person decides to no longer be ruled by fear.

Neuroscience explains this by the way the brain processes threats. The average person lives under the constant dominance of the amygdala—the part of the brain that assesses danger and triggers alarm. This alarm system was essential for survival in evolutionary terms, but in modern societies it reacts to situations that do not pose a real danger. A professional risk, a financial experiment, a new path – all of these trigger the same stress patterns as an encounter with a wild animal once did. The average person follows this alarm and retreats. The two percent have learned to activate the prefrontal cortex – the part of the brain that reflects, soberly assesses risks, and makes conscious decisions. This shifts the inner balance: fear remains, but it loses its power. From a sociological perspective, moving toward the two percent means breaking away from the collective culture of fear. Societies function by rewarding conformity and sanctioning deviation. The average person fears not only personal failure, but also the loss of recognition. They remain average because they want to belong. The two percent dare to be different. They endure the skepticism, the incomprehension, sometimes even the ridicule of others. They know that belonging to the masses comes at a high price: the loss of inner freedom. They would rather stand alone with their clarity than be part of the collective with their captivity. Philosophically speaking, this step is a decision for authenticity. The average person often lives a foreign life. They adopt goals that are not their own—career paths, status symbols, life plans that have been imposed on them from outside.

They chase after something that does not fulfill them internally, just to meet expectations. Opting out means ending this external control. It means asking yourself, "What is my true path?" and having the courage to follow it, even if it doesn't fit the patterns of the majority. This authenticity is at the heart of transformation – and it is the reason why the path of the two percent feels so radically different from the average life. From a spiritual perspective, stepping out is ultimately a step toward truth. The average person lives in illusions: illusions of security, of control, of conformity. They cling to things that have no permanence and call them reality. The two percent have understood that the only true reality is the inner freedom with which one can face any circumstance. Those who take this step stop defending illusions and begin to live in harmony with what is unchanging – the consciousness that lies behind all thoughts, roles, and patterns. It also becomes clear again: The path of the two percent is not a path without fear, uncertainty, or doubt.

It is a path on which one learns to reinterpret these experiences. The exit from the average happens when a person realizes that they no longer have to wait for circumstances to be perfect. It happens when they realize that they can start today, right now, right here – not with grand gestures, but with the simple decision to no longer be ruled by the thinking of the masses. Every step thereafter is a repetition of this decision. Step by step, you remove yourself from the circle of mediocrity – and step by step, you approach the inner freedom that defines the two percent. The path out of mediocrity is not a straight line, but a process full of tension, contradictions, and inner struggles. Those who begin to break away inevitably encounter the power of old patterns that persist because they promise security. Mediocrity thrives on repetition, and any deviation from it provokes resistance—not only from outside, but also from within. This is because the human brain loves the familiar, seeks stability, and wants to save energy by falling back on what it knows. That is why new paths initially feel uncertain, uncomfortable, even dangerous. But it is precisely at this threshold between the known and the unknown that a person decides whether to remain average or take the step toward inner independence.

From a psychological perspective, this threshold moment is of utmost importance. The average person almost automatically interprets the unknown as a threat. Old beliefs reinforce this interpretation: "The risk is too great," "I'm not good enough," "Others can do it, but I can't." These inner voices are nothing more than manifestations of past experiences that have become deeply ingrained. But they are not truths, merely memories that have solidified into patterns. The two percent have learned not to blindly believe these voices. They recognize them as echoes of the past and consciously decide not to give them power over their present. Neuroscience explains this dynamic through the workings of the limbic system, which recognizes danger early on and sounds the alarm, often long before the prefrontal cortex has rationally assessed the situation.

For the average person, the limbic system remains the undisputed ruler: Any uncertainty triggers flight. The two percent, however, train themselves to pause during this phase, to perceive the alarm but not to obey it automatically. They consciously use the prefrontal cortex to reassess whether the danger is real or just a reflex. This ability to open up a space between impulse and action is the key to transformation. From a sociological perspective, this threshold is also reflected in the social environment. The average person remains embedded in structures that confirm their old identity. Friends, family, colleagues—they all often unconsciously keep them in the role they have played up to now.

Those who change hold up a mirror to others, showing them that they too could change – and that creates discomfort. That is why those who step out of the average often encounter resistance. Not because others mean them harm, but because their change challenges their own self-image. The two percent understand this mechanism and do not take it personally. They know that resistance is a sign that they are moving forward while others are standing still. From a philosophical point of view, this threshold is the point at which it becomes clear whether a person is willing to take responsibility. The average person retreats and justifies their decision with external reasons: “It wasn't the right time,” “The circumstances were too difficult,” “Others held me back.”

But in truth, it is always an internal decision. The two percent take radical responsibility. They know that the timing will never be perfect, that circumstances will always remain challenging, that resistance will never disappear. That's why they act anyway. This responsibility transforms them from driven individuals into creators. From a spiritual perspective, this moment is an initiation. Those who stand at the threshold experience confrontation with their own fear. The average person sees fear as an obstacle. The two percent see it as a teacher. Fear shows where growth is possible. It marks the transition from the old to the new identity. Those who avoid fear remain trapped in the old. Those who accept it enter the new. In this sense, leaving the average behind is a spiritual journey: a series of thresholds where you must repeatedly decide whether to give in to fear or follow freedom. At the end of this reflection, it becomes clear that the path of the two percent is not an easy one. It is full of uncertainties, resistance, and inner conflicts. But it is precisely in this discomfort that its power lies. For every step a person takes despite fear, despite resistance, despite uncertainty, strengthens their inner independence. The average person remains trapped in repetition because they do not dare to take these steps. The two percent become free because they are willing to stand at the threshold again and again – and take the step forward. The final departure from the average is not a single event to be celebrated like a victory, but a quiet, steady movement that takes place within. There is no symbolic day when someone wakes up and can say, "Today I belong to the two percent." Rather, it is a process made up of a thousand small decisions, all pointing in the same direction: away from the masses, toward one's own clarity.

The average person looks for visible signs—for status, for proof, for recognition. But the two percent know that the real proof remains invisible. It lies in how you think, how you act, how you live, even when no one is watching. Psychologically speaking, this final step means a profound reorganization of the inner world. The average person remains in a state of constant reactivity. They react to circumstances, to other people, to their own thoughts. The two percent have learned to no longer remain in reaction, but to proactively shape their lives. They recognize that they are the authors of their inner stories. These stories are no longer repetitions of old patterns, but conscious narratives that give them direction. By consciously controlling their thinking, they create a psychological reality that is based on freedom. From a neuroscientific point of view, this means stabilizing new neural patterns. While old pathways are repeatedly activated in the early stages of transformation, the new ones become more solid over time. The brain begins to prefer other connections as the default. Decisions that once required courage become second nature. Thoughts that were once unfamiliar become familiar. Emotions that used to be paralyzing lose their power. Breaking out of the average is thus also a biological reality: a restructuring of the brain that anchors freedom as a new default state. From a sociological perspective, the final departure is evident in the fact that a person is no longer primarily determined by the expectations of others. The average is defined by belonging: they want to be liked, recognized, accepted. The two percent have learned that true belonging does not lie in conformity, but in authenticity. They no longer seek external validation, but live from a place of inner clarity. This attracts a different environment—people who seek and live the same freedom. In this way, an invisible network emerges of those who have detached themselves from the average and are thereby changing the culture itself.

Philosophically speaking, this final step is the transition from necessity to freedom. The average person lives in a mindset shaped by necessity: you have to work, you have to secure your future, you have to conform. The two percent realize that life is not just about necessity, but about possibilities. They discover that freedom does not mean doing everything, but consciously choosing what really makes sense. They make decisions not out of compulsion, but out of clarity. This clarity is the essence of a free spirit. From a spiritual perspective, the ultimate exit is a return to the origin. The average person lives in identification—with thoughts, roles, stories. The two percent have learned that all of this is transient. They have realized that they are not their thoughts, not their successes, not their fears, but the consciousness that perceives all of this. This realization gives them a freedom that no external power can touch. They know that inner independence does not depend on money, status, or possessions, but on the ability not to confuse themselves with the transitory. This brings us full circle: the path of the two percent begins with an inner decision and ends in an inner freedom that is unshakeable. It is open to anyone who is willing to walk it. It requires courage, clarity, and the willingness to stand against the habits of the masses. But in return, it gives a quality of life that the average person will never experience: the experience of being truly free. In the end, one simple truth remains: the difference between the two percent and the 98 percent is no secret. It is not a question of luck, not a question of origin, not a question of education. It is a question of choice. Anyone can start walking the path. Anyone can step out of the average. The only difference is whether they find the courage to start today.

Notes:

Notes:

Closing words:

In the end, one simple but relentless truth remains: life is not a trial run. Every day you live is irretrievable. And every day you spend in mediocrity is a day you have not lived in freedom, in clarity, to your full potential. The two percent are not different because they were luckier, more talented, or had better conditions. They are different because they found the courage to take the step that most people never dare to take: the step out of the crowd, into their own responsibility, into the freedom that no one can give you—except yourself. The average is comfortable. It feels like a warm coat that protects you from uncertainty. But it takes your breath away. It keeps you small when you long for greatness. It feeds you security – and robs you of your freedom. The two percent have shed this coat. They have felt the cold of uncertainty and yet have continued on their way. And that is precisely why they live a life that most people cannot even imagine. There are no guarantees on this path.

There is no guarantee that you won't stumble, fail, or be ridiculed by others. But one thing is certain: if you remain average, you will never discover who you truly are. The price of security is giving up your own greatness. And that is the highest price a person can pay. Perhaps as you read this, you felt something stir within you. A resistance, perhaps even anger. Or a longing, a quiet sigh of relief, a feeling of "Yes, that's what I've always known." All of these are signs that you are not holding this book in your hands by chance. You are here because a part of you has long suspected that mediocrity is not your destiny. You are here because you have the same spark that makes up the two percent. The difference is not in who you are – but in what you are willing to do. In the end, it is not fate that decides your life, nor your background, nor external circumstances. In the end, it is always just one moment that decides: the moment when you say, “I'm starting now.” Not tomorrow, not when it's more convenient, not when the world gives you permission. Now. Breaking out of the average begins with a single decision. It's inconspicuous, it doesn't make headlines – but it changes everything. This book ends here, but your journey begins now. Maybe you'll hesitate, maybe you'll doubt. But remember: the two percent were once in the same place as you. They too faced the question of whether to take the plunge. They too felt fear, uncertainty, resistance. But they went for it. And that step changed their lives forever. It's up to you whether you continue writing the next pages of your life in the book of mediocrity – or whether you start your own book. No one can make this decision for you. No one will make it for you. Only you. Perhaps your path will not be easy.

But it will be true. It will be your path. And it will lead you to a freedom that belongs not only to you, but also to all those who find the courage to break out themselves through your example. Because freedom is contagious. In the end, you will not be asked whether you belonged. In the end, you will only be asked: Did you live? Did you live your truth? Or did you settle for the story of the masses? The two percent are not strangers. They are people like you. The only difference is that they have started. You too can start. Now.

Notes:

Notes:

Concluding sentence:

From a human perspective, it is clear that everyone has the potential to break away from the average.

From a scientific point of view, it has been proven: Our brains are malleable, our patterns are changeable.

From a psychological point of view, it becomes clear: Thoughts are not truths, but programs – and programs can be rewritten.

From a spiritual point of view, it becomes apparent: We are more than our roles, more than our fears, more than what keeps us small.

And from a philosophical perspective, the simple truth remains: freedom is not a question of luck or origin, but of the decision to shape your own life.

Everything leads to one point: whether you remain average or belong to the 2% is up to you – and you alone.

Thinking small means mistaking the limits of your own mind for the limits of the world.

Günther Plamenig

Author, entrepreneur, consultant, and above all, human being.

Notes:

Notes:

Books by the author:

Title: The 2% - You decide

Title: The New Mental Training 2025

Title: Depth and Clarity

Title: The End of Lies - Why the Truth Doesn't Need an Opinion

Title: THE OTHER YOU - Who would you be without your history?

Title: Hypnosis as a path to myself

Title: Charismatic communication

Title: Loyalty - How we recognize who we can trust

Title: The Plamenig self-hypnosis technique

Title: Flash hypnosis

Title: True reality

Title: God Doesn't Have Time for Us Because He Has More Important Things to Do

Title: God Doesn't Need Us

Title: Spirit

Title: The Man with Three Faces

Title: The Mental Coach

Title: The Silent Power – Hypnosis as a Modern Management Tool

Title: The Silent Art of Change – Plamenig Hypnosis

Title: Mentally Strong on the Field – The 5-Step Program for Soccer Players

Title: The Myth of the Battery-Free Car – What Tesla Really Knew

Title: Interest Is the Key to Everything in Life

Title: The Mediator

Title: The New Pope

Title: The Algorithm of Longing – How Machines Read Our Hearts

Title: The Power of the Present – Hypnosis and Mindfulness as a Path to Inner Freedom

Title: Successful Hypnosis – Practice

Title: Modern Hypnosis – Inductions for Addicts

Title: Hypnosis 2025 – New Techniques and Insights

Title: Human 2.0

Title: Heart Time

Title: Who Am I Really?

Title: The Crisis of Meaning in Modernity – Why We Have Everything and Yet Feel Empty

Title: Why Most Relationships End After 9 Months

Title: The First Three Months Unemployed at the RAV

Title: Brain Hacking

Title: 100 Years Young

Title: The Entrepreneur of the Future

Title: How Modern Parents Should Raise Their Children

Title: The Community Advisor

Title: The Board Advisor

Title: The Board Advisor

Title: The True and Right Business Partner

Title: How to Build a Million-Dollar Business in One Year

Title: The Path to Your First Million

Title: The Formula for the Future: AI, Personality, and Business

Title: Unleashing Charisma

Title: The Building Consultant Switzerland

Title: The Construction Site Handbook

Title: A Day in the Future

Title: The Presidential Advisor

Title: The Truth Out There – UFOs, Aliens, and the Silence of the Powerful

Title: Paths to Success

Email: bottomupverlag@gmail.com

Sold out in bookstores:

Title: Paths to Success, 1st edition now available again at: bottomupverlag@gmail.com

Price: CHF 35.50 including shipping.

Publisher: Bottom up

Email: bottomupverlag@gmail.com

Books available: In all bookstores!

https://buchshop.bod.de/catalogsearch/result/index/?q=Günther+Plamenig

Order books directly from the publisher:

https://verlag.bottom-up.ch

Notes:

Notes:

Acknowledgements:

At the end of this book, I am left with one profound word: Thank you. Thank you for reading this far. This book is more than words—it is an invitation. But it is only through your willingness to engage with it that it begins to come to life. Without you, without your questions, your searching, and your courageous insight, it would be nothing more than paper. With you, it becomes a movement that transcends the ordinary. My thanks also go to all the people who have inspired, challenged, and accompanied me—on paths that were not always easy. To those who believed in me, but also to those who doubted. For clarity arose from both voices. Trust and resistance are two forces that drove me to continue – and to complete this work. I thank the teachers of life, visible and invisible, conscious and unconscious. Those who encouraged me to ask questions instead of accepting answers. To those who showed me that freedom is not given, but taken. And to those who taught me that the greatest wealth lies in transforming one's own thinking.

Above all, I thank you, reader. Your courage in opening this book shows that you have already begun to live the difference. Perhaps you still feel like you are at the beginning. Perhaps you still have doubts. But the mere fact that you are allowing yourself not to be part of the 98% as a matter of course, but are considering whether you can be part of the 2%—that is the first step. May this book accompany you, challenge you, remind you: the decision lies within you. Always. Thank you for making it.

Notes:

Notes:

Notes:

Notes: